Meat & Game Cooking

NAOMI WISE
Writer

PEGGY WALDMAN
Editor

CHRIS SHORTEN
Photographer

KAREN HAZARIAN
Food Stylist

MARIA WINSTON
Photographic Stylist

D1408468

CALIFORNIA
CULINARY
ACADEMY

Naomi Wise, a San Francisco based free-lance writer, has written professionally about food for over twenty years. She is a co-author of *Totally Hot! The Ultimate Hot Pepper Cookbook* and the California Culinary Academy book *Regional American Classics.* Winner of several cooking awards, she currently writes a food column for a weekly newspaper and has contributed recipes and restaurant reviews to many other newspapers and magazines. A graduate of the University of Michigan, she has traveled extensively throughout the world collecting recipes.

The California Culinary Academy In the forefront of American institutions leading the culinary renaissance in this country, the California Culinary Academy in San Francisco has gained a reputation as one of the most outstanding professional chef training schools in the world. With a teaching staff recruited from the best restaurants of Western Europe, the Academy educates students from around the world in the preparation of classical cuisine. The recipes in this book were created in consultation with the chefs of the Academy. For information about the Academy, write the Office of the Dean, California Culinary Academy, 625 Polk Street, San Francisco, CA 94102.

Front Cover
Mustard-Coated Roast Rack of Lamb With Tomatoes Provençale (see page 52) makes an elegant, festive, and classic dinner for special occasions that can be prepared in less than an hour.

Title Page
Fresh rosemary dresses up Mustard-Coated Roast Rack of Lamb With Tomatoes Provençale (see page 52), and Pilaf (see page 63) provides an ideal accompaniment.

Back Cover
Upper Left: The spicy short ribs featured in this version of Korean Bulgoki (see page 24) can be either oven-baked or barbecued for a hearty and economical meal.

Upper Right: Leeks, carrots, onions, garlic, and herbs are just some of the ingredients that go into a rich White Veal Stock (see page 17).

Lower Left: Four Cornish game hens are arranged artfully on a platter with baby carrots and green beans. Among the lessons to be learned from professional chefs is that the way food is presented is nearly as important as how it tastes.

Lower Right: Marinated Grilled Pheasant Breasts (see page 119), served in a lively cream sauce, make a savory and easy-to-prepare game-bird treat.

Contributors

Calligraphers
Keith Carlson, Chuck Wertman

Illustrator
Edith Allgood

Additional Photographers
Laurie Black, Academy photography, pages 14, 22, and 101
Alan Copeland, Academy photography, pages 26, 61, 73, 77, 83, and 98
Marshall Gordon, pages 12, 54, 60, 70, 107, and 108
Kit Morris, author and CCA chefs, at left

Assistant Food Stylist
Scott Gill

Copy Chief
Melinda E. Levine

Editorial Coordinator
Cass Dempsey

Copyeditor
Judy Ziajka

Proofreader
Karen K. Johnson

Indexer
Elinor Lindheimer

Editorial Assistants
Andrea Y. Connolly, Tamara Mallory

Composition & pagination by
Laurie Ann's Typesetting Boutique,
Linda M. Bouchard, Stefany Otis

Series format designed by
Linda Hinrichs, Carol Kramer

Production by
Studio 165

Separations by
Color Tech Corp.

Lithographed in U.S.A. by
Webcrafters, Inc.

Acknowledgments appear on page 128.

The California Culinary Academy series is produced by the staff of Ortho Information Services.

Publisher
Robert J. Dolezal

Editorial Director
Christine Robertson

Production Director
Ernie S. Tasaki

Series Managing Editor
Sally W. Smith

System Manager
Katherine L. Parker

Address all inquiries to
Ortho Information Services
Box 5047
San Ramon, CA 94583

Copyright © 1988
Chevron Chemical Company
All rights reserved under international and Pan-American copyright conventions.

1 2 3 4 5 6 7 8 9
88 89 90 91 92 93

ISBN 0-89721-152-9

Library of Congress Catalog Card Number 87-72815

Chevron Chemical Company
6001 Bollinger Canyon Road
San Ramon, CA 94583

Meat & Game Cooking

Made in minutes, sweet-sour Jelly Glazes for Chops are a swift, easy way to brighten the flavors of simple broiled meats for weekday dinners. Recipes on page 11.

The Fundamentals of Meat

Most Americans, if asked their favorite food, will name their favorite meat. The chapters of this book cover each of the meats found in supermarkets and butcher shops, as well as the lean and flavorful game animals and birds that are becoming increasingly available. Along with recipes this book emphasizes the basic information you need to cook consistently tasty and interesting meals. This chapter introduces the basic techniques of meat cookery (see page 6) and presents a wide selection of meat accompaniments including marinades (see page 7), composed butters (see page 9), glazes and toppings (see page 10), quick pan gravies (see page 11), and more elaborate sauces such as béarnaise (see page 14).

WHY COOK WITH MEAT?

Food is as prone to fashions as clothing, but with food, your basic preferences remain with you for life. For many years Americans ate meat almost every day—perhaps too often for ideal nutrition. Then the tide turned, and the virtues of fish, poultry, pasta, and vegetables were discovered.

After a decade of delicate dinners, however, Americans are now returning to their first love. Adventurous chefs also are experimenting more and more with game meats and foods that grow in the wild. Americans have also learned enough about nutrition to be able to make intelligent decisions about how much meat to serve and how often to serve it.

Ranchers and meat processors too have responded to the public's concerns. A well-trimmed Choice-grade steak or roast beef now contains fewer calories per ounce than a chicken drumstick, and today's pork, with 22 percent more protein and 57 percent less fat than the pork of 20 years ago, is comparably lean. Extralean meats are increasingly found in fine markets, and recently the leanest and most flavorful of all meats, those from game animals and game birds, have begun to find their way into the frozen food cases.

Americans have also learned more about what to do with meats in the kitchen, such as trimming them carefully and replacing animal fat with cholesterol-free oils.

Americans have also learned from Asian cooks how to prepare meat dishes that are light but deeply satisfying (such as Galloping Horses on page 78, or Thai Beef Salad on page 31). Cooks have discovered the uses of herbs, wines, and marinades in preparing meats. They have learned to use tough cuts for stews that are hearty without being heavy and to use tender cuts for creations as delicate as the finest fish dish. Today's meat cookery is not about gluttony, but about a full range of flavors.

TECHNIQUES OF MEAT COOKERY

There are many different ways to cook meat, but all methods fall into two basic groupings.

☐ Dry-heat methods (roasting, grilling, broiling, and barbecuing)

☐ Moist-heat methods (sautéeing, deep-frying, poaching, braising, stewing, boiling, and steaming)

The general rule for choosing a cooking method is this: When a cut of meat is tender, use dry heat to cook it quickly and serve it rare (or relatively rare). When a cut of meat is tough, use moist heat to cook it slowly until the tough fibers dissolve and the meat becomes tender.

How can you tell whether a cut of meat is tough or tender? If the meat is from a hard-working muscle, it will be tough. If the meat comes from a muscle that does little work, it will be tender. As you use this book, you'll discover which muscles are tough and which are tender in each of the animals discussed.

Roasting

Although an ideal cooking method for large, tender cuts of meat, not all cuts labeled roast at the store are truly suitable for roasting. Large cuts from the rib or loin of any animal are true roasting cuts. Legs of lamb, veal, pork, and venison also make excellent roasts.

Meats may be marinated before roasting (see page 7), both for extra flavor and to maintain moistness. Lean cuts of meat and poultry can also be kept moist by basting them with their roasting juices, oil, melted butter, or a marinade throughout roasting.

Before carving, meat is left to rest for about 15 minutes on a board or platter in a warm place. This resting period is especially important for red meats, because it allows the meat juices (which were driven toward the center of the roast during cooking) to be reabsorbed throughout the meat.

Meat is roasted uncovered so that it will be cooked by dry heat rather than by the steam that would form under a cover. A rack is usually set in a shallow roasting pan to allow heat to circulate all around the meat.

Choose a roasting pan that fits the size of the meat. If meat extends over the side of the pan, the juices will drip into the oven (causing a mess as well as losing a precious gravy ingredient). If the pan is much too large, however, the juices will burn.

About three quarters of the way through the estimated roasting time, use a meat thermometer to check whether a roast is done. Read it and remove it. Repeat this process when the meat is closer to being done.

The temperature regarded as *rare* has dropped sharply in recent years. In general if you prefer meats rare, cook them to an internal temperature of 120° to 135° F in the thickest part (not 140° F, as older cookbooks suggest). The roasting cuts of most game meats (except boar, bear, and small game animals such as beaver) are considered fully done at 120° F, since these nearly fatless meats will dry out severely if cooked even to medium-rare.

Grilling and Broiling

Quick cooking techniques, grilling and broiling sear the food with very high heat. These methods work best with small, thick cuts of tender, rich meat. (The fat content keeps rich meats from drying out.)

In both grilling and broiling, the meat should be set on a rack, not in a pan, so that it will not stew in its juices. The aim is to cook relatively small cuts through in the time it takes to brown the outside.

Grilling is done directly over the heat of an outdoor grill or barbecue, and broiling takes place under the heat of an oven broiler. (Never attempt to use a charcoal grill indoors, since burning charcoal releases dangerous fumes.) Grilling gives food a smoky flavor; broiling does not.

A broiler should be preheated for 10 minutes before broiling food to make the meat sear properly. A charcoal grill should be prepared at least 30 minutes before cooking begins.

Sautéing (Panfrying) and Deep-frying

In sautéing and deep-frying, the food is rapidly seared by hot fat so that the outer surface browns and forms a light crust, trapping juices and flavors inside. Sautéing calls for just enough fat to film the pan. Deep-frying calls for enough fat or oil (at least ¼ inch) to partly submerge the ingredients.

In both cases food should be dry before it is added to the fat (both to allow proper searing and to prevent dangerous spattering that can occur when liquid encounters hot fat).

In sautéing, food is cooked briefly in a small amount of fat, but with no liquid, over fairly high heat. This is an ideal technique for cooking thin, tender steaks and chops, livers, and scallops of light meats.

Deep-frying can be useful with larger pieces of meat, with cut-up poultry, or whenever a thick coating is desired. It can also be a wonderful technique to use with pieces of meat so thin that any other technique would dry them out.

Poaching, Braising, and Stewing

Poaching, braising, and stewing are the primary moist-heat methods for cooking meats in a liquid other than oil. In all three methods meats are cooked gently in liquid until they are tender. These techniques are ideal for inexpensive cuts of meat, which tend to be tougher, but at the same time more flavorful than more costly cuts.

MARINADES FOR TENDERNESS AND FLAVOR

A marinade is a seasoned liquid that is poured over meat, fish, or vegetables. The marinated food is left to stand briefly at room temperature or is refrigerated overnight (or longer) so that the marinade can permeate it. Marinades prevent lean meats from drying out when roasted and they tenderize at least the outer layers of tough meats when based on an acidic ingredient (such as the alcohol in

wine, beer, or Cognac; vinegar; citrus juice; or yogurt, which contains some lactic acid).

In addition an acidic marinade can help preserve meat. For instance, if a dinner with guests must suddenly be postponed for a week, and an expensive piece of frozen meat has already been defrosted, covering the meat with an acidic marinade will stop the clock on spoilage. Above all, marinating adds extra flavor to any meat. The marinade is often used as the braising or stewing liquid for the meat or is used in the sauce.

Other marinade recipes, in addition to those that follow here, appear throughout this book.

Marinades keep meat moist on the grill and lend rich flavors, too. A Grilled Butterflied Leg of Lamb (see page 55) rubbed with Tandoori Marinade (see page 9) fills the air with the tantalizing fragrance of East Indian spices.

7

Composed butters melting over sizzling steaks or chops can transform simple meals into cosmopolitan treats.

1. If marinating period will be more than 3 days, gently simmer onions, carrots, celery, and garlic in olive oil until tender (about 15 minutes). For a short marinating period, use vegetables raw.

2. Mix with remaining ingredients. Pour half the marinade into a non-reactive bowl large enough to hold meat and liquid. Add meat (either a single piece of meat or meat cut into stewing pieces). Pour remaining marinade over meat. Cover bowl and let stand in a cool place at least 6 hours, or refrigerate at least overnight or up to 1 week. Turn meat several times during marination. Before cooking drain meat from marinade; reserve marinade and use for stewing or braising liquid.

Makes about 5 cups, for about 5 pounds meat.

Variation Substitute white wine for red wine if marinating white meat.

RED WINE MARINADE

This marinade is designed for inexpensive cuts of braising or stewing beef. It also lends an excellent flavor to sweetbreads that are to be braised or grilled or to veal (although both meats will be slightly discolored by it) and is especially useful for keeping delicate sweetbreads from spoiling if there's an unexpected delay between blanching and cooking.

> 1 *cup thinly sliced onions*
> 1 *cup thinly sliced carrots*
> 1 *cup thinly sliced celery*
> 2 *cloves garlic, mashed*
> ½ *cup olive oil*
> 1 *tablespoon fresh thyme*
>   *or 1 teaspoon dried thyme*
> 2 *bay leaves*
> ¼ *cup minced parsley*
> 1 *fifth-sized bottle (about*
>   *3 cups) dry red wine*
> ⅓ *cup Cognac or brandy*

FAJITAS MARINADE

Fajitas are strips of marinated and grilled skirt steak, served with warm tortillas, guacamole, beans, and *salsa cruda*. The marinade is also superb with kid, goat, lamb, or even pork, although for large, thick pieces of meat (such as leg of goat), the recipe must be multiplied.

> 1 *cup olive or peanut oil*
>   *Juice of 2 large, ripe limes*
> 1 *tablespoon chopped cilantro*
> 1 *teaspoon hot-pepper flakes*
>   *or 1 small, fresh, hot chile,*
>   *seeded and minced*
> ¼ *teaspoon each salt and freshly*
>   *ground black pepper*
> ⅛ *teaspoon liquid smoke*
>   *flavoring*

Mix all ingredients. In a bowl place 1½ pounds skirt steak in 1 or 2 pieces (or other meat to be grilled), trimmed of fat; pour marinade over. Cover and marinate, turning occasionally, for 1 to 4 days. (To cook, grill or broil meat, then slice thinly.)

Makes about 1¼ cup, for 1½ pounds thin, porous steak.

HERB AND WHITE WINE MARINADE

This marinade is an adaptation of a French marinade designed both to tenderize wild boar and, conversely, to make domestic pork taste like wild boar. It can also be used for veal, although in that case it's best to omit the coriander and juniper berries. If you have a consistently chilly room, you can try marinating meats at cool (under 65° F) room temperatures; otherwise refrigerate meat.

    ¼ *cup olive oil*
    1 large or 2 medium carrots, thinly sliced
    1 medium onion, thinly sliced
    3 large cloves garlic, peeled and halved
    1 cup dry white wine
    ½ *cup balsamic vinegar or other fine wine vinegar*
    ¼ *cup Cognac or brandy*
    1 teaspoon black peppercorns
    1 teaspoon white peppercorns
    5 coriander seeds
    5 juniper berries, lightly crushed
    8 fresh bay leaves or 4 large, dried bay leaves
    3 sprigs fresh mint, each 6 inches long, or 1 tablespoon dried, crumbled mint
    3 sprigs fresh thyme, each 6 inches long, or 1 teaspoon dried, crumbled thyme

1. In a small saucepan place olive oil, carrot, onion, and garlic. Simmer very slowly until vegetables are softened (about 20 minutes). Add wine, vinegar, Cognac, black and white peppercorns, coriander, and juniper berries; if using dried bay leaves, mint, and thyme, add to liquid.

2. Place meat in bowl and pour marinade over meat, turning meat to coat both sides. If using fresh bay leaves, mint, and thyme, scatter them over meat. Cover bowl and keep in a cool place for 5 to 7 days for wild boar, 3 days for pork, and 1 day for veal, or refrigerate 7 to 9 days for boar and 3 to 4 days for pork or veal. During marinating period turn meat frequently, basting with liquid.

Makes about 2 cups, for up to 6 pounds meat.

Lamb Marinade Substitute red wine for white wine. Add 1 sprig fresh rosemary or 1 tablespoon dried rosemary (or substitute rosemary for bay leaves). Let marinate, refrigerated, about 3 days. Use with leg of lamb to be roasted or butterflied and grilled, or use marinade as braising or stewing liquid for lamb shoulder.

TANDOORI MARINADE

This Indian version of a yogurt marinade is spicy and aromatic, with an exotic flavor. Use it with lamb, goat, pork, or poultry to be grilled, broiled, or roasted.

    ½ *teaspoon cumin seed, toasted and ground*
      Juice of 1 ripe lime
    1 cup plain yogurt
    1 tablespoon grated fresh ginger
    1 tablespoon minced cilantro
    ½ *teaspoon ground anise or fennel seed*
    ¼ *teaspoon ground mustard*
    1 tablespoon cayenne pepper, or to taste
    1 tablespoon paprika
    1 tablespoon minced garlic
    ½ *teaspoon salt*

Mix all ingredients and spread over meat or poultry. Cover and let marinate for up to 3 days (at least overnight) turning occasionally.

Makes about 1½ cups, for 3 to 4 pounds meat or poultry.

SAUCES, TOPPINGS, AND GRAVIES

Even excellent meat can become boring if it is always served plainly roasted, broiled, or grilled. Sauces, toppings, and gravies are the key to presenting an interesting menu.

COMPOSED BUTTERS

Composed butters lend a touch of elegance, as well as a finer flavor, to broiled or grilled meats. Composed butters are made of softened butter mixed with seasonings. The seasonings can include salt, pepper, and any fresh herb in season (parsley, dill, tarragon, cilantro, or chives, for instance) or a combination of herbs. Citrus juice, garlic, and spices can also be used in these butters.

    Composed butter can be refrigerated, covered, for up to one week or it can be frozen. To serve, bring the butter to room temperature and at the last minute, when the food is on a serving plate, spoon butter onto the food it's complementing (meat, poultry, fish, or vegetables served whole, such as asparagus), so that the hot food begins to melt the butter into a sauce just as the dish reaches the dining table. Composed butters may also be stirred into pasta, rice, or chopped vegetables.

ROQUEFORT OR BLUE CHEESE BUTTER

This butter will dress up a good steak—and save one that's disappointing in flavor. It can be used on lamb chops too.

    6 tablespoons unsalted butter, softened
    ¼ *cup crumbled Roquefort or good-quality blue cheese*
    2 teaspoons Cognac or brandy
    1 tablespoon chopped parsley
      Freshly ground pepper, to taste

Beat butter with cheese, brandy, and parsley. Add pepper to taste. Cover and refrigerate for 1 hour to blend flavors. Bring to room temperature before serving with steaks.

Makes about ¾ cup, for 4 to 6 servings meat.

SPICY CILANTRO AND LIME BUTTER

Use this butter to lend a southwestern flavor to steaks, pork chops, grilled sweetbreads, broiled poultry, or vegetables.

6 tablespoons softened, unsalted butter
2 teaspoons lime juice
2 tablespoons minced cilantro
Ground cayenne pepper or hot-pepper sauce, to taste
Salt, to taste

Blend butter with lime juice and cilantro. Add cayenne to taste, a little at a time. Add salt to taste. Cover and refrigerate mixture about 2 hours to blend flavors. Bring butter to room temperature before using.

Makes a generous ½ cup, for 4 servings meat or broiled poultry.

GLAZES AND TOPPINGS

A glaze is a combination of flavoring ingredients, often including some sugar or a sugar-containing element, that is spread over meat that has been broiled on one side. As the glazed side broils, the heat lightly caramelizes the sugar in the glaze, making the glaze adhere as it melts into the meat. A topping for broiled meats can consist of any flavoring ingredient that · will complement the meat and taste good when broiled on top.

For example, a slice of tomato sprinkled with oregano, salt, and pepper can be a delicious topping for a broiled veal chop. Additional glazes and toppings appear throughout this book. (For instance, the mustard, herb, and bread-crumb coating for the roast rack of lamb on page 52 can also be used to coat pork chops, sliced leftover roast beef or lamb, or veal chops. Any of the broiled ham glazes on page 86 can be used for pork.)

FRUIT JUICE GLAZE

Less thick than a jelly glaze, this sweet glaze may drip. To ease clean-up, pour a little water under the rack of the broiler tray before applying it to half-broiled chops.

½ cup fruit juice of choice (such as apple, cranberry, or apricot)
1½ tablespoons cornstarch or arrowroot
1 tablespoon applejack (if using apple juice), brandy, bourbon, or liqueur made from same fruit as juice
1 tablespoon softened, unsalted butter

Mix 2 tablespoons of juice with cornstarch. Set aside. In a small saucepan gently heat remaining juice to bubbling. Stir in cornstarch mixture over medium heat until thickened. Stir in liquor and butter. Spoon sauce over half-broiled chops just after they are turned; continue broiling until chops are cooked.

Makes about ½ cup, for 4 to 6 chops.

CHEESE TOPPING

This topping can be varied to complement any type of broiled chop. Parmesan, mozzarella, or fontina cheese goes well on veal chops; Gruyère, Monterey jack, or Emmenthaler complements pork chops, and Brie or a mild goat cheese provides a delicious topping for lamb chops.

½ cup cheese, freshly grated or crumbled
2 tablespoons whipping cream, or as needed
Salt and ample freshly ground pepper, to taste
1 tablespoon minced fresh herbs (parsley, chives, or tarragon)

Stir together cheese with enough cream to moisten. Stir in salt, pepper, and herbs. Broil chops on one side, turn, and when chops are about 1 minute from being done, spoon on topping. Continue to broil until topping melts.

Makes about ⅔ cup, for 4 to 6 chops.

DEGLAZES

A deglaze is a sauce, or a base for a sauce, made directly in the pan after the meat has finished cooking and has been removed. Deglazing makes use of the meat juices that caramelize on the bottom of the pan during sautéing or roasting. In addition to those that follow here, throughout this book you will find many recipes for sauces made by deglazing, a vital technique in varied, tasty meat cookery. See page 12 for step-by-step photographs explaining this technique.

SIMPLE WINE DEGLAZE

Although this sauce is used most consistently over pan-fried steak, it can also be served with pan-fried lamb, veal, pork, or calf's liver. It's called *sauce Bercy* if made with white wine; or make it with red wine for a dish and *marchand de vin* (wine merchant's style). If calories count, follow the variation, which still makes a fine sauce but uses less fat.

3 to 4 tablespoons unsalted butter (to taste), at room temperature
2 tablespoons minced shallots or whites of green onions
½ cup dry white or red wine
Salt and freshly ground pepper, to taste
2 tablespoons minced parsley or fresh tarragon and parsley

1. Remove cooked steak (or other meat) from skillet. Pour fat out of skillet. Add 1 tablespoon of the butter; stir in shallots and cook over low heat until softened (1 to 2 minutes).

2. Pour wine into skillet and, scraping bottom of skillet constantly, boil wine over high heat until it has reduced to a syrupy glaze. Remove pan from heat.

3. Swirl in remaining butter, a little at a time, until melted and sauce is enriched to your taste. Stir in salt and pepper, then parsley. Spread sauce over meat and serve immediately.

Makes about 1 cup, for up to 2½ pounds meat.

Simpler Wine Deglaze Pour fat out of skillet after panfrying meat and removing it from pan. Add ½ cup dry red or white wine (or a combination of wine and meat stock). Boil over high heat, scraping up browned bits continually with wooden spoon, until liquid is syrupy. With pan off heat swirl in 2 tablespoons unsalted, room-temperature butter, a little at a time. When butter is absorbed spoon sauce over meat.

Makes about ½ cup, for up to 2½ pounds meat.

QUICK PAN GRAVIES

These quick pan gravies are slightly more elaborate than deglazes, although they are based on deglazing techniques.

ZINFANDEL-CURRANT SAUCE

This tart sauce complements sautéed rabbit, venison, wild boar, or even beaver and can certainly be used for pan-fried lamb chops too.

- ¾ cup Zinfandel wine
- 1 tablespoon balsamic or red wine vinegar
- 1 shallot, peeled and minced (about 3 tablespoons)
- ¾ cup Brown Meat Stock (see page 16)
- ⅓ cup fresh or frozen currants or 2 tablespoons red currant jelly
  Sugar, to taste
- 2 tablespoons Cognac or brandy
- 2 tablespoons unsalted butter at room temperature, cut into pieces

1. In a small, nonaluminum (preferably enamel-coated) saucepan, boil together wine, vinegar, and shallot until reduced to 3 tablespoons.

2. In a separate saucepan reduce stock to ½ cup over high heat. Stir reduced stock into wine mixture and add currants (or stir in currant jelly). If using currants taste carefully and add sugar to taste, a little at a time. Sauce should be tart but not mouth-puckering.

3. Over moderately high heat add Cognac to deglaze cooking pan in which meat was cooked, scraping up browned bits. Add wine mixture (or, if meat was roasted, pour deglazing mixture into wine). Bring liquid to a simmer, stirring. With pan off heat swirl in butter. Serve immediately.

Makes about 1 cup, for 1 rabbit or up to 2 pounds red meat.

PIZZAIOLA (HERBED TOMATO) SAUCE

Serve this fresh tomato sauce not just for standard veal cutlets *pizzaiola*, but also with steak, hamburgers, and lamb.

- 2 to 3 tablespoons olive oil
- 1 or 2 large cloves garlic, minced
- 2 large, ripe tomatoes (about 8 oz each), peeled (see Note) and sliced, or 1 can (14 oz) plum tomatoes, drained and roughly chopped
- 1 tablespoon fresh basil leaves, shredded, or 1 teaspoon dried basil or oregano leaves, crumbled
  Salt and ample freshly ground pepper, to taste

JELLY GLAZES FOR CHOPS

The procedure for making jelly glazes is as follows: Dilute jam, jelly, or preserves with another ingredient that will cut the sweetness, then heat the glaze just until it becomes liquid and brush it on nearly broiled chops. If using preserves or a rough jelly, purée briefly in blender or food processor. Turn jelly into a small, heavy saucepan and melt. Stir in secondary ingredient(s). Then broil the chops. After chops have been turned, about 3 minutes before chops are done, brush lightly with glaze. Continue broiling the glazed chops just long enough to flavor them with the sweet, slightly caramelized glaze.

Type	For	Mix	With
Bar le duc	Lamb, veal, game	¼ cup red currant jelly	1 tablespoon orange rind slivers, lime juice, or orange peel liqueur
Orange marmalade	Pork	¼ cup marmalade	1 tablespoon vinegar
Apricot	Pork, ham	¼ cup apricot jam or preserves	1 tablespoon Cognac or bourbon
Jalapeño	Pork, ham	¼ cup jalapeño jelly	2 tablespoons lime juice and 1 tablespoon minced cilantro

Makes about ⅓ cup, for 4 to 6 chops.

---

1. Remove pan-fried meat from skillet. Pour off fat (unless meat was cooked in olive oil; in that case fat can substitute for all or part of oil called for here). Film skillet with olive oil and heat gently, scraping up browned bits from skillet. Add garlic and sauté over low heat until tender (about 1 minute).

2. Add tomatoes, increase heat to very high, and fry, turning frequently, until tomatoes start to fall apart into a thick sauce (about 5 minutes). Stir in basil, salt, and pepper and spoon sauce over meat.

Makes about 2 cups, for 2½ pounds steak, chops, or hamburgers, or 1 pound meatballs.

Note To peel tomatoes drop tomatoes into boiling water to cover. Cook for about 1 minute (water will not have time to return to a boil) or until a knife touched lightly to tomato skin produces a split. Drain immediately under cold running water. Peel will come away easily with fingers or a small knife.

Step-by-Step

DEGLAZING

Deglazes are quick to make, take little forethought (although you'll have the widest range of possibilities if you have some good homemade stocks on hand in the freezer), and do wonders for any meat, whether broiled, roasted, or sautéed. See pages 10 and 11 for deglaze recipes.

1. *The coagulated meat essences, which look like brown bits in the pan, should not be washed out (they are rich in flavor). However, excess fat should be poured out carefully before deglazing begins.*

2. *Add a small amount of liquid to pan. The liquid can be red or white wine, port or Madeira, stock, wine vinegar, citrus juice, or a combination of these. Black coffee is sometimes used for deglazing (especially with ham), and even plain water can be used with highly seasoned meats. Place pan on stovetop. To deglaze a large roasting pan, place pan over two burners. Reduce the liquid in the pan by boiling at highest heat until it thickens slightly, all the while scraping the browned bits from the bottom with a wooden spoon. The reduced liquid is the base for a sauce.*

3. *The liquid can be thickened by stirring in cornstarch or arrowroot or by adding the liquid to a saucepan in which a lightly cooked mixture of flour and fat (called a roux) has already been prepared. It can also be turned into a cream sauce just by adding cream and boiling the sauce until it thickens by itself. When deglazing a roast the deglazing liquid can be poured into a smaller saucepan or a skillet to make this final stage easier to execute. A variety of flavorings, such as tomatoes, herbs, mustard, soy sauce, Worcestershire sauce, or citrus juice, can enhance deglazed sauces.*

4. *The deglazing liquid can also be enriched with a few tablespoons of unsalted, room-temperature butter that is cut into pieces. Swirl butter into the liquid. When butter has melted and the sauce looks glossy and thick, add minced fresh herbs (such as parsley or tarragon) and serve as is, with no further thickening.*

COUNTRY CREAM GRAVY

This flour-thickened "cream" sauce, actually made with milk, is used as a gravy for deep-fried or oven-fried meats or poultry. The key to any flour-thickened gravy is constant stirring to prevent lumps from forming; a small wire whisk is even better than a spoon for this.

- *3 tablespoons rendered bacon or ham fat, or unsalted butter, or oil from frying (see Note)*
- *3 tablespoons flour*
- *1½ cups whole milk Salt, freshly ground black pepper, and cayenne pepper, to taste*

Remove fried meat or poultry from skillet and keep warm. Pour off cooking fat and replace with bacon fat. Heat fat over low heat and stir in flour. Increase heat to medium and stir constantly until raw flour odor disappears (about 1 minute). Slowly whisk in milk and cook, stirring or whisking, until gravy is smooth, hot, and thickened. Carefully add salt, pepper, and cayenne, to taste. Pour over meat or poultry.

Makes about 1½ cups.

Garlic Country Gravy Before stirring flour into fat, add 1 large clove garlic, finely minced (about ½ tablespoonful). Cook garlic in fat over low heat until translucent (about 1 minute). Stir in flour and proceed as above.

Makes about 1½ cups.

Rich, Thin Gravy Decrease flour to 1 tablespoon and replace whole milk with 1 cup half-and-half. Proceed as above. Serve over poultry or veal.

Makes about 1 cup.

Note Many cooks simply use a little frying fat for their sauce base. The sauce then should be quite highly seasoned, or it may be tasteless. For a somewhat more elegant version (for poultry), replace the frying fat with butter, and for a flavorful, smoky version (for meat), use rendered bacon or ham fat, as southern cooks do.

FLOUR-THICKENED PAN GRAVY FOR ROASTS

This slightly unusual technique for making gravy is actually easier than a more conventional one.

> Drippings from roast
> ½ to 1 cup meat or poultry stock, milk, or cream
> Flour, as needed
> Salt and freshly ground pepper, to taste
> Fresh or dried minced herbs, dry sherry, lemon juice, or other flavoring (optional)

1. Remove roast and rack from roasting pan and place roast on carving board. Pour drippings from roasting pan into a roomy heat-resistant glass measuring cup or a medium-sized heatproof bowl and allow to settle for a minute or so, to let fat come to the top. Tip container of drippings and, with a large cooking spoon, skim off fat and reserve.

2. Set roasting pan on stove (over 2 burners, if necessary) and pour in ½ cup stock. Bring to a boil over high heat on both burners, scraping browned bits from bottom of pan. When liquid starts to thicken and has absorbed meat juices from pan, add liquid to drippings.

3. Measure amount of liquid in drippings container; if necessary add more stock to make at least 1 cup.

4. In a small saucepan over a burner set to low, heat 2 to 3 tablespoons of the reserved fat. Stir in flour, using 1 tablespoon per cup of liquid for thin gravy, 2 tablespoons per cup for thick gravy. Stir over low heat until flour loses its raw aroma and starts to color slightly. Stirring constantly and strongly, slowly pour in liquid. Once mixture is smooth increase heat to medium and cook, stirring constantly, until gravy thickens. Season carefully to taste with salt and pepper and stir in flavorings, if desired, just before serving. Juices gathering on cutting board where roast has been resting may be added, if desired, to the gravy. If reheating is needed, do not boil gravy again.

Makes at least 1 cup.

MORE ELABORATE SAUCES

These are the traditional haute cuisine sauces, although some of them are neither hard to make nor time-consuming. They're not just for company but can provide an outstanding midweek lift.

BASIC BROWN SAUCE

This rich sauce is the basis for nearly all brown sauces. It is generally not used as is, but is flavored with wine or other ingredients and then served with red meats. When a piece of meat is beautifully browned, the sauce may be served under it so as not to hide the color of the food.

> 2 tablespoons salad oil
> 2½ tablespoons flour
> 2 cups Brown Meat Stock (see page 16)
> 1 onion, coarsely chopped
> 1 carrot, diced
> 1 tomato, diced
> 1 bay leaf
> 1 sprig fresh thyme or pinch dried thyme
> 5 parsley stems
> 2 teaspoons tomato paste
> Salt and freshly ground pepper, to taste

1. In a medium-sized, heavy saucepan over burner set to low, heat oil. Add flour and cook, whisking constantly, until mixture is golden brown. Be careful not to let it burn. Remove from heat.

2. Gradually whisk stock into flour mixture. Add onion, carrot, tomato, bay leaf, thyme, and parsley. Bring mixture to a boil, stirring constantly. Reduce heat to low. Simmer, uncovered, stirring frequently, for 1 hour.

3. Stir tomato paste into sauce, season lightly with salt and pepper, and simmer 1 minute. Strain sauce through a fine sieve. If not using sauce at once, dab top with butter to prevent a skin from forming. Sauce can be refrigerated, covered, up to 3 days, or it can be frozen.

Makes about 1½ cups.

MADEIRA SAUCE

Madeira Sauce may be served with grilled or sautéed steaks or with roast beef, veal, chicken, or turkey.

> 1½ cups Basic Brown Sauce (recipe at left)
> 4 tablespoons Madeira
> Salt and freshly ground pepper, to taste
> 1 tablespoon butter (optional)

1. Bring Basic Brown Sauce to a boil in a medium-sized, heavy saucepan over medium heat, whisking often.

2. Whisk in 2 tablespoons of Madeira, add salt and pepper, and simmer, uncovered, over medium-low heat for 10 minutes.

3. Add remaining 2 tablespoons Madeira and bring sauce just to a simmer. Remove pan from heat and stir in butter, if desired. Taste and add more salt and pepper, if needed. Serve hot.

Makes about 1½ cups.

DEVILED SAUCE

This tart sauce goes well with broiled or grilled meats.

> ⅔ cup white wine
> 1 tablespoon wine vinegar
> 1 tablespoon minced shallot or white of green onion
> ¼ teaspoon dried thyme leaves, crumbled
> 1 small bay leaf
> 1 cup Basic Brown Sauce (recipe at left)
> 1 teaspoon minced parsley
> Freshly ground black pepper and cayenne pepper, to taste

1. In a small, nonaluminum saucepan, boil together wine, vinegar, shallot, thyme, and bay leaf until liquid is reduced by two thirds (to about ¼ cup). Stir in Basic Brown Sauce, return mixture to a gentle boil, and reduce for about 5 minutes over moderately high heat, stirring.

2. Strain sauce and add parsley, pepper, and cayenne.

Makes about 1 cup.

QUICK BÉARNAISE SAUCE

Béarnaise sauce, a more elaborate version of the familiar hollandaise, is flavored with tarragon, vinegar, wine, and shallots. Most people now make it with white wine (which gives it a golden color), but if you are drinking a fine red wine with dinner, you can certainly use some in the sauce. The sauce will then be rosy. Serve béarnaise sauce over broiled steak or top-quality lamb chops and with broiled fish or poached eggs.

- 1½ tablespoons finely minced shallots or whites of green onions
- 2 teaspoons wine vinegar or fresh lemon juice
- ¼ cup dry wine, white or red
- 1 tablespoon fresh tarragon leaves, minced, or ½ tablespoon dried tarragon, crumbled
- 1 tablespoon fresh chervil leaves or ½ tablespoon dried chervil
- ¼ teaspoon freshly ground white pepper or cracked black pepper
  Pinch salt
- ½ cup unsalted butter (clarified butter will give finest texture)
- 3 egg yolks

1. In a small, heavy, nonaluminum saucepan, mix shallots, vinegar, wine, tarragon, chervil, pepper, and salt. Cook over medium heat until reduced to about 2 tablespoons (mixture will be very thick, with little liquid). Strain, pushing hard on solids with a spoon to extract all liquid, and let glaze cool.

2. In separate pan melt butter over burner set to medium; then remove pan from the heat.

3. *To prepare in a blender or food processor:* Place egg yolks in container. Cover and whirl long enough to break yolks. Add glaze, blend, and very gradually pour in hot melted butter in a thin, steady stream (see Note). Cover and blend for about 1 minute, then let mixture rest about 30 seconds. Repeat until sauce is as thick as mayonnaise. *To prepare in a*

saucepan: Return strained glaze to saucepan and whisk with egg yolks over low heat until mixture is creamy and thick. Be careful not to let sauce get too hot, or yolks will curdle or scramble. Remove pan occasionally from heat, still beating, to make sure it does not get too hot. When mixture thickens remove from heat and whisk for 30 seconds longer. Then whisk in butter drop by drop at first, until sauce starts to thicken, and then in a very thin stream, whisking constantly and briskly (see Note).

4. Serve as soon as possible. Sauce may be kept warm in a thermos bottle or may be placed on a rack set above warm water and whisked frequently.

Makes about ¾ cup.

Note The key to béarnaise sauce, as with any egg yolk–based sauce (including mayonnaise and hollandaise) is to add the fat (in this case butter) very slowly, letting each addition be absorbed fully before adding more. Sometimes, despite your best efforts, a béarnaise sauce will separate. To save it whisk 1 tablespoon sauce with 1 tablespoon cold water until mixture is smooth. Gradually whisk in remaining sauce. If this does not work, start again by whisking 1 egg yolk and 1 tablespoon water together in a small, heavy saucepan over low heat until thick, then slowly pour in remaining sauce, whisking constantly.

MEAT AND POULTRY STOCKS

Stock is a term that refers to the basic building block of most soups and many sauces: a clear, nearly unseasoned bouillon made by simmering meat and bones together with some vegetables until their essential flavors have cooked into the liquid.

Meat and poultry stocks made at home are vastly superior to canned stocks. They are often the difference between a superb sauce and one that tastes just a little "off." If you look at the ingredients listed on the labels of canned stocks, you'll find salt in a prominent position—whereas stocks for cooking should barely be salted at all, since they will later become part of mixtures that will be seasoned as needed.

Sugar is also used in canned stocks, whereas in home-cooked stocks sweet vegetables (carrots and onions) lend the stock as much natural sugar as it needs. In addition the high temperatures required for sterile commercial canning and packaging in metal do the flavors of canned stocks no good at all.

Making poultry stock takes just a few hours and very little work. Meat stocks can be prepared at leisure over a weekend in quantities to ensure a three- to six-month supply, and can be kept in the freezer until needed.

STOCK-MAKING SECRETS

Stock is allowed to boil just once, if at all, at the very beginning of cooking. The scum that rises to the top is carefully skimmed off, and the stock is then simmered at length. If it boils again the fat and scum rising to the surface during simmering will be reabsorbed into the liquid.

Never fully cover a stock until it has cooled. If hot stock is covered, it will turn as sour as vinegar. Do not salt stock. In many recipes for sauces, soups, stews, and braises, stock will be reduced, and any salt will be concentrated. It is better to salt foods during the last stages of preparation, when all ingredients are in their final proportion.

THICKENERS FOR SAUCES

There are numerous ways to thicken sauces. In some methods a self-effacing thickener pulls together a sauce at the last minute without changing the taste, and in others the thickener adds a special flavor.

Arrowroot, cornstarch, potato starch, and water chestnut starch All of these produce a translucent sauce with a glossy finish. Cornstarch is the coarsest starch, creating a slightly glutinous texture familiar to anyone who has eaten at a family-style Chinese-American restaurant. The other three starches are preferable for delicate sauces.

To avoid lumping always add starch in paste form—mixed with liquid. Mix 1 tablespoon starch with 2 tablespoons water to thicken 1 cup liquid into a heavy sauce, or 4 teaspoons starch to 2 tablespoons water to thicken 2 cups liquid into a somewhat lighter sauce.

Flour When flour thickens a sauce, it makes the sauce opaque. Flour paste may be added directly to a sauce then simmered long enough to let the unpleasant raw-flour taste cook completely away.

To thicken 1 cup liquid into a thick sauce, use 2 tablespoons flour mixed with 2 tablespoons cold water, stock, or cream. For a lighter sauce halve this quantity. In many countries (including England), rice flour is preferred to wheat flour as a paste-type thickener for delicate sauces.

Roux A roux consists of roughly equal parts wheat flour and fat, cooked over low or medium heat to form a grainy paste. Roux adds body and flavor, as well as thickening, to sauces. Roux may be made in advance and stored, refrigerated, up to two weeks.

To make roux heat fat carefully (do not let it brown) or use clarified butter or oil. Whisk in flour vigorously to blend, then cook mixture over medium heat, stirring constantly, 2 to 3 minutes to let raw flour aroma dissipate. Roux may be left white, for a cream sauce; it may be cooked golden (for blond roux or peanut butter roux) to add a little color; or it may be cooked to a brown, nutty color for deeper brown sauces.

The more (and darker) a roux is cooked, the less it will thicken a sauce, and the more painful and sticky will be any spatters that touch the cook's hand. For most sauces made with roux, 2 tablespoons each of fat and flour will thicken 1 cup liquid to a heavy sauce or will make 2 cups liquid into a light sauce.

Beurre manié An uncooked paste of equal amounts of butter and flour, beurre manié is kneaded together with the fingers or mashed with a fork. It is used to lightly thicken a sauce that is too thin or to lend body to braising sauces that have been reduced but have not otherwise been thickened.

Stir beurre manié into the sauce and simmer, stirring, for a few minutes in order to cook the flour and thicken the sauce. It is easiest to make beurre manié with butter that's at cool room temperature. Extra beurre manié can be wrapped well and refrigerated for about 10 days.

Whipping cream, sour cream, and yogurt Whipping cream is used both as a thickener and an enrichment for sauces. When boiled it thickens itself. Sour cream may be used to thicken a sauce when the distinctive flavor is desirable.

Have sour cream at room temperature, beat a little hot sauce into sour cream, then whisk mixture back into the rest of the sauce. Never allow sauce to boil, or sour cream will curdle and make the sauce very unappealing. When the sourness of yogurt will complement a sauce, it may be used in place of sour cream with fewer calories and no danger of curdling.

Egg yolks An excellent choice for thickening refined sauces, egg yolks are used in *velouté* (velvety) sauces and in Greek *avgolemono* (egg-lemon) sauce, which consists of stock and lemon juice thickened with egg.

To use egg yolks beat yolks lightly and while beating pour a little hot liquid into yolk. Whisk well. Beat in a little more hot liquid, and when mixture is smooth, pour it back into sauce and heat gently. Do not allow sauce to boil, or egg will hard-cook and separate from the sauce. Use 1 yolk to lightly thicken 1 cup sauce, 2 to 3 yolks to thicken sauce more.

Vegetable purées Although used primarily to thicken soups, vegetable purées were the basis for low-calorie sauces during the brief vogue of France's *cuisine minceur* ("skinny" cooking). Some of the vegetables from a stew may be puréed as a thickener for the sauce of the stew, and wherever beans are present, some of them may be mashed or puréed and returned to the dish as a highly effective and flavorful thickener.

Reduction Thickening a sauce by the process of reduction is simple: Cook the sauce uncovered until volume decreases and flavor is concentrated. Deglazes are high-heat reductions, but some other reductions are done slowly, at a simmer. Seasoning should be added only after sauce is fully reduced, since it, too, will concentrate during the reduction process.

Butter swirls As well as adding flavor and lending an elegant appearance, butter swirls will thicken a sauce slightly. Cut butter into small pieces and bring to room temperature. Add butter bit by bit to sauce at the end of cooking, with pan off heat, and swirl the pan to create spirals.

Flavorful homemade meat and poultry stocks are the bases of soups and sauces. For greatest convenience, spoon chilled and degreased stock into small freezer bags, seal, and freeze until needed.

STORING STOCKS

After they are skimmed, stocks may be stored, covered, and refrigerated, for about a week. The life of refrigerated stock may be extended by bringing it just to a boil and letting it cool before refrigerating it again. (This should be done every five days, for up to about one month.)

The most convenient method for long-term storage is to partially fill heavy-weight, zip-top freezer bags with stocks in convenient quantities (use some 1-pint bags, some 1-quart bags) and freeze them. (Do not fill bags entirely, or, as the liquid expands into ice, it will break bags.)

Stocks will keep, frozen, almost indefinitely. To defrost, simply turn frozen stock out of the bag into a saucepan and heat it until it is melted. If you have defrosted too much stock, reheat stock to just the boiling point, let it cool, and then refreeze it.

BROWN MEAT STOCK

This long-cooked stock is indispensable in many richly flavored soups, braising liquids, and sauces.

> 5 *pounds bony, tough beef (such as knuckles, shanks, shins)*
> 3 *pounds cracked beef and veal bones with some meat clinging*
> 2 *large carrots, pared, and halved lengthwise and crosswise*
> 2 *large onions, peeled, trimmed, and halved*
> 2 *cups hot water*
> 4 *large leeks, well-cleaned, and coarsely sliced (optional)*
> 2 *stalks celery with leaves*
> 2 *cloves garlic, peeled*
> *Bouquet garni (6 sprigs parsley, 1 sprig thyme or ¼ teaspoon dried thyme leaves, 1 bay leaf, and 2 whole cloves, wrapped and tied in a piece of cheesecloth)*

1. Preheat oven to 450° F. In a large roasting pan, place meat, bones, carrots, and onions. Roast, turning pieces every 10 minutes until well browned (about 40 minutes). Remove meat, bones, and vegetables to large stockpot. Pour fat out of roasting pan. Place pan over 2 burners set to high heat. Add water and boil, using a wooden spoon to loosen all browned bits. Pour liquid over ingredients in stockpot.

2. Add more water to cover ingredients and bring to a simmer. Skim off scum. Add leeks if used, celery, garlic, and bouquet garni. Partly cover and simmer at least 4 hours. Add boiling water if needed. Skim surface occasionally. Cool stock uncovered. Strain into large container, cover, and refrigerate overnight. Remove fat from surface and correct seasonings. If stock seems weak, boil down.

Makes 6 to 8 quarts.

Brown Game Stock Make Brown Meat Stock using meaty bones from the saddle or meaty shanks and knuckles of venison, bison, or wild boar. (It is best to make separate stocks from each species, though.) Add 12 whole peppercorns to liquid as it cooks.

WHITE VEAL STOCK

Use this delicate stock as a braising liquid and sauce for white meat dishes, such as veal, sweetbreads, and rabbit. Since veal unleashes a large amount of white, foamy scum, the bones and meat are parboiled and rinsed at the start.

> 4 pounds veal shanks
> 4 pounds veal bones with some meat on them
> 2 carrots, pared, trimmed, and coarsely sliced
> 2 large onions, peeled, trimmed, and halved
> 2 stalks celery with leaves
> 2 large leeks, well-cleaned, and sliced (optional)
> 2 cloves garlic, peeled
> Bouquet garni (6 sprigs parsley, 1 sprig thyme or ¼ teaspoon dried thyme leaves, 1 bay leaf, and 2 whole cloves, wrapped and tied in a piece of cheesecloth)
> Salt, to taste (optional)

1. In a large (at least 8 quarts) stockpot place veal shanks and bones. Cover with cold water and then bring to a boil. Let boil about 5 minutes, then strain liquid through a colander into sink, discarding the water. Run cold water over contents of colander to rinse well.

2. Return shanks and bones to pot, add cold water to cover veal by 2 inches, and bring to a simmer. Skim again. Add carrots, onions, celery, leeks if using, garlic, bouquet garni, and salt (if desired). Simmer, partly covered (with cover well askew) for at least 4 hours, and preferably 8 hours. Strain stock and refrigerate, covered, overnight. Remove sheet of fat from top of stock. Taste stock; correct seasonings. If stock is weak (or storage space is at a premium) boil stock down until satisfactory. Store cooled stock as desired.

Makes 6 to 8 quarts.

POULTRY STOCK

This rich stock has many uses, ranging from the chicken soup that cures all ills to the most elegant sauces. Chicken feet thicken and enrich the soup with gelatin. Include them if you can, along with the head, if available.

> 5 pounds (approximately) poultry spare parts (wing tips, necks, backs, gizzards, hearts, heads, and bones) or 1 stewing hen (5 lb), cut up
> 2 to 4 cleaned chicken feet, if available
> ½ to 1 pound trimmed, pared carrots, coarsely chopped (these sweeten the stock, so adjust quantity to taste)
> 2 large onions, peeled and quartered
> 3 stalks celery with leaves
> 6 sprigs parsley
> 2 small cloves garlic, peeled

1. Place poultry, including feet, if used, in a large (at least 8 quarts) stockpot and cover with 2 inches of cold water. Bring to a boil. Lower heat immediately to a simmer and carefully skim surface scum until very little additional scum arises (about 5 minutes).

2. Add carrots, onions, celery, parsley, and garlic. Simmer, uncovered, until stock develops flavor (about 3 hours). Add boiling water if too much liquid evaporates, but do not thin stock too much.

3. Let stock cool, then strain, pressing on solids in strainer to extract their juices. Refrigerate, covered, overnight. Remove fat from surface (it may be saved for use as a cooking fat). Taste and correct seasonings and, if stock is too weak, boil it down until satisfactory. Store cooled stock as desired.

Makes 4 to 6 quarts.

BROWN POULTRY STOCK

Here is a stock for waterfowl and game birds and for pan sauces for any roast bird. The amount made by this recipe will rapidly produce a concentrated broth for a sauce to be served the same night, with the rest of the bird. It can also be made in larger quantities than described here if you've saved and frozen the carcasses (raw or cooked) and spare parts of several other birds.

> Neck, gizzard, heart, wing tips, bones, and scraps from at least 1 bird (include cooked or raw carcasses, if available)
> 1 sliced onion
> 1 sliced carrot
> 1 tablespoon rendered poultry fat (chicken, duck, goose, game bird) or cooking oil
> 2 sprigs parsley
> 1 tiny bay leaf
> Pinch dried thyme leaves
> 12 whole peppercorns (if making game bird stock)
> 2 cups Poultry Stock (recipe at left) or canned chicken broth

1. Chop the parts and scraps of the birds into small, 1½-inch pieces. In a heavy, medium-sized (about 2 quarts) saucepan place poultry pieces, onion, carrot, and fat. Over medium heat brown pieces and vegetables, stirring occasionally.

2. Pour out fat and add parsley, bay leaf, and thyme. If making a stock with game birds, add peppercorns. Pour in stock and, if necessary, enough water to cover contents by ½ inch. Simmer, partly covered (with cover well askew), until stock is very richly flavored (about 1½ hours), skimming if needed. (If making stock in larger quantities, cook until richly flavored, about 2 to 3 hours.) Strain stock and skim off fat (if for immediate use) or refrigerate and then degrease.

Makes about 1 cup.

Cooking is one way to express affection. For instance, serve a lavish Old English Roast Beef Dinner to special evening guests. Recipes start on page 34.

Beef

Beef has long been America's favorite meat. Its assertively meaty flavor and dense, chewy texture make it, for many, the very definition of "good eating." Nearly every part of the steer finds its way onto our tables, whether as a tender Roast Rib of Beef au Jus (see page 34), a hearty Broiled Steak (see page 26), or a savory stew such as Basic Boeuf en Daube (see page 29). This chapter also presents recipes for lighter dishes such as Thai Beef Salad (see page 31), Singapore Satay (see page 32), and Carpaccio (see page 32). Begin by reading about beef grading, aging, and the new light beef (see pages 21 and 22). There's also a special section on ground beef and "second helpings," with recipes such as Basic Roast Beef Hash (see page 34).

CUTS OF BEEF

Chuck
1. Stew
   Ground beef
2. Chuck roast
   Blade roast and steak
3. Boneless shoulder pot roast
   and steak
   Arm pot roast and steak
4. Cross-rib roast
   Short ribs

Rib
1. Standing rib roast
   Rib steak
   Rib-eye (Delmonico) roast
   and steak
2. Short ribs

Short Loin
1. Top loin steak
   Club steak
2. Top loin steak
   T-bone steak
   Filet mignon
   (tenderloin)
3. Top loin steak
   Porterhouse steak
   Filet mignon

Sirloin
1. Pinbone sirloin steak
   Boneless sirloin steak
2. Flatbone sirloin steak
3. Wedgebone sirloin steak
4. Tip steak
   Tip roast
   Cube steak
   Kebabs

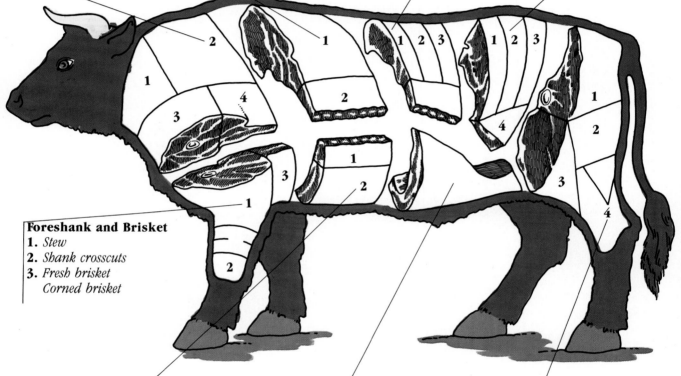

Foreshank and Brisket
1. Stew
2. Shank crosscuts
3. Fresh brisket
   Corned brisket

Short Plate
1. Short ribs
   Stew
2. Stew
   Skirt steak rolls
   Ground beef

Flank
Flank steak
Flank steak rolls
Ground beef

Round
1. Boneless rump roast
2. Round steak
   Top round steak
   Bottom round
   steak and roast
   Eye of round
   Cube steak
3. Tip roast
   Tip steak
   Cube steak
   Kebabs
4. Heel-of-round roast
   Ground beef

There are eight primal or wholesale cuts on a side of beef.

Short Loin, Sirloin, and Rib

The short loin, sirloin, and rib primal cuts contain the tenderest meat and are usually the most costly. From these areas come the expensive and highly desirable steaks and roasts that are cooked by dry heat: rib roast and rib steaks; club steaks; and T-bone, porterhouse, filet mignon, and sirloin steaks.

There is also a portion of the blade chuck roast that is actually an extension of the tender rib-eye muscle, and it, too, can be cooked quickly as a steak. The top round is also sold as a roast or a steak for dry-heat cooking, but it is not tender enough for all tastes, and many people prefer to braise this cut.

Less Tender Cuts

The lower-priced, less tender meats come from the chuck cut of the front shoulder and breast as well as from all the primal cuts on the lower half of the steer. The pot roast cuts include the chuck, blade roast, shoulder, arm, cross-rib roast, brisket, flank, and nearly all parts of the round, ranging from the relatively tender top round to the very tough eye of round (with the bottom round midway between them in tenderness). Stewing cuts include the entire chuck cut, the top of the foreshank, the short plate, and, again, most of the round. The favored cut for stir-frying is the flank steak, followed by the top round. The most popular cut for well-marinated *fajitas* (Tex-Mex marinated and barbecued steak) is skirt steak, but the flank or brisket also serves well.

Ready-made beef kebabs are usually cut from the round, but the long, thin kebabs favored in Thai cookery are sliced from flank steak. In areas where Asian cooking is popular, the price of flank steak has risen until it equals that of porterhouse—but at least there's virtually no waste.

TODAY'S BEEF

At fashionable restaurants diners have rebelled against tiny plates of "art" and are demanding more substantial, satisfying dinners. As one of the most satisfying foods available, beef is experiencing a resurgence of popularity. On both coasts, old-fashioned steak houses have returned to favor—and at home, cooks, seeking balance and variety in their main dishes, now include meat in their diets several times a week. Retailers are responding to increased demand with improvements both in the kinds of beef available and in the way it is packaged for the consumer.

In recent years health-conscious consumers have grown concerned about the calories and cholesterol in red meat, and many consider beef a particular risk. In response the meat industry has turned to leaner breeds and less fattening feeds. The tender but caloric Prime grade is now a rarity; today you'll find the leaner but no less flavorful Choice grade predominating in most meat markets and nearly all supermarkets.

Ounce for ounce, even Prime beef has fewer calories than salmon and less cholesterol than a chicken drumstick with skin. The calorie content of Choice beef is lower than that of white-meat chicken with skin, and its cholesterol is equal to skinned chicken breast. Beef graded USDA Select, used for house brands in some supermarket chains, is even leaner.

In many regions even healthier alternatives are becoming available. As naturally lean strains of beef cattle (such as Italy's *Chianina* and France's white Charolais) are imported to U.S. rangelands for breeding, the consumer increasingly encounters specifically identified light (or lite) beef. To be labeled light, beef must legally contain at least 25 percent less fat than typical beef—and the fattest typical beef, Prime grade, contains less than 11 percent fat. Several brands of light beef are calorically equivalent to skinned white-meat chicken and turkey.

And in many supermarket meat cases, "natural beef," raised to maturity without growth hormones, can be found alongside more conventionally raised beef. Natural beef, too, is consistently leaner than the beef of yore, with just half the fat of unskinned chicken breast and far fewer calories for the weight-conscious diner.

WHAT MAKES BEEF CHOICE

The choiceness (how tender, juicy, and flavorful the meat is) of any piece of meat depends on where it comes from on the animal and the quality or *grade* of an individual meat carcass.

The choicest cuts of meat come from the parts of the animal that do the least work. Just as in humans, the hard-working lower leg of an animal develops a strong, tough muscle, full of sinewy fibers and connective tissues. Meanwhile, the well-protected and rarely exercised small muscle in the middle of the back (the filet mignon) remains tender. Tougher cuts are just as tasty and nutritious as tender ones, if they're cooked using a method that tenderizes them.

Aging The aging of a piece of beef also affects its tenderness and flavor. During aging, beef is hung in large primal or wholesale cuts or in smaller subprimal cuts (such as the entire rib roast) at a cool temperature and allowed to develop its full flavor. Virtually all beef is aged to some extent before it reaches the retail market, but the length of aging varies and may considerably affect the local retail price.

Since meat shrinks during aging (and since a coating of harmless mold develops on the outer portion of the meat that must be trimmed away before the meat is sold), well-aged meat is more expensive than briefly aged cuts. Prime beef sold in specialty meat markets (especially the rib and short loin wholesale cuts) is usually aged longer than the lower grades sold in supermarkets.

Marbling The degree of marbling in a cut of meat also affects its tenderness. Marbling refers to the small, paper-thin veins of fat that crisscross a piece of meat. Hard-working muscles (such as those of the flank and shin) have very little marbling, whereas tender cuts, such as the rib and the loin, are finely marbled all over. Marbling is an important factor in determining the grade of beef.

Grading All meat sold in the United States is checked by government inspectors for wholesomeness. The United States Department of Agriculture (USDA) also inspects most meat to determine its quality, or grade. Meat is graded according to its tenderness, juiciness, and flavor. The top grades in beef are USDA Prime, Choice, and Select.

Prime The highest grade of meat, containing the greatest degree of marbling, is Prime. Prime beef is produced in very limited quantities and is generally sold at premium prices to finer restaurants and specialty meat markets. Prime cuts, because they are already expensive, also tend to be aged the longest.

Choice This is the grade generally sold at retail stores. Choice meat is preferred by consumers because it contains sufficient marbling for taste and tenderness, but is less costly and less fattening than the higher grade Prime beef.

Select A lower-priced grade of meat with less marbling than USDA Choice, Select beef is as nutritious as the higher grades of beef, but less juicy and flavorful. Some supermarket chains sell Select meat under their own quality designation rather than a USDA grade name. Select-grade cuts are also used commercially in many canned meat items.

LABELING

Many retail stores recently have adopted the National Livestock and Meat Board's recommendations for standardizing meat labels. However, the names of retail cuts still can vary sharply from region to region and store to store. For instance, London broil may be a flank steak in one market, a thick-cut top round steak in another.

On the new form of label, the primal or wholesale cut (chuck, rib, and so on) is listed along with the kind of meat (beef, pork, and so on) and the retail cut name. This information gives the consumer all the data required to determine what method to use to cook a particular piece of meat.

COOKING METHODS

Since the tenderness of beef varies with the part of the animal a cut comes from, the cut you buy should determine your cooking method.

Tender cuts of meat are usually cooked by dry heat: roasting, broiling, panfrying, grilling, and barbecuing. These cooking methods enhance flavor but tend to toughen meat fibers.

When roasting meat, it is important to use a meat thermometer to check whether the roast is done. An instant-read meat thermometer is generally more accurate than those that remain in the meat throughout cooking. Insert it at least 2 inches into the meat in the thickest part (not into fat, bone, or stuffing) and leave it about 10 seconds.

When panfrying or sautéing meat, a hot pan is essential to keep food from sticking and absorbing too much fat. A heavy skillet is required to heat the fat evenly and prevent scorching. The pan should be large enough to hold all the food easily, with enough space between pieces so that they can be turned easily.

When barbecuing meat, allow the coals to burn until they are covered with white ash before oiling the rack lightly and adding the food. Most meat should be grilled 4 to 6 inches above the coals, or the same distance below the broiler's heat source. Use tongs to turn broiling or grilling meats in order to avoid puncturing them and losing their juices.

Less tender cuts require moist-heat cooking—stewing, braising, or poaching—in which meat is cooked in a liquid that helps to tenderize it and break down tough connective tissue. The gelatin that dissolves out of connective fibers helps to thicken and enrich the cooking liquid.

Marinating, pounding, cubing, and grinding can also be used to tenderize tough cuts. Commercial tenderizers such as papain, which partially "predigest" raw meat, are also employed by many cooks, although these may affect both flavor and texture.

Certain relatively tough cuts of beef are also used for stir-frying (usually following a brief marinating period) and, after more prolonged marinating, for barbecue. In both cases, the meat seems tender because it is sliced very thinly across the grain (before cooking in a stir-fry and after cooking in a barbecue).

TRIMMING

Kebabs and stewing beef cut at the market often include a thick line of fat and sinew running through their centers. If calories and cholesterol are important considerations, more scrupulous trimming can be assured by purchasing a whole roast (such as a top round roast or chuck roast) and taking a few minutes to chop and trim it at home. Cutting meat is easy to do, and is an economical way of ensuring that each chunk of beef you use is lean.

ROAST BEEF

The most sought-after cut of beef for roasting is the prime rib. Prime rib has come to refer to a cut of beef (the long ribs just behind the shoulder of the steer) rather than a grade; often such roasts aren't genuine USDA Prime beef, but the leaner, less marbled Choice grade.

Several less costly cuts can do double-duty as pot roasts and oven roasts. Sirloin tip, rump roast, and top round (the latter being the cut of most delicatessen roast beef) can be roasted creditably, although they contain more gristle and are less finely marbled (and thus less tender) than the rib. A thick, tough steak (such as chuck) can be marinated overnight in an acidic liquid and roasted slowly for about one hour, as well.

At the opposite extreme are the tenderloin (the cut used for that continental cuisine war-horse, beef Wellington) and Chateaubriand cuts. Their flavor is rather bland, however, and calls for the help of a rich sauce and sapid garnishes.

Whichever cut you prefer, choose an evenly marbled roast that is closer in color to maroon than orange; the darker meat is likely to have been aged longer or to have come from an older animal; in either case it will have a richer flavor. (For special occasions you may want to contact a butcher shop, rather than relying on the supermarket meat case, and ask that the roast receive extra aging; the difference in flavor can be remarkable.)

For flavor and tenderness (as well as to make the Yorkshire Pudding on page 34 or Franconia Root Vegetables on page 35), the roast should have a layer of fat at least ½ inch thick on top, whether the fat is its own or a sheet of suet tied on by the butcher.

Count on at least ½ pound of boneless beef per person, or 1 pound of bone-in roast, if you want any second helpings and some leftovers.

Do not salt beef before roasting; salt draws out the juices, making the meat dry and tough. (However, the tougher roasting cuts can be rubbed with vinegar, wine, or oil to help tenderize them, and any roast can be rubbed with a generous coating of fresh or dried herbs or black pepper.)

Roasting slowly just to rare will maximize the tenderness of most roasting cuts. The exceptions are tenderloin and Chateaubriand, which are cooked quickly, like steaks. They should be browned in a heavy skillet filmed with oil, then roasted at 450° F for just 10 minutes per pound to be eaten rare.

Rolled roasts should be placed on a rack; a standing rib roast can rest on the ends of its bones directly in the roasting pan. Bone-in roasts will cook about 5 minutes per pound more quickly than rolled roasts. Roasts should be allowed to stand for a few minutes after they're removed from the oven; this allows the juices to retract into the meat before the meat is sliced.

While roasts stand they will continue to cook (checking with an instant-read meat thermometer after 5 minutes will prove this), so keep this in mind when determining the doneness of a roast. Lovers of rare beef may remove roasts from the oven when the meat thermometer reads 120° to 130° F, rather than 140° F, to allow for this extra cooking.

Drippings rendered by roast beef can be strained and stored in the freezer for up to 6 months; they are indispensable in making gravy, Franconia Root Vegetables (see page 35) to serve with roast lamb (since lamb fat isn't a desirable medium), and the many forms of suet pudding (such as mincemeat and persimmon pudding) served during the Christmas season. You can use beef drippings to make Basic Roast Beef Hash (see page 34).

HOT-WEATHER ROAST BEEF

This odd but amazingly effective method of roasting seems to have originated on the Louisiana "Cajun Prairie," where for much of the year there's good reason to minimize the time that the oven is hot. Most home ovens are sufficiently well-insulated that, after the gas is turned off, their heat diminishes gradually over several hours; thus, in this recipe, roasting begins at a searing temperature, and then, when the oven is turned off, the beef cooks very slowly to a perfect medium-rare.

> *1 medium-sized boneless beef roast (such as rolled prime rib, sirloin tip, or top round), 3½ to 5 pounds Cracked black pepper (optional)*
>
> *4 to 6 cloves garlic, peeled and slivered (optional)*

1. One or two hours before starting to cook, remove beef from refrigerator to allow it to come to room temperature. If desired, coat beef with cracked black pepper and insert garlic slivers between the fat layer and the meat. Place roast on a rack, fat side up.

2. Preheat oven to 500° F. Place roast in center of oven and sear for 15 minutes. (For a roast over 5 pounds, sear 20 to 30 minutes; the larger the roast, the longer it should be seared.) Turn off oven and let roast remain there, undisturbed, for two hours. Do not open oven door. When roast is done, remove from oven and let stand for 10 minutes before slicing. The roast will be warm, not hot.

Serves 6 to 10.

Sesame-sprinkled Korean Bulgoki makes a welcome change from winter stews. Hearty, economical beef short ribs soak up an Asian-style marinade before being baked or grilled.

KOREAN BULGOKI
Marinated baked short ribs

Salty, spicy, grilled Korean short ribs have attained worldwide popularity in recent years. Since grilling over wood is difficult in winter, just when the heartiness of this dish seems most welcome, this version is oven-baked.

¾ cup soy sauce

1 cup rice wine (such as sake or Shaoxing) or dry sherry

1 teaspoon dark sesame oil

2 or 3 small jalapeño or serrano chiles to taste, stems trimmed, sliced thinly

1 teaspoon freshly ground black pepper

5 green onions (including crisp greens), trimmed and sliced thinly

1 tablespoon minced garlic
Thumb-sized piece of fresh ginger, peeled and finely minced

4 pounds meaty, thickly cut short ribs

¼ cup sesame seed

2 tablespoons minced fresh coriander

1. Mix soy sauce, wine, oil, chiles, black pepper, green onions, garlic, and ginger in large roasting pan. Add ribs, turning them several times in liquid. Cover pan with foil or plastic wrap and let ribs marinate 3 hours at room temperature or overnight in refrigerator, turning several times to coat meat thoroughly.

2. *To bake:* Preheat oven to 375° F. Remove and reserve ribs and pour marinade into bowl. Return ribs to pan, bone side down, leaving some space between them. Bake until tender (40 minutes to 1 hour, depending on thickness), brushing with reserved marinade every 10 minutes. *To barbecue:* Scatter a layer of wood chips (such as hickory or, if available, kiawe wood) on top of white, ashy charcoal. Place rack high above coals and barbecue ribs slowly, turning and basting frequently. Add more wood chips as needed, until ribs cook through (about 40 minutes).

3. At the final basting, sprinkle ribs with sesame seeds. When done remove from grill or oven, sprinkle with coriander, and serve immediately.

Serves 3 or 4.

24

STEAKS

Which steak to buy? The cut that makes the "best" steak varies sharply from region to region as a result of differences stemming from the source of the meat, including the breed, growing conditions, and aging done at the meat packinghouse. Only by sampling the different cuts will you discover your favorite. Most people prefer a cut from the top half of the steer. Generally New Yorkers feast on sirloin, San Franciscans savor porterhouse, and Texans relish the T-bone.

Popular Cuts

In all regions the costly filet mignon (the most cosseted portion of the tenderloin) is the tenderest steak of all. However, it's far from the most flavorful. Filet mignon is best accompanied by a powerful sauce (such as Madeira Sauce or béarnaise; see pages 13 and 14). Tournedos and the thicker Chateaubriand are also cuts from the tenderloin and call for a deluxe treatment to boost their flavor.

The tasty but tough long-muscled cuts from the bottom half of the steer (flank, brisket, skirt steak, cube steak, round steak, and London broil, a thick cut of round), along with chuck from the hard-working front shoulder, are usually braised or stewed, but they can also be regarded as steaks—especially when they're tenderized by an acidic marinade (such as Fajitas Marinade on page 8), barbecued over charcoal and wood, and then sliced very thin (if from a long, thick cut). They can also be marinated overnight and then roasted slowly at 300° F for about 25 minutes per pound.

Tender steaks up to about 1½ inches thick may be panfried or broiled; very thick steaks (such as London broil, Chateaubriand, and "butterball") are best broiled and then sliced. Before cooking trim excess (or all) fat from outer edge of steak and trim off (or slash small cuts in) the gristly connective tissues around the steak, which when left intact make the meat curl up into a half-shell and cook unevenly. Do not salt steak before cooking, since salt draws out the juices and dries out the tender meat.

Serving Size

Count on 6 to 7 ounces of boneless, untrimmed steak per person for light eaters, 8 to 9 ounces for moderate eaters, at least 1 pound for serious eaters, and 4 to 5 ounces for dieters or when filet mignon in a rich sauce is the steak of the evening. The bones in T-bone, porterhouse, and rib-eye steaks weigh approximately 1 ounce for each ½ inch of the steak's thickness, so calculate accordingly.

Judging Doneness

Very thin steaks (under ½ inch thick) will cook to rare over high heat in as little as 10 seconds per side. Generally, though, for each ½ inch of thickness, about 2 minutes of rapid cooking per side will produce a perfectly rare steak.

When droplets of red liquid form on the top side of a steak that has been turned, and when the steak just begins to bounce back when pressed with a fingertip, it is medium rare. (For well-done steak, just keep cooking it longer.)

Another, more intuitive way to judge doneness is to listen carefully to the sizzle: Uncooked steak sizzles loudly; as soon as the sizzle quiets down (indicating that the meat has rendered most of its juices), it has probably cooked to medium rare. The surest way to determine the state of the steak is to cut a small slit halfway through it when you suspect it's nearly done to your taste.

Light Beefsteaks

Whereas normally marbled beefsteaks are cooked very rapidly over (or under) high heat, light beef (because it has very little marbling) should be cooked only over medium heat and never to more than medium rare. (If well-done meat is preferred, it is better to braise this cut in a liquid.) Light steaks benefit from a day in an oil-containing marinade, which may restore a few of the calories of normal beef, but none of the cholesterol.

PAN-FRIED STEAK

Like broiled steak, pan-fried steak is cooked rapidly and briefly (for rare or medium rare), but here, some fat is necessary. The tastiest medium for panfrying steak is the steak's own fat.

Fat trimmed from side of steak or 2 tablespoons cooking oil
1½ pounds tender beefsteak, trimmed of fat
Salt and freshly ground pepper, to taste

1. Cut trimmed fat into 1-inch pieces, place in a heavy skillet large enough to hold steak, and cook over moderate heat until enough fat has been rendered (about 2 tablespoons) to film skillet. Remove the solid chunks of fat and discard. Skillet may also be filmed with low-cholesterol cooking oil (such as sunflower, corn, or peanut oil).

2. Heat fat until it begins to smoke (this will seal the meat, making additional fat unnecessary) and place steak in pan. Sear steak on first side for 2 to 3 minutes for a steak up to 1 inch thick; season seared side with salt and pepper, if desired, then turn and continue cooking at high heat until done as desired (see Judging Doneness, at left).

3. For a very thick steak (over 1 inch), a bacon press (or a brick or heavy can placed in a pie pan and laid on top of the steak) will keep the steak flat and the temperature hot. Alternately, turn steak again and cook for another 2 to 3 minutes until finished.

4. Remove steak from pan as soon as cooked to desired doneness. Serve with a deglazed pan sauce (see pages 10 and 12) made from the caramelized juices of the cooked steak.

Serves 3 or 4.

SHORT-ORDER STEAK AND ONIONS

Steak and onions is one of the most popular of the quick and easy pan-fried steak dishes. This hearty main dish is especially welcome on a cold winter day.

> *Fat trimmed from steak or 2 tablespoons cooking oil*
> 1 *pound tender steak, trimmed of fat*
> 1 *clove garlic, halved*
> *Generous sprinkling of freshly ground pepper, to taste*
> 1 *large sweet onion (such as red or Walla Walla), sliced*
> *Salt, to taste*
> ¼ *cup water or beef stock*

1. Melt fat trimmed from beef in a very large (preferably 12 inches), heavy skillet. Pick out and discard solids. Alternatively, film skillet with cooking oil.

2. Rub steak with a cut clove of garlic, highly season with black pepper, and let stand to come to room temperature and absorb seasonings. Meanwhile, add onion to skillet and sauté over low heat until well wilted, stirring frequently. Push onion to far side of skillet, off direct heat, and place steak in pan. Increase heat to high and cook steak on both sides as directed in Pan-Fried Steak recipe (see page 25), salting browned side. (Onion slices will continue to cook slightly and will brown a little, releasing their sugar as caramel, which will color and flavor the gravy.)

3. Remove steak and onions to a warm plate and deglaze pan with the ¼ cup water or beef stock. Pour liquid over steak and serve.

Serves 2 or 3.

BROILED STEAK

Broiled steak is the lowest-calorie version of a steak dinner.

> 1½ *pounds tender steak (such as rib, T-bone, porterhouse, or sirloin)*
> 1 *clove garlic, halved (optional)*
> *Dried herbs of choice (optional)*
> *Salt and freshly ground pepper, to taste*
> *Composed Butter (see page 9), Quick Béarnaise Sauce (see page 14), Madeira Sauce (see page 13), or other topping of choice (optional)*

1. Preheat broiler (even in a gas oven) for about 10 minutes before starting steak.

2. If desired rub steak with garlic or herbs. Place steak on a lightly greased rack over broiling pan; do not salt before starting to cook. Set steak 4 inches under heat source. For steaks up to 1 inch thick, broil about 5 minutes on first side; season top side with salt and pepper, then turn and broil about 3 minutes on second side for medium-rare. For steaks 1½ inches thick, broil 7 minutes, season and turn, and broil 5 minutes more. To serve, top with a Composed Butter or a sauce, if desired.

Serves 3 amply, 6 lightly.

BARBECUES

Tender cuts of beef may be barbecued simply, but marinating and then barbecuing allows the cook to experiment with economical but flavorful cuts of beef, which stand up well to a strong marinade.

For long, thick steaks (skirt steak, flank, round), marinate meat in Fajitas Marinade (see page 8) and barbecue at least 4 inches from well-burned, white, ashy charcoal (preferably mesquite charcoal or other charcoal topped with a layer of mesquite chips). Slice thin and serve with guacamole, warmed flour tortillas, and Salsa Cruda (see opposite page).

For thinner steaks marinate as for *fajitas* (see page 8) or Korean Bulgoki (see page 24) and cook very quickly, close to heat source, over wood or charcoal with a topping of wood chips.

The recipe for Santa Maria BBQ Beef that follows is an excellent barbecue treatment for a tender cut of beef.

SANTA MARIA BBQ BEEF

The Santa Maria Valley of California's central coast has a tradition of outdoor barbecues going back to the early Spanish rancheros. Valley cooks serve simply seasoned slabs of beef cooked over oak fires, accompanied by fresh tomato Salsa Cruda (a Mexican-style chunky hot sauce) and barbecued beans. Chef and grilling expert Jay Harlow makes this version with a boneless sirloin tip roast in place of the traditional thick sirloin steaks. Serve with homemade frijoles or canned ranch-style pinto beans.

> 1 *large sirloin steak or small roast (about 3 lb)*
> 1 *teaspoon each salt and garlic salt*
> ½ *teaspoon freshly ground pepper*

Salsa Cruda

1 pound fresh ripe tomatoes, seeded and cut into ¼-inch dice (about 2 cups)

⅓ cup finely minced sweet red onion or white of green onion

4 fresh jalapeño or serrano chiles, trimmed, seeded, and minced finely

¼ cup minced cilantro

1 small clove garlic, peeled and minced finely
Juice of 1 lime
Salt and freshly ground pepper, to taste

1. Trim meat of excess fat and tough membranes. If using a sirloin tip roast, remove strings and butterfly (cut across grain almost through, then open like a book). Overall thickness should be 2½ to 3 inches. Combine salt, garlic salt, and pepper and rub generously all over meat. Set aside to season for up to 2 hours at room temperature, or longer in the refrigerator.

2. Two to three hours before serving time, build a fire of oak or other hardwood and allow to burn down to red-hot coals. Or, build a charcoal fire 1½ hours before serving time and, when most of the charcoal is burning, add small chunks of oak. Sear meat over hottest part of fire, then move it to a slightly cooler part and cook to taste. Total cooking time depends on size of meat, heat of fire, and type of grill (open or covered); thinner cuts over a hot fire may be medium-rare in 8 to 10 minutes per side, but with a slower fire or a larger piece of meat, allow 15 to 20 minutes per side.

3. Carve thin slices of meat on a cutting board with grooves to catch juices. Transfer slices to a warm platter and moisten with juices. Garnish with salsa; serve immediately.

Serves 6.

Salsa Cruda Combine all ingredients in a small bowl. Taste and correct seasoning if needed. Let stand at room temperature about 30 minutes. Serve the same day, or tightly cover and refrigerate for up to 2 days.

Makes about 3 cups.

Santa Maria BBQ Beef is a tempting favorite from the central California coast, where Mexican flavors liven up traditional American cookery.

Basic Boeuf en Daube, a hearty French beef stew, can be varied from dinner to dinner: add sautéed mushrooms, olives, or any tempting fresh vegetable, or substitute orange juice and rum for the wine and Cognac.

BRAISES AND STEWS

Few foods are as comforting, economical, and convenient as a rich pot roast or stew—a balanced, flavorful meal for a crowd emerging from a single casserole. At today's rushed tempo such a dish cooked over the weekend (or started alongside a quicker dinner and allowed to simmer until bedtime) is a wonderful treat later in the week.

Nearly all braises and stews benefit in flavor by mellowing overnight or longer in the refrigerator. Chilling also simplifies the degreasing process.

The principles of cooking braised beef (cooked in a single, large piece and sliced before serving) and stewed beef (cut in chunks before cooking) are similar, and recipes are virtually interchangeable.

In either case the meat used is from a lean, flavorful, but relatively tough cut, such as round, chuck, or brisket. Vegetables may be included, not only to provide that convenient one-pot meal, but also to add their flavor to the sauce.

Both braises and stews are cooked long and slowly (whether on the stovetop or in the oven) in a large, heavy, covered pot, often with some relatively acidic ingredient (wine, brandy, beer, vinegar, tomatoes, citrus juice) in the liquid to give the beef tenderness.

Beef cooked in a single large piece absorbs less liquid. Thus, many braised-beef recipes call for marinating before cooking, and many pot roasts call for merely 1 or 2 cups of water for each 3 pounds of meat. Beef pot roasts normally require somewhat longer cooking (about 3 hours) than beef stews (2 to 2½ hours) until the meat is tender.

Degreasing and Thickening Pot Roast and Stew Liquid

Excess fat should be trimmed from meat before cooking. Nonetheless, braising or stewing liquid should be degreased before serving.

A simple way to degrease liquid is to chill it overnight. This not only deepens the flavor of a braise or stew, it also congeals fat into a thin, solid sheet on top of the liquid that can be lifted off easily and discarded before the dish is reheated.

If the dish is to be served the same day as it's cooked, it can be degreased moderately well by tilting the pan and spooning off the fat layer from the top of the liquid. For thorough degreasing pour off liquid into a wide-mouthed bowl, place bowl in the freezer for 20 to 30 minutes, and carefully remove partially congealed fat from top. If desired thicken liquid (as described below); then return it to the original pot and warm all ingredients together.

To thicken the cooking liquid into a gravy, refrigerate it separately. After degreasing, boil it over high heat, stirring, until it is reduced by about half, or bring it to a simmer and stir in Beurre Manié (see page 15).

The recipes that follow are classics within their own ethnic areas, but feel free to look upon braises and stews as unfinished canvases that you may complete with your own designs by varying the liquid, the vegetables, and the herbs and spices.

GREEK STIFADO WITH FETA CHEESE CRUST

This thick, slightly exotic stew is subtly spiced and deliciously enriched with tangy feta (sheep's milk) cheese and nuts. Serve with rice.

- 2 tablespoons olive oil
- 3 tablespoons butter
- 3 pounds lean beef stew meat (such as round), cut into ½- by 1-inch cubes
- 1 medium onion, minced
- ½ cup tomato paste
- ½ cup dry white wine
- ¼ cup red wine vinegar
- ¾ cup water
- 2 tablespoons minced garlic
- 1 bay leaf
- 1 teaspoon dried oregano leaves, crumbled
- 1 teaspoon ground cinnamon
- ½ teaspoon ground cumin
- ½ teaspoon sugar
- ¼ teaspoon cayenne pepper, or to taste
  Salt and freshly ground black pepper, to taste
- 16 small white boiling onions, peeled
- ½ cup pine nuts (or pecan or walnut halves)
- ½ pound feta cheese, crumbled or grated
- ½ cup minced parsley
  Hot-pepper sauce (such as Tabasco), optional

1. In a large, heavy skillet, heat oil and butter over moderate heat. Raise heat to high and brown meat, one third at a time, removing meat to a large, heavy casserole (preferably with an enamel or porcelain coating) as it browns. Add minced onion to skillet, sauté just until wilted, and spoon into casserole.

2. Add tomato paste, wine, vinegar, the water, garlic, bay leaf, oregano, cinnamon, cumin, and sugar to the casserole. Stir well and add cayenne, salt, and pepper, to taste. Bring just to a boil, cover tightly, lower heat, and simmer 1 hour. Add white boiling onions and simmer, covered, until meat is very tender (about 1 hour longer).

3. Degrease stew if necessary and carefully correct seasonings; stir in nuts. Sprinkle feta cheese over stew, pushing it gently into top of liquid with a wooden spoon. Cover and simmer to melt cheese (about 5 minutes longer). Sprinkle parsley on top and serve stew in deep soup bowls, making sure that everyone gets some nuts and cheese, but leaving some room in each bowl for rice to be added. Have hot-pepper sauce on hand, to be added as desired.

Serves 4 to 6.

BASIC BOEUF EN DAUBE
French wine-stewed beef

France's wine-based beef stews are popular nearly everywhere beef is eaten. Many variations spring from this basic version: Add blanched vegetables of your choice just before serving; vary the cooking liquid; or sprinkle with fresh garden herbs.

- ¼ pound sliced bacon
- 3 pounds beef round or chuck, cut in stewing pieces
- 2 large onions, minced
  Bacon fat or cooking oil, if needed
- 2 tablespoons Cognac, Armagnac, or brandy
- 2 pounds carrots, peeled, trimmed, and cut in thick, diagonal slices
- 4 cloves garlic, crushed and peeled
- 3 veal bones or 1 calf's foot (optional)
  Bouquet garni (3 sprigs parsley, 1 bay leaf, and 1 sprig thyme or ¼ teaspoon dried thyme leaves, wrapped and tied in a piece of cheesecloth)
- 3 cups dry red wine
- 1 cup Brown Meat Stock (see page 16) or canned beef bouillon, preferably low-salt
  Salt and freshly ground pepper, to taste
- 6 to 8 small, scrubbed or peeled boiling potatoes or 6 slices French bread and 1 clove garlic, halved
- 4 tablespoons Beurre Manié (optional)

1. Cut bacon slices horizontally into strips about ¼ inch by 1 inch. In a very large, heavy skillet, sauté bacon until lightly browned but not crisp. Remove bacon with a slotted spoon and reserve.

2. Reheat bacon fat and over high heat brown about one third of the beef. (If beef is crowded it will release its juices and boil rather than brown.) Remove with a slotted spoon to a large, heavy casserole or Dutch oven and brown remaining beef in two more shifts, transferring it to casserole when it is done. Over moderate heat sauté onion until wilted (adding additional fat or oil to skillet if necessary), then transfer it to the casserole.

3. In a small saucepan over low heat, warm Cognac; have a long match ready. Warm casserole over low heat. Pour Cognac into casserole, warm for a minute, and very carefully (making sure nothing flammable is near stove) set Cognac aflame. When flame dies down add reserved bacon, carrots, garlic, veal bones or calf's foot (if used), bouquet garni, wine, and stock. Stir, carefully season to taste with salt and pepper, cover, and simmer very slowly (or slowly bake in oven at 250° F) until beef is very tender (2 to 2½ hours).

4. Meanwhile, boil potatoes (if used) in salted water to cover until tender (25 to 30 minutes).

5. When stew is done, remove and discard veal bones and bouquet garni. Degrease stew (see page 28). If desired, liquid may be poured off into a saucepan and boiled over a high heat until reduced by half, or it may be thickened and enriched with Beurre Manié (see page 15). Return liquid to stew along with potatoes, if used. Correct seasonings and reheat together gently for a few minutes.

6. Toast French bread (if used) and rub while hot with cut sides of garlic. Float toast on top of stewing liquid.

7. Serve stew hot in broad soup bowls with a piece of garlic toast (if used) topping each bowl.

Serves 6.

OXTAILS JARDINIERE

Oxtails require patience, and they're less economical than they seem, considering the portions yielded—but they're also, arguably, the tastiest cut of the steer. This American version of a French classic is best cooked on a lazy afternoon because it takes some time—but it's worth the effort.

>   4   tablespoons flour
>   1   teaspoon salt
>   ½   teaspoon freshly ground pepper
>   ¼   teaspoon dried thyme or basil leaves, crumbled, or ground dried thyme
>   ⅛   teaspoon ground dried savory
>   1   tablespoon paprika
>   3 to 4 pounds oxtails, cut in serving-size pieces
>   2   tablespoons cooking oil, plus more as needed
>   1   tablespoon unsalted butter
>   1   large onion, peeled and chopped (about 1¼ cups)
>   1   tablespoon minced garlic
>   1   jigger (about 2 tablespoons) brandy (optional)
>   1   bay leaf
>   ½   cup dry white wine
>   1   cup water, plus more as needed
>   1   cup tomato juice
>   1   tablespoon Worcestershire sauce
>   12 small white boiling onions, peeled
>   6   carrots, scraped, cut in 2-inch diagonal slices
>   12 small boiling (new) potatoes, scrubbed or pared, or 6 large boiling potatoes, pared and quartered
>   1¼ cups fresh shelled peas or 1 package (10 oz) frozen peas
>   ¼   cup minced parsley

1. Mix flour, salt, pepper, thyme or basil, savory, and paprika in a paper bag. Add oxtails to mixture and shake to coat lightly, shaking off any excess. Heat oil and butter in a large, heavy casserole or Dutch oven (one with an enamel or porcelain coating is best). Over moderately high heat brown oxtails on all sides in two or three shifts, so that they are not crowded in the pot; with a slotted spoon remove them when browned and reserve.

2. Add onion to fat remaining in casserole (adding more oil, if necessary) and sauté over moderate heat until wilted. Add garlic and stir well for a minute or so. Add brandy, if used, and stir well, scraping bottom of pan; then stir in bay leaf, wine, the water, tomato juice, and Worcestershire sauce. Return reserved oxtails to casserole, cover tightly, and simmer until oxtails are somewhat tender (2 to 2½ hours). Check occasionally and add more water if needed to keep stew from sticking.

3. Add boiling onions, carrots, and potatoes and simmer until meat separates easily from bone and vegetables are tender, about 1 hour longer. (Stew may be prepared to this point, then refrigerated until needed, degreased, and gently reheated to a simmer.)

4. About 20 minutes before stew is done, drop peas into boiling, salted water to cover and boil just until barely tender (about 2 minutes for frozen peas, 5 minutes for fresh). Drain and reserve.

5. Remove oxtails and vegetables from sauce with a slotted spoon and keep warm in a heated serving dish. Degrease sauce (if not already done) and pour over oxtails. Scatter peas on top and sprinkle with parsley. Serve in deep bowls.

Serves 3 or 4.

CARBONNADE FLAMANDE

An oniony Belgian beef stew Carbonnade Flamande uses beer, rather than wine, to tenderize the beef. Serve in deep plates over or next to noodles.

>   3   pounds boneless beef pot roast (round, brisket, chuck)
>   2   tablespoons unsalted butter
>   1   tablespoon oil
>   6   medium onions, chopped coarsely
>   ½   teaspoon flour
>   2   teaspoons sugar
>   ¼   cup brandy or Cognac
>   ¼   cup Brown Meat Stock (see page 16) or canned consommé
>   1   cup light beer
>   1   bay leaf
>   Salt and freshly ground black pepper, to taste
>   6   slices fresh French bread Dijon-style mustard

1. Trim beef of excess fat and slice meat into rectangles about ½ by 2 by 3 inches.

2. In a large, heavy casserole (at least 2½ quarts) over moderate heat, warm butter and oil. Increase heat and brown beef one third at a time, removing and reserving meat as it browns.

3. Add onions to casserole, lower heat to medium, and sauté, stirring, until onions are slightly browned. (Browning releases the sugar in the onions.) Stir in flour and sugar and cook together over medium-low heat until well browned. Stir in brandy and heat briefly, scraping browned bits from bottom of pan.

4. Gradually stir in stock; add beer. Return beef to casserole; bring liquid to a boil. Add bay leaf, season to taste with salt and pepper, and cover tightly. Lower heat; simmer until meat is tender (about 2½ hours). Degrease liquid, if needed.

5. Spread each slice of French bread with a thin coat of mustard and float slices on top of stew. Simmer, uncovered, until bread dissolves into a coating on top of stew.

Serves 4 to 6.

LIGHT BEEF RECIPES

Beef need not always be a hearty main-course dish. It can serve just as well as an appetizer or as the entrée in a light supper.

THAI BEEF SALAD

This appetizer is found on the menu of almost every Thai restaurant in the United States. Sometimes the beef is stir-fried in a minimum of oil, and the salad is served while the beef is still warm. (See Carpaccio, page 32, for techniques for slicing beef thinly.) Sometimes it's served cold, using thinly sliced rare roast beef.

- 2 tablespoons peeled, minced garlic
- 3 tablespoons minced fresh hot chiles (serrano or jalapeño)
- ½ teaspoon firmly packed dark brown sugar
- ¼ cup fresh lime juice
- 1 tablespoon finely chopped unsalted roasted peanuts
  Salt (optional)
- 12 medium-sized leaves of romaine or iceberg lettuce
- 1 medium red onion, diced fine
- 4 green onions, chopped
- 1 tablespoon peanut or corn oil (optional)
- 1 pound very lean steak (flank or round), trimmed of fat and gristle, very thinly sliced (⅛ by ¼ by 1 in.), or rare roast beef, sliced in thin strips
- 1 tablespoon freshly ground black pepper, or to taste
- 4 tablespoons chopped fresh coriander
  Mint leaves (optional)

1. Mix garlic, chile, brown sugar, lime juice, peanuts, and salt (if desired) and reserve.

2. Wash and dry lettuce leaves and arrange on a flat serving platter. Top with diced red and green onion.

3. If using raw beef heat a wok or large, heavy frying pan over high heat for 30 seconds. Add peanut oil and heat until fragrant. Add raw beef

and, stirring and flipping constantly, fry until browned all over. With a slotted spoon or spatula, remove beef from pan.

4. Scatter stir-fried or roasted beef over lettuce and grind over it a very liberal quantity of black pepper. Pour sauce over beef, sprinkle evenly with coriander, and garnish (if desired) with mint leaves.

Serves 4.

When it's too hot to cook, a quick, spicy Thai Beef Salad appetizer is a perfect start to a light dinner. It can even be a main course as the temperature soars.

SINGAPORE SATAY

Asian satays gain their flavor from their exotic marinades and the rapid cooking that chars the glaze. The meat, cut into small pieces, is threaded on thin bamboo skewers that have been soaked in water for several hours to prevent burning (the skewers are available in Asian groceries and souvenir shops and in some cookware stores). Thin metal skewers (or even lengths of metal wire) can be substituted.

> 1 pound tender beef (or lamb)
> 4 small red onions, chopped (about 3 cups)
> 2 large cloves garlic, chopped (about 2 tablespoons)
> 3 stalks fresh lemongrass, chopped, or 1 tablespoon fresh lemon juice
> 1 teaspoon ground cumin
> 1 teaspoon ground ginger
> 1 tablespoon ground turmeric
> ½ teaspoon freshly ground pepper
> ½ teaspoon salt
> 1½ teaspoons firmly packed brown sugar
> 3 tablespoons soy sauce (preferably Chinese thin soy)
> Peanut or corn oil, as needed

1. Cut meat into 1-inch cubes, carefully trimming away all fat and gristle. Place in a nonreactive container (stainless steel, plastic, or glass).

2. Purée remaining ingredients, except oil, in a blender or food processor and pour over meat. Marinate at least 3 hours at room temperature or overnight in refrigerator. Meanwhile, soak bamboo skewers (if used) in water for at least 3 hours.

3. Thread meat cubes on skewers, reserving any unabsorbed marinade. *To cook indoors:* Preheat broiler for 10 minutes and broil as close as possible to heat, basting with reserved marinade or with oil and turning every few minutes, until meat is well browned (about 12 minutes). *To barbecue:* Place grill close to heat source over a wood fire or a charcoal fire with wood chips scattered on top and cook rapidly, turning and basting frequently.

Serves 4 as an appetizer, 2 as an entrée.

CARPACCIO

Carpaccio, an appetizer of thinly sliced, tender raw beef, was popularized among sophisticated Americans by Harry's American Bar, Ernest Hemingway's famous hangout in Venice, Italy. Carpaccio is currently enjoying a resurgence in trendy restaurants, whose chefs (no matter how various their recipes) all claim to have re-created Harry's original. Both of the "Harry's" sauces that follow are delicious, whether authentic or not; for an especially amusing appetizer, coat half the beef on each plate with one sauce, half with the other. For a California-style variation, nap raw beef with Mexican-style Salsa Cruda (see page 27) instead.

> 1½ pounds very lean, very tender raw beef (filet, sirloin, shell steak) or beef scallops cut by the butcher
> 24 slices fresh French bread, toasted lightly (optional)

"Harry's" Creamy Sauce

> 1 cup mayonnaise (preferably homemade, with lemon juice)
> 1 tablespoon Worcestershire sauce
> ½ teaspoon dry mustard, or to taste
> ½ teaspoon Louisiana-style hot sauce (such as Tabasco), or to taste
> ⅓ cup strong beef stock (preferably homemade)
> Salt (optional)

"Harry's" Piquant Sauce

> 1 can (12 oz) flat, oil-packed anchovies, drained
> ½ teaspoon coarse-ground mustard
> 2 tablespoons drained capers
> ¼ cup peeled, minced shallots or onion
> 1 tablespoon Worcestershire sauce
> Juice of 1 medium-sized ripe lemon
> 1 cup chopped parsley leaves (no stems)
> 3 tablespoons olive oil
> 1 tablespoon red wine vinegar
> ½ teaspoon cracked (or freshly ground) black pepper
> Salt, to taste

Slice meat as thinly as possible (no more than ⅛ inch thick). Meat may be partially frozen first (to aid in slicing), or it may be sliced ¼ inch thick and then pounded with the flat side of a meat mallet (or any flat, heavy object) between two sheets of waxed paper until half as thick. Cut slices into rectangles, about 2 by 3 inches. Arrange on individual appetizer plates (on a bed of toasted French bread, if desired) and nap with sauce.

Serves 6.

"Harry's" Creamy Sauce Whisk mayonnaise and Worcestershire sauce together. Whisk in dry mustard. Add hot sauce, a little at a time, tasting and adjusting. Whisk in beef stock by tablespoonfuls until sauce is the consistency of heavy cream. Taste and, if needed, add salt.

Makes about 1½ cups.

"Harry's" Piquant Sauce Blend all ingredients in a blender or food processor until a grainy but creamy mixture forms. (This tangy sauce can also dress halved, ripe avocados or be judiciously mixed into mayonnaise for a salad dressing.)

Makes about 1¾ cups.

GROUND BEEF AND "SECOND HELPINGS"

As any supermarket shopper knows, ground beef, unlike other ground meats, comes in several grades and prices determined by the amount of fat ground with the meat. The cheapest grade, usually just called ground beef, contains 30 percent fat (as much as sausage). It's often identified as chuck, but other parts may be included in the grind.

Ground chuck can be used in dishes (such as spaghetti sauce) where the meat is browned first and the fat poured off; however, considering the loss of nearly one third of the meat's volume, its economy is moot. It can also be used in meat loaf recipes that contain a high proportion of bread crumbs (which will absorb the fat) if calories and cholesterol aren't a problem.

The middle grade (often called lean ground beef, lean ground chuck, or ground round) contains about 20 percent fat and is the grade usually used for hamburgers, meat loaf, meatballs, and more elaborate ground beef dishes. The leanest grade (usually identified as ground sirloin or extralean ground beef) contains approximately 15 percent fat. Although somewhat dry when cooked, it is the dieter's favorite for lower-calorie hamburgers.

In many recipes cooked beef can be used interchangeably with ground beef—solving the problem of what to do with the rest of that delicious roast or the last slice of that tasty braise.

Leftover roast beef, cut in thin shreds, can also be used in salads (such as Thai Beef Salad on page 31). For the old favorite—open-faced hot roast beef sandwiches—leftover beef can be placed on slices of bread on a lightly buttered baking pan, covered with Basic Brown Sauce (see page 13) or a more adventurous sauce, and heated in a 400° F oven. Sliced cooked beef can also be deviled—coated with Dijon mustard, fresh bread crumbs, and a drizzle of melted butter—and reheated under the broiler.

BEEF PIROSHKI
Russian beef and mushroom turnovers

The unusual, luscious filling of these savory Russian turnovers is especially designed to restore the moisture to cooked beef.

    4   tablespoons butter
    3   medium onions, minced
        (about 3 cups)
    ¼   pound mushrooms, wiped
        clean and chopped in fine dice
    1½ cups finely diced rare roast
        beef or ¾ pound lean
        ground beef
    1   teaspoon salt
    ½   teaspoon freshly ground
        pepper
    ¼   cup sour cream, at room
        temperature
    2   hard-cooked eggs, chopped fine
    ¼   cup finely minced fresh dill or
        2 tablespoons dried dill,
        crumbled
        Oil, for greasing baking sheet
    1   egg, lightly beaten with
        3 tablespoons water

Sour Cream Pastry

    1¾ cups flour
    ½   teaspoon salt
    ½   teaspoon baking powder
    4   tablespoons butter, chilled
        and cut into small pieces
    1   egg
    ½   cup sour cream

1. Prepare and chill pastry dough.

2. In a large skillet melt butter. Add onions and sauté, stirring over moderate heat, until onions are wilted. Add mushrooms; continue stirring until lightly browned. If using ground beef add it to skillet and sauté, stirring and breaking it up with a fork, until it loses its redness.

3. Remove pan from heat and stir in cooked beef (if using), salt, pepper, sour cream, chopped eggs, and dill. Let cool.

4. Preheat oven to 400° F. Lightly grease a baking sheet. On a floured board or between sheets of waxed paper, roll out pastry to a large, very thin sheet. Using a 4-inch cookie cutter (or the lid of a 40-ounce peanut butter jar), cut pastry into rounds. Set aside in one layer on sheets of waxed paper. (For larger piroshki, suitable for lunch rather than hors d'oeuvres, mark dough with an 8-inch pie plate and cut with a knife. Double quantity of filling when stuffing.) Gather trims into a ball, cover with plastic wrap, and freeze or refrigerate.

5. The dough will shrink after cutting. Take one round of pastry and roll it out again or carefully stretch by hand until thin. Place 1½ to 2 tablespoons filling (for small-sized piroshki) in a lump on half the circle of dough. Brush the rim of the circle with egg-water mixture, fold the other half of the dough over to enclose filling, and squeeze the edges of the dough shut with fingers or press with the tines of a fork. Brush top with egg mixture to seal. Repeat until all pastry circles have been filled. Remove ball of trimmed dough from refrigerator, roll out again, cut another set of rounds, and repeat the assembly process until this set of rounds has been filled. (If desired, piroshki may be frozen until ready to use. Thaw at room temperature for 3 hours before baking.)

6. Place piroshki on prepared baking sheet. Bake 25 minutes (or 35 minutes for large-sized piroshki). Serve immediately.

Makes about 18 small or 8 large piroshki.

Sour Cream Pastry

1. *To make in a food processor:* Mix all ingredients until blended thoroughly. *To make in a mixing bowl:* Combine flour, salt, and baking powder. Cut in butter with pastry blender or rapidly crumble with fingers until mixture forms a coarse meal. Using a fork, blend in egg and sour cream.

2. Shake or scrape mixture onto a lightly floured board or a sheet of waxed paper. Gather together and knead just until flour becomes smooth and elastic. Flatten dough with the heels of the hands into a pancake and wrap well in plastic wrap. Chill for at least 2 hours, or overnight.

BASIC ROAST BEEF HASH AND DECORATIONS

Roast beef hash is delicious all by itself, but this recipe also includes a range of decorations.

- 2 large baking potatoes (about 24 oz), pared
- 5 tablespoons oil (peanut, corn, or sunflower), or as needed
- 1 large or 2 medium onions (about 12 oz; preferably red onions), peeled and chopped
- ½ tablespoon minced garlic
- 1½ cups cooked roast beef, trimmed of fat and gristle, cut in ½-inch dice
  Salt and freshly ground pepper, to taste
  Pan gravy, to moisten (optional)

1. Drop potatoes into a deep saucepan of cold salted water to cover. Over high heat bring to a boil. Remove from heat, let cool, pat outsides dry, and cut in ½-inch dice.

2. In a large (12 inch) heavy skillet, heat oil until fragrant. Add onions and garlic and, stirring over moderate heat, sauté until wilted. Add potatoes, turning and stirring to coat each piece equally with oil. (Add more oil by tablespoons, stirring, if there is not enough.) Sauté mixture over moderate heat, stirring and flipping with a spatula frequently, until potatoes are browned all over and tender within (about 20 minutes).

3. Stir in roast beef and season liberally with salt and pepper. Add enough pan gravy to moisten, if desired. Cook, stirring over moderate heat, until meat is heated through.

Serves 3 or 4.

Horseradish Mustard Hash Stir horseradish mustard to taste (a tablespoon at a time) into hash just after beef. Soften flavor with a few tablespoons whipping cream, if desired.

Barbecue Hash Stir about 1 cup barbecue sauce (or to taste) into hash when beef is added.

Ranchero Hash Moisten hash with bottled salsa to taste. Top with one poached egg per person.

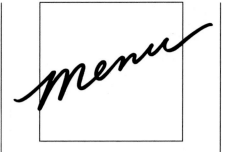

OLD ENGLISH ROAST BEEF DINNER

Roast Rib of Beef au Jus With Yorkshire Pudding

Franconia Root Vegetables

Green Salad of Choice

Tipsy Syllabub

A Fine Red Wine (such as Bordeaux or Cabernet) or a Well-Chilled French Sauternes

This celebratory feast is a modern re-creation of the English country manor dinner, where a haunch roasted on a spit in the hearth, its drippings flavoring pudding and vegetables. Although this modern version is hardly a calorie-conscious (or cholesterol-free) meal, it's a splendidly convivial one for special occasions. Accompany the roast with a fine red wine or, in the decadently luxurious style of fin de siècle Paris, consider a well-chilled French Sauternes. The menu serves six.

ROAST RIB OF BEEF AU JUS WITH YORKSHIRE PUDDING

A Yorkshire pudding is a high, light pancake (which, unfortunately, may partially deflate as soon as it's cut) served as a savory bed for slices of roast beef. In this recipe, which recreates the flavors of an earlier age, the pudding bakes under the roast until it begins to puff, absorbing the tasty drippings. When the roast is removed, the oven temperature is increased to finish off the pudding.

- 6 to 8 cloves garlic (to taste)
- 1 boneless rib roast of beef (about 6 lb)

Yorkshire Pudding Batter

- 1½ cups sifted flour
- 1½ teaspoons salt
  Pinch ground nutmeg
- 3 eggs
- 1½ cups milk

1. One hour before starting to roast, remove meat, eggs, and milk from refrigerator to allow each to reach room temperature.

2. Preheat oven to 450° F. Drop unpeeled garlic into a small saucepan of boiling water and boil until it starts to soften (10 minutes) to mellow the flavor. Peel garlic, halve one clove, and rub halves all over beef. Quarter each remaining clove lengthwise and insert slivers between fat and meat on top of roast and between veins of fat and meat at both front and back of roast. Use a small, sharp knife to make slits in meat, if necessary.

3. Place roast on a rack in a roasting pan, set pan in lower third of oven, and immediately lower oven thermostat to 300° F. Roast for about 20 minutes per pound for rare, 25 minutes for medium-rare, and 30 to 35 minutes per pound for well-done, or until an instant-read meat thermometer inserted for 10 seconds into the center of the roast reads 120° to 130° F for rare or 140° F for medium-rare. (Meat will continue to cook after it's removed from the oven. If some of the people at the table prefer well-done meat, roast to 140° F and serve them slices from the ends of the roast.)

4. One hour before beef is done, pour all fatty drippings from roasting pan into a dry, heatproof 2-cup measuring cup (or heatproof bowl). Reserve a generous half cup of the drippings for Yorkshire Pudding; the remainder will be used for Franconia Vegetables. Return roast to oven.

5. Make Yorkshire Pudding Batter.

6. About 20 minutes before beef is done, carefully remove rack and roast from baking pan (using a double set of thick potholders). Pour the reserved half cup of drippings into a heavy, 12-inch ovenproof skillet (such as a cast-iron skillet) or a flameproof rectangular baking pan (about 1 by 8 by 12 inches). Heat drippings on top of stove until fragrant and then add pudding batter (see Note). Position rack and roast over skillet or pan and return to oven, letting roast drip into pudding. After 20 minutes remove roast (and rack) and let stand before slicing.

7. Increase oven temperature to 400° F, move pudding to top third of oven, and bake until pudding puffs above pan lip and is lightly browned (about 15 minutes longer). As pudding finishes slice roast; place slices on serving platter and top with juices rendered during slicing. When pudding is done, cut it into equal portions, letting each serve as a bed for a portion of roast beef.

Serves 6.

Yorkshire Pudding Batter In a large bowl mix flour, salt, and nutmeg. In a separate bowl, beat eggs and whisk in milk; then pour into flour mixture. Whisk batter just until smooth, with large bubbles forming on top; do not overbeat or pudding will be tough. Batter may be refrigerated if not used immediately; briefly whisk again just before cooking.

Note Yorkshire pudding may also be cooked at 400° F for 30 to 35 minutes.

FRANCONIA ROOT VEGETABLES

This variation on traditional Franconia potatoes, roasted in drippings until the outsides are crisp and the insides are meltingly tender, adds carrots, onions, and turnips to provide a complete and handsome vegetable course. If you're using a small rack and a large roasting pan for the beef (or if you're roasting a standing rib roast without a rack), the vegetables can nestle around the edges of the roasting pan; otherwise, the vegetables will need a separate pan so they can be turned as they roast.

> 6 *large boiling potatoes (3 to 4 lb)*
> 1½ *pounds small carrots, trimmed and scraped (or large carrots, cut carefully into ovals)*
> 1 *pound small turnips, peeled, sprout end trimmed (or large turnips, trimmed carefully into ovals)*
> 12 *small, white boiling onions, peeled*
> *Drippings rendered from roast beef*
> 1 *teaspoon dried thyme leaves, crumbled*
> *Salt and freshly ground pepper, to taste*
> ¼ *cup minced parsley*

1. Peel potatoes and drop into a saucepan of cold, salted water. Over high heat bring water to a boil, lower heat to medium, and cook potatoes 12 minutes. Drain, let cool for a few minutes, pat dry, and cut into quarters (or halve horizontally and trim each half into ovals). Meanwhile, drop carrots, turnips, and onions into boiling salted water to cover. Lower heat to medium, cover, and cook until barely tender (10 to 15 minutes, depending on size). Drain, instantly cool under running water, and set vegetables aside.

2. About one hour before beef will be served, place potato quarters in drippings (at least ½ cup) rendered by roasting beef and turn them to coat. (If beef hasn't rendered enough drippings, supplement with cooking oil and a little unsalted butter.) Place in oven (wherever there's room,

including the bottom shelf) and roast for 45 minutes, turning every 10 minutes or so to brown all sides evenly. Add carrots, turnips, and onions and sprinkle with thyme, salt, and pepper. Continue roasting and turning frequently until vegetables are tender and evenly browned (about 15 minutes longer). Using tongs (or a slotted spoon) and draining off excess fat, remove to serving dish; sprinkle with parsley.

Serves 6.

TIPSY SYLLABUB

In seventeenth-century England syllabub was a beverage: a shockingly rich "milkshake" combining foamy cream with fruit juice. Today it's an elegant, simply made dessert, with the cream whipped so that one cup serves six diners rather than one drinker. Start making Tipsy Syllabub early in the day, but do not assemble it more than an hour or two before serving, since it will separate slightly if it is allowed to stand.

> ¼ *cup dark rum, bourbon, Scotch, brandy, or medium-dry sherry*
> ⅓ *cup strained fresh lemon juice*
> 1 *tablespoon finely grated lemon rind*
> 2 *pints whole, trimmed berries of choice (fresh or frozen without syrup and defrosted)*
> ¼ *cup superfine sugar*
> 1 *cup whipping cream*

1. Combine liquor with lemon juice and lemon rind. Cover and let stand at room temperature at least 4 hours or overnight.

2. Shortly before serving divide berries among 6 large wine goblets (or place in bottom of a glass serving bowl). Stir sugar into liquor mixture. Beat cream to soft peaks, gradually adding liquor mixture once cream starts to thicken. Spoon mixture over berries and refrigerate for up to two hours, until ready to serve.

Serves 6.

CUTS OF VEAL

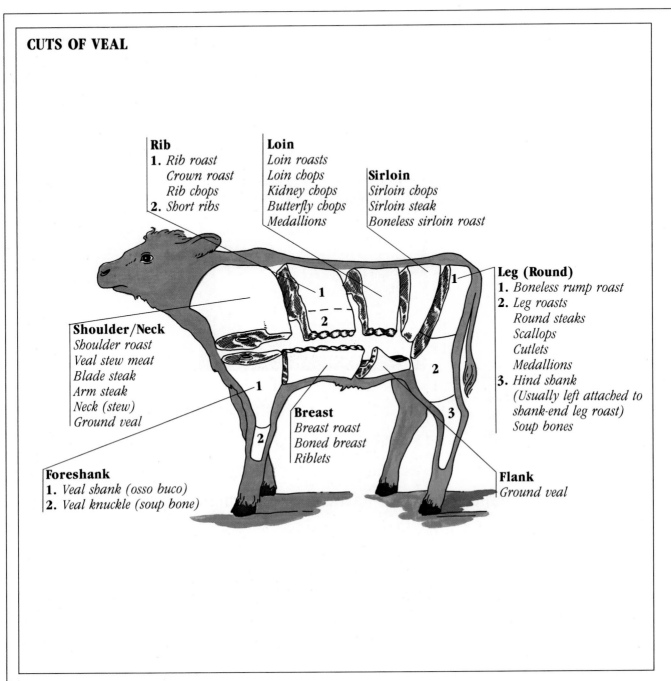

Rib
1. *Rib roast*
   Crown roast
   Rib chops
2. *Short ribs*

Loin
Loin roasts
Loin chops
Kidney chops
Butterfly chops
Medallions

Sirloin
Sirloin chops
Sirloin steak
Boneless sirloin roast

Leg (Round)
1. *Boneless rump roast*
2. *Leg roasts*
   Round steaks
   Scallops
   Cutlets
   Medallions
3. *Hind shank*
   (Usually left attached to
   shank-end leg roast)
   Soup bones

Shoulder/Neck
Shoulder roast
Veal stew meat
Blade steak
Arm steak
Neck (stew)
Ground veal

Breast
Breast roast
Boned breast
Riblets

Foreshank
1. *Veal shank (osso buco)*
2. *Veal knuckle (soup bone)*

Flank
Ground veal

The primal, or wholesale, cuts of veal are similar to those of a full-grown beef steer (see page 20), but there are fewer of them. The rump, round, and hind shank, for instance, are all considered a part of the leg, and the breast is a single cut.

Shoulder/Neck

Tenderer by far than the corresponding part of a steer, although tougher than the rib, loin, or leg, veal shoulder makes excellent stewing and braising meat. Although the shoulder cut contains many thin membranes, these seem to disappear with long, slow cooking.

Boneless shoulder is often sold as a roast as well (sometimes in a single piece, but sometimes as several pieces stuffed into a cylinder of butcher's netting—a nasty surprise when one starts to carve). It makes a passable roast if it's cooked with liquid as an oven pot roast, rather than as a genuine roast.

Veal neck is another cut from the shoulder; it is quite tough and must be cooked slowly by moist heat. Shoulder of veal is sometimes cut into steaks. Despite the name *steak*, veal shoulder steaks should be braised slowly, rather than grilled.

Foreshank

Veal foreshank is usually sold under its Italian name, *osso buco*. Although tougher than the hind shank (which is often sold as part of the leg) and full of membranes, it's perhaps the richest-flavored cut of veal when cooked slowly in liquid for long enough to dissolve the sinews. The bones also yield delicious marrow.

Veal foreshank is indispensable in making meat stocks (and the sauces and soups based on meat stocks), yielding the gelatin that makes good stocks rich and substantial. This cut is usually sold at a reasonable price, but it has a high ratio of bone to meat. As meat for stock (where the bones play a major role in thickening the broth), however, it's a superb and cost-effective choice.

Breast

Veal breast is tough, bony, and (for veal) rather fatty, but it's always an economical buy. With the bone in, the breast can be cut into riblets and grilled. More popular are boned breasts, with a pocket cut in them for stuffing. Ground veal is usually made from this cut. It is much less fatty than other ready-made ground meats.

Rib

Occasionally an entire rack, or crown roast, of veal rib is sold as a roast. More often the rib section is cut into tender, flavorful chops.

Loin

The loin (or hind saddle) of veal includes numerous smaller cuts, not all of them available from a typical meat case. Loin chops are the most familiar, and these can be sautéed, broiled, braised, or baked.

The next most common cut from the loin section is the boneless, rolled loin roast. This and several cuts from the leg are perhaps the most suitable cuts of veal for genuine roasting (but with a liquid baste).

The rolled loin can be unrolled, filled with stuffing, and rerolled—tied in several places with kitchen twine—for an elegant roast. A bone-in loin includes the T-bone and is a V-shaped cut that's also suitable for roasting.

Sirloin Less common in butcher shops is the veal sirloin (the portion of the loin next to the leg). It's a delicious cut, but since a calf is so much smaller than a steer, it's a bony one (thus yielding relatively little meat for its premium price).

Veal sirloin chops are high priced and delicious. Many butchers also cut the boned sirloin into veal scallops, although the meat for genuine veal scaloppine comes from the center of the leg.

Leg (Round)

Most commonly leg of veal is boned and sold as a roast. Butchers also divide the leg into its separate muscles and then slice the muscles thinly to make cutlets and scallops; the center cut of the leg (which is often labeled round) is probably the major source of these prized cuts. (To obtain veal scallops at a reasonable price, buy the boned leg and slice it thinly at home.)

Occasionally you may find other versions of leg of veal. Veal round roasts may actually be from the leg (rather than the shoulder), as are bone-in rump roasts (cut from the area where the leg joins the hip). These, and the center-cut leg, are more tender than the shank-half leg that's occasionally sold as a roast, but which really should be a pot roast.

Flank

Meat from the breast or shoulder, as well as from the flank, goes into meat-case ground veal. Unless it has been mixed with beef suet, ground veal contains 20 percent fat or less. It is relatively difficult to make ground veal at home (the meat is too slippery to shred well in a food processor, so an old-fashioned grinder is needed).

BUYING VEAL

True veal is the meat of calves between eight and twelve weeks of age, fed on nothing but milk or formula and weighing between 150 and 250 pounds. Their firm, fine-grained meat ranges from white to a very light pink, and has a very small amount of white fat. Their bones are small and filled with bright red marrow.

The best veal of all is the milk-fed Prime-grade veal of free-range calves from ranches specializing in organic meat. Its flavor is greatly superior to (and its meat firmer than) the meat of calves fed on formula. Such meat is available from specialty butchers—at a high price.

When a calf passes the age of a true "vealer," it's fed on grass and grain, like its parents, and starts to turn into beef. Calves that are slaughtered when they are nearly five months old and weigh 350 pounds or more may still be sold as veal. Veal that is a dark pink to red, with yellowish fat in significant quantities and dark marrow in grayish bones, probably comes from calves that have started to graze.

Between the ages of seven and ten months, calves are not yet mature, but are too old to be called veal. Meat from such calves is sold as baby beef. This meat is light red and has a milder flavor and less fat than mature beef. It's still fairly tender, but its flavor requires a strong boost, whether from a marinade or a strong, distinctive sauce.

Veal contains very little marbling (and what there is, is almost invisible if the meat is white). Because veal is tender and delicate, it is not aged for any appreciable length of time by butchers or meat wholesalers. On the contrary, it is sold as soon as possible.

For the centerpiece of a special dinner, treat a lavish veal roast tenderly and it will be tender in return. The sophisticated Hazelnut Cream Sauce brings out the best in roast veal.

COOKING VEAL

Veal's very blandness and leanness pose certain problems that good cooks over the centuries have learned to solve creatively. The meat is mild-flavored not only because the animal is young (and has not lived long enough to develop a strong flavor), but also because it contains more water and less fat than beef.

This means that veal needs "something else" to replace the fat and lend the meat flavor. (Nearly every dieter has, at some time, attempted to make a meal of a plain, broiled vealburger, but few have attempted it twice.) The something else can be as suave as a cream gravy or a cheese sauce, or as tartly animated as lemon juice with capers or a biting tomato sauce.

Veal is generally cooked by moist-cooking methods (sautéing, braising, or stewing), because it does not have enough fat to keep the meat moist during dry-cooking. Even when roasted, veal is either basted with a liquid or else cooked in a covered pot so that the meat is really steamed, rather than roasted.

In a great many recipes, veal is paired with a sauce based on butter, oil, or cream to compensate for lack of flavorful fat in the meat. (Veal is very low in calories—but like potatoes, it's often dressed up quite calorically.) Thin cuts of veal (such as scallops and chops) are often cooked very quickly, but the thicker cuts usually require long, slow cooking that allows them to absorb the liquid they're cooked in.

ROAST VEAL

Veal is a tender enough meat to roast very quickly, but since the unmarbled meat is so lean, most successful veal roasts actually are closer to braises: Either some liquid is added to the pot for an uncovered roast, or the veal is roasted covered to steam in its own juices or in added liquids.

The leg, loin, and rack are all good, lean roasts, whether rolled or bone-in. The hind shank of the leg and the boneless shoulder may also be sold as roasting cuts, but these are tougher than the loin and upper leg and should be roasted more slowly and with more liquid.

Boned breast of veal makes an economical (if untender) roast, cooked very slowly and usually covered. With a pocket cut in and filled with a tasty stuffing, it makes a nice entrée.

Dishes such as Spinach-Stuffed Breast of Veal (see page 42), a large and dramatic-looking main course, are cooked covered for part of the time to keep the meat moist. Accompanied by a salad or green vegetable, such dishes will serve a large group economically and well.

ROAST VEAL IN HAZELNUT CREAM SAUCE

A cream "massage," a bed of vegetables to release some steam, and frequent basting with wine lends lean veal the moisture it needs to be roasted successfully. This elegant dish with its subtle, nut-flavored sauce goes well with fresh pasta, white beans, or potatoes, along with steamed and buttered spinach, chard, or beet greens as a vegetable.

> 1 boneless veal roast from leg or loin (3 lb)
> ½ teaspoon freshly ground pepper, plus more to taste
> 1¼ cups whipping cream
> 1 cup hazelnuts
> 3 tablespoons unsalted butter
> 1 medium onion, minced
> 1 stalk celery with leaves, finely diced
> 1 medium carrot, pared and finely diced
> 2 cloves garlic, crushed and peeled
> 1½ cups dry white wine
> Salt, to taste
> 2 tablespoons minced parsley

1. With kitchen string tie veal into a cylinder, tying at ends and middle. Rub veal all over with the ½ teaspoon pepper and about ¼ cup of the cream. (If veal has come from the butcher packed in netting with a layer of suet tied on, slip off netting to remove suet, rub with cream and pepper, then pack back into netting.) Cover meat loosely and let come to room temperature (or wrap with foil and refrigerate up to 24 hours).

2. Preheat oven to 400° F. Place hazelnuts on a baking sheet and bake about 12 minutes, shaking pan frequently to turn nuts, until skin turns black and nutmeats are golden and fragrant. Remove nuts from oven and turn oven down to 325° F. When nuts cool slip off skins. Coarsely chop

¼ cup nuts and grind remainder to a paste (in an electric minichopper or clean coffee grinder or with a rolling pin). Reserve chopped and ground nuts separately.

3. In a heavy baking dish just large enough to hold veal, melt butter over medium heat. Add onion, celery, and carrot. Sauté, stirring frequently, until mixture begins to brown. Add garlic and sauté about 30 seconds longer. Push vegetables to sides of pan, add veal to center, and brown veal lightly on all sides. Lift veal, push vegetables back to center, and set veal on vegetables.

4. Transfer baking dish to oven and roast 20 minutes, then pour 1 cup of the wine over veal. Continue to roast, basting every 10 minutes with pan juices, until veal reaches an internal temperature of 140° to 150° F for rare to medium-rare or to taste (40 to 50 minutes). At the final basting (or sooner, if liquid has evaporated and vegetables are starting to blacken), add ¼ cup of the remaining wine.

5. Remove baking dish to top of stove. Transfer veal to serving platter and keep warm. Pour pan juices through a strainer into a saucepan, pressing the solids with a wooden spoon to extract as much juice as possible. Add reserved finely ground nuts and remaining ¼ cup wine and over high heat boil down to a thick glaze (about 5 minutes). Stir in remaining 1 cup cream·and boil until sauce is thick enough to coat a spoon (5 to 8 minutes). Season to taste with salt and pepper.

6. Slice veal thinly. Coat lightly with sauce and pour remaining sauce into a gravy boat. Sprinkle veal with chopped nuts and minced parsley and serve immediately.

Serves 6.

SPINACH-STUFFED BREAST OF VEAL

This baked veal breast with its meaty stuffing is mostly Italian.

> 1 breast of veal (3 to 3½ lb), with pocket cut for stuffing
> 2 tablespoons olive or salad oil, for brushing
> 1 cup each chicken stock and dry white wine

Ground Beef and Spinach Stuffing

> ½ pound ground beef
> 1 medium onion, chopped
> 1 clove garlic, minced or pressed
> 2 oz small fresh mushrooms, wiped dry and thinly sliced
> 1 package (9 or 10 oz) frozen chopped spinach, thawed and squeezed dry
> ½ cup soft bread crumbs
> 1 cup grated Monterey jack cheese
> 1 egg, slightly beaten
> ½ teaspoon each salt and dried basil
> ⅛ teaspoon seasoned pepper

1. Preheat oven to 325° F. Fill pocket with Ground Beef and Spinach Stuffing; fasten open end with small metal skewers. Place meat in a large roasting pan. Brush with oil. Pour on ¾ cup each of stock and wine. Cover with aluminum foil and bake until meat is very tender (2 hours). Increase oven temperature to 350° F and continue baking, uncovered, 25 to 30 minutes more. Brush occasionally with pan drippings. Remove meat to heated platter and keep warm.

2. To loosen pan drippings add remaining ¼ cup each stock and wine, stirring over high heat until reduced by a third. Serve sauce separately. To carve veal, cut between rib bones.

Serves 6 to 8.

Ground Beef and Spinach Stuffing Crumble ground beef into large frying pan and brown. Add onion, garlic, and mushrooms. Cook, stirring occasionally, until onion is soft. Remove pan from heat; add spinach, bread crumbs, cheese, egg, salt, basil, and pepper; mix lightly.

BRAISES, SOUPS, AND STEWS

Cooked slowly in liquid, even the toughest cuts of veal become meltingly tender, and the mild-flavored meat mirrors the tastes of the ingredients it's cooked with. Unlike stewing beef, veal needs little trimming, since veal isn't fatty and the membranes between muscles seem to vanish during cooking. (In fact, veal is extremely difficult to trim, since these membranes are very slippery.)

However, veal yields quite a lot of scum into its cooking liquid. To avoid extensive skimming, veal is usually browned (often with a thin coating of flour) before braising or stewing. Do not crowd the skillet, or the veal will boil instead of brown, and the problem will remain.

VEAL STEW WITH SORREL AND PEAS

The delicious sourness of sorrel (sometimes called sourgrass), a large-leafed herb dear to French and Russian cooks, is an exquisite complement to the mild flavor of veal. If you have a garden, note that sorrel is an undemanding plant grown rapidly from seed.

> 1 cup (about ¼ lb) fresh sorrel
> 3 tablespoons corn, sunflower, or light olive oil
> 4 tablespoons unsalted butter
> 3 pounds boneless veal stew meat, cut into 1½-inch cubes
> 2 medium onions, minced
> 3 medium carrots, pared and finely diced
> ½ pound fresh mushrooms
> 1 cup dry white wine
> 1 cup chicken stock
> 1 sprig parsley
> 1 bay leaf
> 1 sprig fresh thyme or ½ teaspoon crumbled dried thyme leaves
> Salt and freshly ground pepper, to taste
> ½ cup whipping cream
> 1 cup frozen tiny peas
> Plain potatoes, rice, or noodles, for accompaniment

1. If sorrel is homegrown, soak for about ½ hour in several changes of cold water. Shake dry and reserve. If sorrel is storebought, just rinse well, shake dry, and set aside.

2. In a very large skillet, heat 2 tablespoons of the oil and 1 tablespoon of the butter until butter melts. Over medium-high heat sauté veal in several uncrowded batches until golden (about 4 minutes per side). With a slotted spoon remove veal to a heavy, medium (about 1½-quart) flameproof casserole.

3. Add remaining 1 tablespoon oil and 2 tablespoons of the butter to the skillet. Sauté onions and carrots over low heat until tender (about 7 minutes). Trim mushrooms, wipe off grit with a paper towel, and slice. Add mushrooms and sauté until they change color (5 minutes longer). Remove vegetables to casserole. Add wine to skillet and deglaze briefly over high heat, scraping up browned bits. Pour wine into casserole.

4. Pour stock into casserole. If needed add water to barely cover ingredients. Add parsley, bay leaf, thyme, and salt and pepper to taste. Cover and simmer on low heat until veal is very tender (1½ to 2 hours). While veal cooks tear sorrel leaves off stems. Stack leaves on cutting board, roll up, and slice thinly across roll. In a medium skillet melt remaining 1 tablespoon butter, add sorrel shreds, and cook over low heat until sorrel "melts" into butter (about 5 minutes), stirring occasionally. Put aside and save.

5. Place a large strainer over a bowl and, with a slotted spoon, remove veal to strainer. Remove bay leaf and parsley sprig from liquid in pot. Pour veal juices from bowl back into casserole and reserve veal. Skim fat from surface with a cold, large spoon. Over high heat reduce cooking liquid until well-thickened and intense in flavor (about 12 minutes). Stir in sorrel and cream. Return veal to casserole with peas and cook over low heat a few minutes, until peas are cooked and veal is warmed. Serve with potatoes, rice, or noodles.

Serves 6.

SLICED VEAL BRAISED WITH WILD MUSHROOMS

This exquisite braise includes a built-in starch course and needs only a green salad or a delicate green vegetable (such as peas, zucchini, or artichoke hearts) to accompany it. The mushrooms are available in specialty food stores and the gourmet aisle of some supermarkets.

> 3 ounces dried wild mushrooms of at least 3 types (porcini, cèpes, morels, chanterelles, shiitake, or oyster mushrooms)
> 1 boneless veal roast from leg or loin, not shoulder (about 2½ lb)
> 5 tablespoons olive oil
> Salt and freshly ground white pepper, to taste
> ⅓ cup minced shallots
> 2 medium carrots
> ¼ teaspoon ground nutmeg
> 1 pound new potatoes, pared and thinly sliced, soaked in cold water for 20 minutes
> 1 cup white wine
> 1½ cups whipping cream
> 2 teaspoons crumbled dried sage leaves

1. Combine mushrooms in a medium-sized bowl. Cover with hot water and soak 15 minutes (20 minutes if shiitake are used). Drain, reserving soaking liquid. Remove stems from shiitake and oyster mushrooms, if used. Cut mushrooms in slices.

2. Cut veal into thin slices and halve each slice. In a large, heavy skillet, heat 2 tablespoons of the olive oil. Over medium-high heat sauté veal in several batches just until slices turn pale. Remove veal as it is sautéed to a large (4-quart), heavy, ovenproof casserole and sprinkle each layer with salt and white pepper. Layer half the mushrooms over the veal.

3. Add 1 tablespoon of the oil to skillet. Add shallots and carrots, sprinkle with nutmeg and a little more salt and white pepper, and cook for 1 minute. Remove to casserole with a slotted spoon. Drain potatoes and pat dry with paper towels. Add remaining 2 tablespoons oil to skillet and quickly sauté potatoes lightly on both sides. Layer potatoes over vegetable mixture and cover with remaining mushrooms.

4. Preheat oven to 350° F. Pour wine into skillet and deglaze quickly over high heat, scraping up browned bits and vegetables. Add ½ cup of the mushroom juices plus cream and sage. Bring to a simmer and pour sauce into casserole. Cover casserole; bake until veal is tender (1½ hours).

Serves 4 or 5.

VEAL CHOPS

Veal chops may be cut from the loin, sirloin, or rib. Loin and sirloin chops are expensive but have little waste; with less expensive rib chops, the buyer pays for bone and some fat, but the meat is no less tasty.

Old-fashioned thick-cut rib and sirloin chops (weighing about 10 ounces per chop) are favorites in bistros and grills. A third kind of chop you may find is the large kidney chop cut from the loin (which may or may not actually have a piece of veal kidney in the center).

Although veal benefits from moist cooking, veal chops may be seasoned as desired and broiled or grilled, for about 5 minutes per side, about 4 inches from the heat source. (A slice of bacon wrapped around the chop and attached with toothpicks or turkey skewers will add flavor.)

Broiled or grilled chops may be dressed up with a pan gravy (see page 11), any composed butter (see page 9), or a squirt of lemon or lime juice and a sprinkling of minced fresh herbs or even fresh hot chiles. Veal chops may also be grilled over a fire made with aromatic, smoky chips to add flavor.

More commonly veal chops are sautéed, braised, or cooked in the oven in papillote, as described in the recipe at right. The varied treatments for veal scallops described on page 44 can also be applied very successfully to sautéed veal chops. (Increase cooking time from the mere seconds required for scallops to about 5 minutes per side for chops or longer for very thick chops.)

VEAL CHOPS IN PAPILLOTE WITH SUN-DRIED TOMATOES AND OLIVES

In this quickly prepared, hearty, bistro-style dish, thick veal chops are anything but bland when paired with tangy, smoky-flavored sun-dried tomatoes and brined black olives.

> 4 veal sirloin or rib chops, approximately ¾ inch thick (10 to 14 oz each)
> Olive oil, for brushing chops
> Salt and freshly ground pepper, to taste
> 1 jar (3 oz) sun-dried tomatoes in olive oil
> 1 cup black olives (preferably brined olives, such as Kalamata), pitted and coarsely chopped
> 4 tablespoons chopped fresh basil or 2 tablespoons chopped fresh sage leaves or 1½ tablespoons dried, crumbled basil

1. Preheat broiler for about 10 minutes. Trim any fat from outsides of chops and brush chops on both sides with a little olive oil. Broil chops about 4 inches from heat for 5 minutes. Salt and generously pepper cooked side, then turn and broil 5 minutes longer. Remove from broiler and let chops cool until they can be touched safely.

2. Drain sun-dried tomatoes, reserving oil. (If jar is cold and oil has congealed, seal jar tightly and place in a bowl of very hot tap water until oil loosens.) Chop tomatoes coarsely.

3. Set oven temperature at 450° F. Cut 4 sheets of aluminum foil to lengths about 2½ times longer than the chops at their widest point. Brush centers of foil sheets with olive oil from tomatoes and place chops on the oiled sections. Brush chops lightly with more oil from tomatoes. Distribute tomatoes evenly over chops, then scatter olives over tomatoes. Scatter basil over all. Fold foil loosely toward center and roll all edges to seal completely. Place packages in a baking pan, set in upper third of oven, and bake for 20 minutes. Serve immediately.

Serves 4.

Veal scallops are easy on the waistline—and have no waste at all. A bold, lemony Veal Scaloppine Piccata is an elegant dinner when time is short and calories are a concern.

SCALLOPS, CUTLETS, AND MEDALLIONS

Veal scallops, cutlets, and medallions are almost interchangeable in recipes. However, each cut comes from a different part of the calf and requires a slightly different treatment before cooking begins.

Veal scallops are nearly always cut thinly from the leg. Trim off or slash the membrane that surrounds each scallop, or the meat will curl up in the pan. In most recipes scallops are pounded before cooking to flatten them into the thinnest possible pieces.

Place scallops between two sheets of waxed paper and pound with the flat side of a meat mallet (or any other flat, heavy object) until they've doubled in size and are almost paper-thin (⅛ inch). Mere seconds of cooking time are sufficient.

Veal cutlets (also called veal round steak) come from the center of the leg and usually include a center marrow bone. Veal "birds" are just boneless cutlets. These are left thicker than scallops, as are medallions,

which are usually cut from the loin and are very tender. To prepare any of these cuts in a recipe that normally calls for scallops, just increase the cooking time long enough to cook these thicker pieces through.

Besides making the recipes in this chapter, you can serve veal scallops, cutlets, and medallions with pan gravies (see page 11) varied with such seasonings as fresh chives, roasted caraway seed, crumbled Roquefort cheese, or poached garlic and with such additional ingredients as sautéed mushrooms (especially wild mushrooms, such as morels) or poached frozen artichoke hearts.

Madeira Sauce (see page 13) is also superb with tender veal, as is the apple accompaniment in Pork Chops With Apples in Cider Sauce (see page 74). Veal cutlets may also be sautéed with tomatoes and onions, along with bell peppers, mushrooms, or ripe olives. They may be floured or breaded, sautéed in oil, and then finished off in the oven coated with homemade tomato sauce and slices of mild cheese.

VEAL SCALOPPINE PICCATA

This lovely, tart dish from Italy takes almost no time to cook and may just be the finest treatment of all for excellent veal. It's also relatively low in calories.

- ½ cup flour, or enough to coat veal
- 1 pound veal scallops, cut approximately 3 inches across and ¼ inch thick, trimmed and pounded (see page 44)
- 4 tablespoons unsalted butter
- 2 tablespoons mild-flavored cooking oil, such as light olive oil, corn oil, or sunflower oil
  Salt and freshly ground pepper, to taste
- 2 tablespoons lemon juice
- 1 tablespoon drained capers
- 2 tablespoons finely minced parsley
- ½ lemon, thinly sliced (optional)

1. Warm a serving dish in low oven or microwave. Spread flour in a plate and lightly dip both sides of scallops in it, shaking off excess. Meanwhile, in a large, heavy skillet over medium-high heat, warm 2 tablespoons of the butter with the oil until very hot and fragrant. Add scallops (you may have to work in several batches to keep them uncrowded) and brown lightly on both sides (about 1 minute per side). Remove immediately to warmed serving dish, sprinkle with salt and pepper, and tent with foil to keep warm.

2. Pour oil out of skillet. With pan off heat add lemon juice, scraping up browned bits. Stir in remaining 2 tablespoons butter plus capers and 1 tablespoon of parsley. Return veal to sauce and warm briefly over medium heat, turning veal in sauce to coat. Return veal and sauce to serving platter, garnish with remaining 1 tablespoon parsley and lemon slices (if desired). Serve immediately.

Serves 4.

VEAL SCALOPPINE WITH MUSHROOMS AND MARSALA

Here is a classic Italian veal recipe as it's lovingly prepared in New York's Neapolitan community. It goes especially well with pasta dressed in cream and Parmesan cheese and a green vegetable.

- 4 tablespoons unsalted butter
- 2 tablespoons olive oil, or more as needed
- ½ pound small mushrooms, wiped clean and thinly sliced
- 1 pound veal scallops, trimmed and pounded (see page 44)
  Salt and freshly ground pepper, to taste
- ½ cup flour, or enough to coat veal
- ½ cup Marsala or a good dry sherry
- ½ cup white veal stock or chicken stock (preferably homemade)

1. In a large, heavy skillet over a medium temperature, heat 2 tablespoons of the butter with the oil until foam dies down. (Reserve remaining butter at room temperature.) Add mushrooms and sauté over medium-high heat, stirring frequently, until lightly browned. With a slotted spoon remove mushrooms and reserve. If necessary add a little more oil to pan.

2. Lightly season veal with salt and pepper, dip in flour, and shake and pat off excess. Brown veal in skillet (in batches, if necessary) about 1 minute per side. Remove to hot platter and pour off fat from skillet.

3. Pour wine and stock into skillet. Over high heat, scraping up browned bits, rapidly reduce liquid to a glaze. Return veal and mushrooms to pan; heat very briefly (about 15 seconds). Remove from heat and add remaining 2 tablespoons butter, working it into sauce with a wooden spoon. Serve immediately.

Serves 4.

GROUND VEAL AND "SECOND HELPINGS"

The first recipe to follow is designed for use with cooked (braised or roasted) veal. The second recipe uses ground veal or cutlets.

LIGHT VITELLO TONNATO
Chilled veal in lightened tuna sauce

This lightened California version of Italy's famous chilled veal platter is very subtly flavored with tuna. It makes a lovely appetizer or, accompanied by a green salad, a light summer supper.

- 1 pound cold, cooked veal (roasted or braised), thinly sliced
- ¼ large dill pickle or 2 small cornichons
- 1 large stalk celery
- 1 green onion (white part only)
- 3¼ ounces (half a 6½-oz can) water-packed tuna, drained
- 1 teaspoon anchovy paste or 2 anchovies, drained
- 4½ teaspoons capers, drained
- 1½ tablespoons fresh lemon juice
- 1 cup homemade mayonnaise made with lemon juice
  Salt and freshly ground pepper, to taste
  Sliced green olives, pimiento slices, rolled anchovies, and thinly sliced hard-cooked egg, for garnish

Arrange veal slices on a serving platter. In blender or food processor, purée pickle, celery, green onion, tuna, anchovy paste, and ½ teaspoon of the capers. Transfer mixture to a medium bowl and stir in lemon juice, mayonnaise, remaining 4 teaspoons capers, salt, and pepper. Spread sauce over veal and garnish as desired. Serve cold or at cool room temperature. (Platter may be covered and refrigerated for up to 4 hours; with longer refrigeration sauce will separate slightly.)

Serves 4 as a main course, 6 to 8 as an appetizer.

CHICKEN-FRIED VEAL BIRDS IN COUNTRY GRAVY

This quickly prepared dish is a favorite in the South, where fat rendered by bacon and ham is always saved to flavor gravies. (Frozen, the fat will keep for many months.) Serve with French-fried or mashed potatoes or corn bread and any vegetable.

> *Cooking oil, such as corn, peanut, or sunflower oil, for frying*
> 1½ *pounds veal cutlets, put through butcher's tenderizer to score, or ground veal*
> ½ *teaspoon poultry seasoning*
> ½ *teaspoon salt, plus more to taste*
> 1 *teaspoon freshly ground pepper, plus more to taste*
> 1 *cup flour*
> 2 *eggs*
> 2½ *cups milk*
> 3 *tablespoons rendered bacon or ham fat*

1. In a large, heavy skillet over high heat, warm at least ½ inch oil until hazy (to about 360° F).

2. Meanwhile knead ground veal with poultry seasoning, salt, and pepper to taste and form into patties about ¼ inch thick. (If using veal cutlets, merely rub with seasonings.) In a medium bowl mix flour with the ½ teaspoon salt and the 1 teaspoon pepper. Reserve 3 tablespoons of mixture for gravy. In another medium bowl beat eggs with 1 cup of the milk. Dip steaks in liquid, then dredge in seasoned flour, shaking off excess. (If a very thick coating is desired, repeat.)

3. Fry veal birds until browned (about 3 minutes per side). Remove to serving dish and keep warm. Pour fat out of skillet and replace with bacon fat. Melt fat, then over low heat stir reserved flour mixture into pan liquid. As soon as the aroma of raw flour disappears, slowly add remaining 1½ cups milk, stirring constantly. Increase heat to medium-low and stir until gravy is smooth and thickened. Correct seasoning and pour gravy over veal birds.

Serves 4 to 6.

A DINNER FROM PROVENCE

Osso Buco in Citrus Wine Sauce

Fettuccine With Butter, Garlic, Parmesan, and Black Pepper

Young Zucchini in Tarragon Butter

Cherry Clafouti

Red Côtes-du-Rhône or Côtes-de-Provence wine

This menu, full of the sunny flavors of southern France, with its hillsides of wild herbs and its bounteous vegetation, progresses from an intriguingly flavored main course of orange-scented tender veal shanks to a light and extremely popular dessert. The meal is economical, elegant, and easy to assemble, although the osso buco needs one day's advance preparation. The menu serves four, with plenty of dessert for all.

OSSO BUCO IN CITRUS WINE SAUCE

Osso buco is the front shanks of the calf, bony but wonderfully rich and flavorful. Here, an overnight marinade and slow braising in a lively sauce makes them light and flavorful. If possible, use the same type of wine for cooking and drinking.

> 4 *veal shanks, bones sawed but not separated*
> 2 *medium carrots*
> 1 *large bulb garlic (about 20 cloves), cloves separated*
> 1 *large onion, thickly sliced*
> 3 *cups dry red wine (preferably Côtes-du-Rhône, Côtes-de-Provence, or Petite Sirah)*
> 1½ *cups veal, beef, or poultry stock (preferably homemade) Juice of 4 large, ripe juice oranges Juice of 3 small limes*
> ½ *teaspoon freshly ground pepper*
> 2 *tablespoons flour*
> 2 *tablespoons light olive or peanut oil*
> 1 *teaspoon freshly grated orange zest*
> ¼ *teaspoon finely minced garlic*
> 1 *tablespoon minced parsley*

1. Place veal shanks in 1 layer in the bottom of a large (about 4-quart) enameled casserole (or casserole made out of some other nonreactive material, such as glass). Quarter carrots lengthwise, then cut into 2- to 3-inch slices. Crush garlic cloves with the side of a heavy knife and peel. Scatter carrots, garlic, and onion over veal. Add wine, veal stock, three fourths of the orange juice and two thirds of the lime juice, and pepper. Cover and refrigerate 24 hours.

2. Preheat oven to 300° F. Remove veal shanks from liquid, pat dry with paper towels, and sprinkle all over with flour to coat lightly. In a large, heavy skillet over high heat, warm oil until fragrant. Reduce heat to medium-high, add veal shanks, and brown on all sides (about 4 minutes per side; a spatter shield is desirable). Meanwhile bring marinade to a simmer in an ovenproof casserole.

3. Place veal shanks in casserole in marinade. Cover and bake in oven until meat falls off bones (2 hours). Remove to stovetop and transfer shanks temporarily to a plate or bowl, pouring liquid back into casserole. Place casserole over high heat and boil for 10 minutes to reduce sauce. With a slotted spoon remove all solids from sauce into a food processor or blender; then pour in about 1 cup of the liquid. Blend to a fine purée (about 2 minutes).

4. With a wooden spoon push purée through a strainer back into sauce; discard any remaining solids. Add remaining juice and return to high heat for 2 minutes. Correct seasonings to taste. Return veal to casserole and sprinkle orange zest, minced garlic, and parsley on top. Heat together for 1 or 2 minutes to reheat veal and blend flavors. Serve from casserole.

Serves 4.

FETTUCCINE WITH BUTTER, GARLIC, PARMESAN, AND BLACK PEPPER

This delicious pasta dish is quick to prepare and can give a festive touch to many everyday meals.

- *3 quarts well-salted water*
- *1 tablespoon (approximately) olive or cooking oil*
- *8 to 12 ounces dry fettuccine or 1 pound fresh fettuccine*
- *3 tablespoons unsalted butter*
- *2 large cloves garlic, finely minced*
- *4 tablespoons Parmesan cheese, or to taste*
  Salt and freshly ground pepper, to taste

1. In a large (at least 4-quart) saucepan, bring salted water to a boil. Drizzle in oil. Stir in fettuccine and cook until firm-tender (about 2 minutes for fresh, 7 minutes for dried), tasting single strands frequently. Do not allow pasta to become mushy. Drain as soon as done and place in serving dish.

2. While pasta cooks melt butter in a small saucepan over low heat. Add garlic and cook until garlic is transparent but not browned. Pour garlic butter over pasta. Stir in cheese to taste 1 tablespoon at a time and season with salt and a liberal quantity of freshly ground black pepper (8 to 12 grinds). Serve immediately (or cover and keep warm, if necessary, in a low oven for up to 20 minutes).

Serves 4.

YOUNG ZUCCHINI IN TARRAGON BUTTER

You can cook this delicate, summery vegetable dish on top of the stove or bake it along with the veal.

- *3 tablespoons clarified unsalted butter*
- *1 pound small, young zucchini, trimmed and sliced*
- *1 tablespoon snipped fresh tarragon leaves or 1 generous teaspoon crumbled dried tarragon leaves*
  Salt and freshly ground white pepper, to taste

To prepare in oven: Preheat oven to 300° F. In a large, heavy ovenproof skillet over medium heat, warm the butter until fragrant. Add zucchini slices a handful at a time, turning to coat all sides. Lower heat to simmer, cover, and cook 5 minutes. Turn zucchini, cover, and cook 5 more minutes. Uncover, stir in tarragon, and sprinkle with salt and white pepper. Move skillet to oven and bake about 20 minutes without stirring. *To cook on stove:* Prepare as above, but leave skillet on stovetop. Increase heat to medium-low and turn zucchini frequently until crisp-tender but not soggy (about 10 more minutes).

Serves 4.

CHERRY CLAFOUTI
French deep-dish cherry custard pie

In this immensely popular and quickly made French dessert, the batter forms a tender custard with a pancake-like crust at the bottom and succulent fruits generously scattered throughout. Small blue plums, halved and pitted, are also delicious in clafouti. Bake the dessert before the veal goes into the oven.

- *3 tablespoons unsalted butter*
- *¼ cup flour*
- *¼ cup sugar*
  Pinch salt
- *4 eggs*
- *1½ tablespoons whipping cream*
- *1½ tablespoons sour cream*
- *½ cup plus 2 tablespoons milk*
- *1 teaspoon vanilla extract*
- *1 pound fresh Bing cherries, stemmed and seeded, or 1 package (14 to 16 oz) frozen cherries, defrosted, or 1 can (14 to 16 oz) pitted cherries, drained*

1. Preheat oven to 350° F. Thoroughly grease a 9-inch slanted-side pie plate or ovenproof skillet with 1 tablespoon of the butter. Melt remaining 2 tablespoons butter and let cool. In a food processor or electric mixer, blend flour, sugar, and salt. One by one beat in eggs, scraping bowl between additions. Add whipping cream, sour cream, milk, and vanilla and blend well. Blend in reserved melted butter and beat for about 1 minute with mixer or 30 seconds with food processor. (Mixture may also be made by hand, with a handheld electric beater or a whisk, using longer beating times.)

2. Pour batter into prepared pan and scatter cherries evenly over it. (They will sink in.) Place pie in oven and bake until puffed and golden brown (about 30 minutes). Cool on a rack for 5 to 10 minutes. Serve at room temperature. (If preparing clafouti far in advance, cover with plastic wrap, refrigerate, and return to room temperature before serving.)

Serves 6.

An authentic Armenian Shish Kebab Dinner is easy to prepare with a well-trimmed leg of lamb and a good marinade. Recipes start on page 62.

Lamb & Goat

A favorite of those with discerning palates, lamb becomes lyrical when complemented by herbs and spices as in Greek Easter Lamb (see page 51) or by a tasty marinade as in Grilled Butterflied Leg of Lamb (see page 55). This chapter also presents more elegant fare such as Mustard-Coated Roast Rack of Lamb (see page 52). Goat and kid are suited to many of the same cooking techniques as lamb. Try Cabrito al Pastor (see page 52), roast kid done Tex-Mex style. Or for an exotic meal, try the Armenian Shish Kebab Dinner starting on page 62. There are step-by-step photographs on boning and butterflying leg of lamb on page 54 and making lean ground lamb on page 60.

CUTS OF LAMB

Shoulder
1. *Neck slice*
2. *Shoulder roast*
   Blade chops
   Arm chops
   Stew
   Ground lamb

Rib
Rack of lamb
Rib chops

Loin
Saddle
Loin chops
Loin roast

Leg
1. *Sirloin*
   Lamb steak
   Sirloin chops
2. *Leg of lamb roast*
   Lamb steak
   Lamb kebabs
3. *Hind shank*

Foreshank and Breast
1. *Shank*
2. *Spareribs*
3. *Riblets*
4. *Breast*
   Stew meat
   Ground lamb

Lamb has fewer retail cuts than beef, but many of the same rules apply: The parts that do the least work are the most tender. However, a lamb is a smaller, younger animal than a steer, and even the "tough" parts are usually more tender than the corresponding section of beef.

Shoulder

The shoulder is the hardest-working muscle of the lamb, with the most fat and plentiful bone. It is best suited for braising or stewing.

The neck section of lamb is a stewing cut taken from the front of the shoulder. Boneless shoulder is sometimes sold as a roasting cut (although it is probably better braised).

Chops cut from the shoulder (including both the blade chop, with a long bone down the center, and the arm chop, with a round bone near the end) are fatter than the higher-priced rib and loin chops, but can be treated much the same way (baked, broiled, or panfried).

Rib

Lamb ribs make up the fine rib roasts sold as rack of lamb or, curled into a circle, as crown roast. Chops from the rib are tender and juicy, whether cut whole or, more elegantly, frenched (with fatty meat scraped away from the bottom of the bones).

Rib chops can be broiled or panfried, and double rib chops can be rapidly baked as well, with a pocket cut for stuffing if desired. Like the loin, the rib portions of lamb are right at home with rich sauces.

Loin

The whole loin roast (and the even less common whole saddle of lamb) are found at the butcher's only occasionally. Chops cut from the loin are more frequently available. These extremely tender chops can be broiled or panfried and richly sauced.

Foreshank and Breast

Shanks are always cooked in liquid, at length, until the meat starts falling off the bones. Boneless rolled breast or bone-in breast is sometimes roasted (often with a stuffing inserted into a pocket cut in the center), but it is more often braised, since it's rather fatty and not especially tender.

Economical lamb spareribs and riblets from the breast can be barbecued or braised and are sometimes even roasted, but they are not wholly a bargain since the buyer is paying for a great deal of bone and not very much meat.

Supermarket lamb stew meat, kebabs, and ground lamb are usually cut from the shoulder, but kebabs cut from the leg are far superior in leanness and tenderness.

Leg

The back leg of the lamb is significantly more tender than the back leg of a steer. It may be cut into a whole leg (with the sirloin attached), a short-cut leg (with the sirloin trimmed off), a shank portion of the leg, and a center leg roast. These cuts, used primarily for roasting and grilling, can be butterflied for barbecuing or cut off the bone for top-quality kebabs.

Lamb steaks (to broil, panfry, or barbecue) are usually cut from either the center of the leg or from the more tender sirloin just above the leg. Occasionally lamb sirloin roast and sirloin chops can be found; these are both lean and tender. The hind shank, like the foreshank, is braised.

LOVELY LAMB

Lamb, a beloved meat in many parts of the world, surprisingly is less accepted in the United States. Although lamb (and even mutton) are relished throughout Great Britain, in sheep-raising areas of the Americas (whether in Montana or southern Argentina), lamb is a relative rarity at the table.

Those who know their lamb best know how to trim it and treat it well. Often they replace lamb fat with gentle-flavored, aromatic oils and cut the grease with the tang of citrus. All around the Mediterranean (including southern France, Italy, Spain, and North Africa) and in the Aegean area, the Balkans, the Middle East, and India, superb recipes have developed for nearly greaseless, rich-flavored lamb, often sparked with savory herbs and spices to complement the deep-flavored meat.

ROAST LAMB AND KID

Old-fashioned American meat thermometers still specify 170° F as the proper internal temperature for roast lamb—but in the sun-splashed countries where lamb is the staple meat, it's roasted as rare as a fine roast beef to maintain its tender juiciness. Noted cookbook author James Beard, a convert to the Mediterranean style of lamb cookery, specified a mere 125° F internal temperature (quite red); a greater number of cooks and diners may find lamb cooked to 135° F less alarming—and far more tender than well-done lamb.

The speed at which lamb is roasted depends on the cut. A dense leg of lamb does best started at high heat to sear it, then finished at moderate heat, whereas tender, bony rack of lamb is best roasted briefly (half an hour) in a hot oven.

Kid and goat remain "goaty" when rare and are seldom cooked to an internal temperature of less than 140° to 150° F. Since goat meat is almost fatless, it is best to "tame" and tenderize it with an assertively flavored marinade containing both oil and acid and to baste the meat frequently while it roasts.

GREEK EASTER LAMB OR KID

A savory herb crust forms over a leg of lamb or kid marinated and roasted in this celebratory Greek fashion.

- *1 leg of lamb, kid or goat (about 5 lb)*
- *1 teaspoon salt*
- *2 tablespoons fresh oregano leaves or 2 teaspoons dried oregano leaves, crumbled*
- *2 tablespoons fresh basil leaves or 2 teaspoons crumbled dried basil leaves*
- *2 tablespoons fresh mint leaves or 2 teaspoons crumbled dried mint leaves*
- *3 tablespoons fresh rosemary leaves or 1½ tablespoons dried rosemary*
- *1 tablespoon fresh thyme leaves or 1 teaspoon crumbled dried thyme leaves*
- *4 large cloves garlic, crushed, peeled, and coarsely minced*
- *1 cup olive oil*
  Juice of 2 large lemons

1. Two to four hours before roasting, remove meat from refrigerator. Trim all outside fat and prominent sinews. In a food processor, blender, or electric mincer purée together salt, oregano, basil, mint, rosemary, thyme, and garlic. (Add 1 or 2 spoonfuls olive oil if needed.) If no electric appliance is available, mince herbs and seasonings and pound in a mortar. Rub herb mixture on lamb. Stir together olive oil and lemon juice and paint some generously on meat, reserving remainder. Let meat stand at least 2 hours.

2. Preheat oven to 475° F. Place leg on rack in roasting pan in center of oven. Lower heat to 350° F. Brush meat with reserved oil mixture every 10 minutes. Roast until internal temperature at thickest part registers 135° F on an instant-read meat thermometer (20 minutes per pound) for rare, 150° F for medium, and 165° F for medium well-done. Let meat rest before slicing across grain.

Serves 6 to 8.

MUSTARD-COATED ROAST RACK OF LAMB WITH TOMATOES PROVENÇALE

The rack of lamb, a tender rib cut, is roasted quickly at high temperatures and served rare or medium-rare. (It's too expensive and gentle-flavored a cut to serve well-done.) Mustard-parsley coating is a classic, and tomatoes are the perfect accompaniment. To obtain bread crumbs, trim crusts from good-quality white bread and coarsely crumb the slices in a food processor or blender.

1 eight-chop rack of lamb or
  4 two-chop racks (about
  1½ lb each after trimming),
  trimmed (see Note)
¼ cup olive oil, for brushing
  lamb
1½ cups slightly coarse fresh
  bread crumbs
½ cup minced parsley
2 tablespoons dried rosemary
  leaves, finely chopped
½ teaspoon dried crumbled basil
  leaves
2 teaspoons minced garlic
1 teaspoon minced shallots
½ cup Dijon-style mustard
¼ pound unsalted or clarified
  butter, melted

Tomatoes Provençale

3 tablespoons (approximately)
  olive oil
4 tomatoes, halved horizontally
  Salt and freshly ground
  pepper, to taste
6 cloves garlic, minced
½ cup fresh white bread crumbs,
  or as needed
¼ cup minced parsley
2 tablespoons chopped fresh
  basil leaves or 2 teaspoons
  dried basil

1. Preheat oven to 425° F. Brush meaty areas of lamb with olive oil. Place rack, fat side up, in a roasting pan large enough to hold it.

2. Roast about 30 minutes for rare (125° F on an instant-read meat thermometer) or 40 minutes for medium-rare (135° F). Meanwhile, prepare Tomatoes Provençale. Remove lamb and let rest while preparing coating. Turn on broiler.

3. To prepare coating, in a large bowl toss together bread crumbs, parsley, rosemary, basil, garlic, and shallot. Brush mustard thickly over meaty topside of racks, then sprinkle bread crumb mixture over mustard and pat on gently to set in place. Drizzle melted butter lightly over the crumbs.

4. Place Tomatoes Provençale in oven and set lamb under broiler. Broil lamb 6 inches from heat source until crumb coating is golden and sizzling (about 2 minutes). Remove tomatoes and lamb at the same time. Carve racks into serving pieces and serve hot with Tomatoes Provençale.

Serves 4.

Tomatoes Provençale

1. Heat 1 tablespoon of the oil in a heavy skillet over high heat. When oil begins to smoke, add tomatoes, cut side down, and fry quickly until browned. Turn tomatoes and cook for a few seconds. Remove tomatoes and place cut side up in an ovenproof pan (such as a pie plate); sprinkle with salt and pepper. Keep warm.

2. Heat 1 tablespoon of the oil in a small skillet and gently sauté garlic over low heat until tender but not browned. Sprinkle garlic over tomatoes. Lightly sprinkle tomatoes with bread crumbs and then with parsley and basil. Drizzle a very small amount of olive oil over each.

Serves 4.

Note When buying a rack of lamb, ask the butcher to crack the chine bones to facilitate carving. Either have the butcher remove all but a thin (no more than ¼ inch) layer of fat from the outside, and french the ribs, or trim the meat yourself. (To french the ribs, scrape the last 2 to 3 inches of the bones with a sharp knife to remove the fatty meat between them.)

CABRITO AL PASTOR
Tex-Mex roast kid, shepherd style

Goat and kid are almost fatless, so they dry out if roasted too harshly. Although kid leg may be roasted in a home oven, goat leg is too strongly flavored for this treatment, requiring mesquite smoke to counter the goatiness. This version of Cabrito al Pastor includes a side dish of puréed black beans since *cabrito* is always served with black beans on the border.

2 or 3 legs of kid (cabrito) or
  1 leg of goat (about 6 lb)
4 recipes Fajitas Marinade,
  but use only 1 teaspoon chile
  (see page 8)
  Sliced ripe avocados sprinkled
  with lime juice and cilantro or
  guacamole, for garnish
  Salsa Cruda (see page 27), for
  accompaniment
  Warmed flour tortillas, for
  accompaniment

Black Bean Purée

6 cups cooked black beans
2 or 3 pickled jalapeño chiles,
  trimmed
½ tablespoon cumin seed,
  ground
1 tablespoon minced fresh
  epazote leaves or ½ teaspoon
  crumbled dried epazote leaves
  (see Note) or dried summer
  savory
  Salt, to taste (optional)
2 to 3 tablespoons bacon fat
  or lard
3 ounces soft goat cheese,
  crumbled

1. Remove fatty skin from kid or goat leg and trim any remaining fat, prominent membranes, and sinews. Place meat in a container (or doubled plastic bags), pour in Fajitas Marinade, cover (or seal bag), and marinate 24 to 72 hours in refrigerator, turning several times.

2. Preheat oven to 300° F. Drain meat, reserving marinade. Roast each leg for about 12 minutes per pound to rare (125° F on an instant-read meat thermometer inserted in the thickest part), basting frequently with reserved marinade. (Meat can now be reserved in refrigerator for up to 3 days.) Save any leftover marinade.

3. Prepare charcoal grill using mesquite charcoal or mesquite chips over other charcoal, placing charcoal at edges of barbecue, not in center. Place meat on an oiled grill 5 to 6 inches above heat source. Cover grill and cook leg 30 to 45 minutes, turning and basting frequently, until browned all over and smoky-flavored. During the last 20 minutes, grill meat directly over coals to brown (about 10 minutes per side). Let meat stand for a few minutes before slicing thinly.

4. Garnish serving dish with avocado and serve with Black Bean Purée, Salsa Cruda, and tortillas.

Serves 6.

Black Bean Purée

1. Drain cooked beans, reserving liquid. Purée beans, chiles, cumin, and epazote in a blender or food processor, adding some reserved liquid if paste is too dry. (Mixture should cohere but not be pasty.) Taste and add salt if needed.

2. In a large skillet heat bacon fat until fragrant. Add purée; stir, and fry over low heat until mixture is heated through, stirring occasionally. When beans are hot, add goat cheese, cover, and continue simmering until the cheese is melted.

Serves 6.

Note Epazote is a Mexican herb available in Latin food stores.

Classic French fare need not take all day: Mustard-Coated Roast Rack of Lamb With Tomatoes Provençale mingles rich and tangy flavors—and takes less than one hour to prepare.

BONING AND BUTTERFLYING LEG OF LAMB

Whether a whole leg with a pocket or a butterflied leg is desired, boning a leg of lamb is far easier than it looks. With a sharp boning knife, even your first attempt at boning will take a mere 20 minutes or so, and your speed will improve as you get more practice.

1. *Wear a full apron to protect your clothes. Place lamb on a cutting board and have ready a newly honed boning knife and, if desired, a larger, equally sharp chef's knife for the coarser cutting. Begin by chopping off the fatty "tail" at the pointed (shank) end and carving around and removing the bony plate that may be attached to the wide (sirloin) end. Remove excess or all fat by slipping boning knife between the fat-covered membrane and the meat at the wide end and cutting down toward the shank. Repeat until lamb has been stripped down to meat all around the thicker part of the leg. (If you remove all fat, rub lamb with oil or melted butter before cooking to keep it moist. It will still be much lower in calories than a 1-inch-thick sheath of lamb fat and will taste better.)*

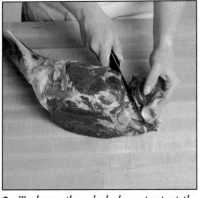

2. *To bone the whole leg, start at the wide end. The first bone you'll encounter is a flat bone attached to a round bone. Work boning knife around flat bone until it's detached. Remove the streaks of fat you encounter. Work knife down along the round, knobby bone until it's freed from the surrounding meat. About 5 inches down into the leg, this bone is attached to the shank bone.*

3. *After completing steps 1 and 2, if leaving the leg whole, stand the meat on end, and cut downward carefully, working knife all around the leg bone. When the round leg bone can be wiggled, push back the meat around the bone to view the shank and the small, flat bone attached to the knee. Remove this knee bone, using the point of the boning knife. Lay the leg on the cutting board and, just to the side of the shank bone, cut a long slit so that the bone is exposed. Slip the boning knife all around it and remove leg and shank bones together. Carefully cut away the pockets of fat inside the leg.*

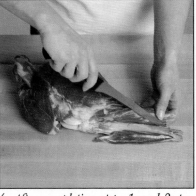

4. *After completing steps 1 and 2, to butterfly leg, turn lamb so its leaner side is up. Starting at the butt end, work knife into meat and along bone, cutting down to shank bone. This will expose all remaining bones. Remove them. Open up the meat like a book, cut side up, so that it lies flat on the board. Cut away fat and some of meat from center of leg, so remaining meat forms a thick, relatively flat and even piece. (Meat removed can be used for kebabs, stir-fries, or homemade ground lamb.)*

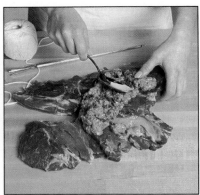

5. *Butterflied leg may be marinated and grilled, or stuffed for roasting. To stuff, spread stuffing in center and sew meat closed with strong white thread or with kitchen string and a larding needle. If you have not butterflied leg, insert stuffing in cavity left by removal of bones and sew up opening.*

GALLIMAUFRÉE PROVENÇALE
Spring leg of lamb stuffed with basil and mushrooms

Gallimaufrée is a famous hearty dish from the Burgundy area of France. The original Burgundian recipe seems rather heavy to modern palates, but this equally traditional herb-spiked variation from southern France tastes like it was invented yesterday. It's a springtime dish, when the lamb legs are small and fresh basil appears in the market. It goes well with Tomatoes Provençale (see page 52) and Pilaf (see page 63) or small new potatoes sautéed in butter.

> 1 boned small leg of lamb (about 4 lb before boning) or 1 boned shank half of a larger leg
> 1 quart water
> 4 ounces bacon, sliced crossways into rectangles about ¼ inch wide (about ½ cup)
> 2 medium shallots, peeled and minced
> ¼ pound fresh mushrooms (preferably chanterelles), stemmed and finely diced
> 1 tablespoon (approximately) olive oil (optional), plus olive oil for rubbing lamb
> 1 tablespoon minced garlic (about 3 cloves)
> 3 tablespoons minced fresh basil
> 2 tablespoons minced parsley
> 4 tablespoons soft bread crumbs, or as needed

Wine and Garlic Pan Sauce

> 12 large cloves garlic, unpeeled
> 1 cup dry white wine
> Juice of ½ lemon
> ¼ cup meat stock (preferably homemade)
> Salt and freshly ground pepper, to taste

1. Remove lamb from refrigerator 2 hours before cooking to allow it to come to room temperature. Trim off all exterior fat, if not already done.

2. Preheat oven to 400° F. Bring the water to a boil. Drop in bacon, lower heat to medium, and blanch at a low boil for 5 minutes. Drain. Pat bacon with paper towels to dry, scatter in a medium skillet, and fry over medium-high heat, flipping frequently with a spatula until very lightly browned but not crisped. With slotted spatula transfer bacon to a food processor or blender, reserving fat in the skillet.

3. Add shallots and mushrooms to bacon fat. If there is not enough fat, add the 1 tablespoon olive oil. Sauté rapidly, stirring constantly, until mushrooms are lightly browned. Remove from heat and reserve.

4. Add to the food processor or blender the garlic, basil, and parsley and process until finely minced. Pour mixture into a bowl and stir in mushroom mixture. One tablespoon at a time, stir in enough bread crumbs to make mixture cohere.

5. Stuff mixture into the hole in the lamb created by boning it. Sew up opening over stuffing (ideally with a larding needle and kitchen string). Rub lamb all over with olive oil and place on an oiled rack over a shallow roasting pan. Roast lamb about 30 minutes, total, for very rare (125° F on an instant-read meat thermometer inserted into the thickest part), 45 minutes for rare, or 55 minutes for medium-rare with some well-done portions. Allow lamb to rest for a few minutes before slicing. Then place on serving platter and pour Wine and Garlic Pan Sauce over sliced lamb.

Serves 4 to 6.

Wine and Garlic Pan Sauce Drop garlic into boiling water to cover. Lower heat and simmer 25 minutes. Drain, cool briefly, and squeeze garlic out of its peels into a small bowl. Reserve. When lamb is done pour any excess fat out of roasting pan.

Deglaze roasting pan over top of stove (using 2 burners if necessary) with wine and lemon juice, scraping up browned bits. Pour liquid into a small, nonreactive saucepan. Add stock and over high heat reduce by about half, until moderately thickened. Season to taste with salt and pepper. Add reserved garlic cloves, squashing some of them into the sauce by pressing them against the side of the pan with a wooden spoon. Heat garlic briefly in sauce.

Makes about ⅔ cup.

GRILLED OR BROILED BUTTERFLIED LEG OF LAMB

Butterflied leg of lamb, flavored and moistened with a marinade, is an ideal cut for rapid grilling on a barbecue.

> 1 butterflied whole leg of lamb (about 5 lb)
> 1 Shish Kebab marinade (see page 63), Greek Easter Lamb marinade (see page 51), Tandoori Marinade (see page 9), or other marinade of choice
> Fresh Mint Sauce (see page 58), for accompaniment (see Note)

Steep lamb in marinade for at least 2 hours at room temperature or, preferably, overnight in refrigerator. Bring meat to room temperature, remove meat, and reserve marinade. Preheat broiler or burn coals in grill to white ash. Place lamb about 3 inches from heat source and broil 8 to 10 minutes per side for medium-rare, basting every few minutes with reserved marinade. Serve with Fresh Mint Sauce on the side.

Serves 8 to 10.

Note Fresh Mint Sauce is not recommended to accompany the meat if the Tandoori Marinade is used.

LAMB CHOPS, STEAKS, AND MEDALLIONS

In most recipes lamb loin chops, lamb steaks, and lamb medallions are virtually interchangeable—all are highly tender pieces that can easily be trimmed of all fat. Lamb steaks are usually cut from the sirloin or sometimes from the leg, and noisettes or medallions are usually just loin lamb chops from which the bones and fat have been removed. Paillards are usually ½-inch-thick lamb steaks cut from boned leg of lamb. You can easily cut your own noisettes, medallions, and paillards from the appropriate parts, if the butcher seems to be charging for the French nomenclature rather than merely for well-trimmed meat.

Lamb chops may be cut from the rib, loin, or shoulder of lamb. Both the rib and loin chops are tender, easily trimmed of fat, and suitable for cooking quickly or slowly by dry heat (broiling, baking, or panfrying in a small amount of fat). They are well suited to the most aristocratic recipes.

Shoulder chops, on the other hand, may be more economical, but they are not only far less tender but unfortunately have fat embedded in them as streaks in the meat attached to tough connective tissue. Shoulder chops are least greasy when rapidly broiled or grilled, especially if they've been prepared with Tandoori Marinade (see page 9), which will tenderize the meat and, with its tartness, cut the fat. Trimmed meat from shoulder chops makes fine, economical home-ground lamb, however (see page 60).

Lamb kebabs are best cut from the leg, and lamb strips for stir-frying or Singapore Satay (see page 32) are equally good when cut from the leg or the sirloin. Lamb shoulder is sometimes used for such dishes in inexpensive restaurants, with less-than-satisfactory results.

BAKED MARINATED STUFFED LAMB CHOPS

This recipe has elements in common with many more elegant lamb dishes. It uses mushrooms, Dijon mustard, and an enticing oil and lemon marinade, but it is simple fare that comes out with its own unique and delicious taste.

- *4 double rib lamb chops (see Note)*
- *2 tablespoons olive oil*
- *2 tablespoons lemon juice*
- *½ teaspoon freshly ground pepper*
- *¼ teaspoon dried crumbled oregano*
- *1 clove garlic, finely minced*
- *2 tablespoons butter*
- *1 tablespoon cooking oil, such as peanut or sunflower oil*
- *2 small shallots, peeled and minced*
- *8 medium mushrooms, trimmed, wiped, and minced*
- *2 tablespoons minced parsley*
- *4 tablespoons (approximately) soft bread crumbs*
- *1½ teaspoons Dijon mustard*
- *1 tablespoon white wine vinegar*
- *2 teaspoons water*

1. Trim lamb chops of excess fat. Cut a large pocket in center of chops by inserting a sharp small knife (such as a boning knife) in the meaty side and cutting to within ½ inch of the edge all around. Mix together olive oil, lemon juice, pepper, oregano, and garlic. Spread mixture on both sides of chops, cover tightly, and refrigerate overnight (or let stand at room temperature for at least 1 hour).

2. Preheat oven to 425° F. In a heavy medium skillet over moderate heat, melt butter with cooking oil. Add shallots and mushrooms and stir until lightly browned (about 6 minutes). Add parsley and enough bread crumbs to absorb butter. Stir in 1 teaspoon of the Dijon mustard.

3. Open pockets of marinated chops and insert stuffing. Close openings with turkey skewers or toothpicks. Mix together vinegar, the water, and remaining ½ teaspoon mustard. Place chops bony side down in a shallow baking pan, pour vinegar mixture over them, place pan in center of oven, and bake about 30 minutes for rare, 40 minutes for medium.

Serves 4.

Note This recipe can be prepared with thick shoulder lamb chops trimmed of fat. Proceed as above, but place chops on a rack in a baking pan and bake at 350° F until medium well-done (1 to 1¼ hours).

LAMB CHOPS VILLANDRY

Here is an all-out recipe for company, with roots in the Loire River château district of France. Although the wine component of the sauce is flexible (you can use a California Fumé Blanc or Sauvignon Blanc as well as a French Vouvray or Muscadet), it's not worth making the dish if canned beef stock has to substitute for homemade veal stock. Serve this gala entrée with the same wine used in the cooking, well chilled.

- *½ cup White Veal Stock (see page 17) or Brown Meat Stock (see page 16) made with veal*
- *8 frozen artichoke bottoms*
- *½ pound fresh mushrooms, finely minced*
- *8 tablespoons unsalted butter*
- *1 tablespoon cooking oil*
- *2 tablespoons minced shallots*
- *3 tablespoons finely chopped fresh tarragon or 1½ tablespoons dried crumbled tarragon leaves*
- *4 thick rib lamb chops or 8 thick loin lamb chops or noisettes, trimmed of all fat*
- *¾ cup fruity, dry white wine Salt and freshly ground pepper, to taste*

1. In a small, heavy pot, bring stock to boil and reduce by half. Meanwhile cook artichoke bottoms according to package directions. Drain, place on ovenproof serving dish large enough to hold lamb chops as well, and keep warm (in oven turned to lowest temperature).

2. Squeeze out excess moisture from mushrooms, a palmful at a time. In a small, nonreactive skillet over moderately high heat, melt 2 tablespoons of the butter with the oil. Add mushrooms and shallots and sauté, stirring frequently, until mushrooms begin to brown (about 5 minutes). Fill cooked artichoke bottoms with mushrooms and keep warm.

3. Mash 2 tablespoons of the butter with one third of the tarragon. Form into as many small balls as you have lamb chops. Make a small but deep slit in the side of each chop, insert the ball of seasoned butter, and fasten the slits shut with turkey-trussing skewers or toothpicks.

4. In a large, heavy skillet over high heat, melt 3 tablespoons of the butter. Add chops and quickly sear on both sides (4 to 5 minutes per side for rare). Remove chops to a plate. Pour wine into skillet and deglaze over high heat, scraping up browned bits. When wine is reduced to a glaze, add half of remaining tarragon. Return chops to skillet and gently reheat over medium heat.

5. Remove skewers from chops and arrange chops on serving platter with stuffed artichoke bottoms. Season to taste with salt and pepper. With pan off heat swirl remaining 1 tablespoon butter into sauce. Pour sauce over lamb and stuffed artichoke bottoms and sprinkle with remaining tarragon. Serve immediately.

Serves 4.

Lamb Chops Villandry are lovely at a candle-lit dinner when there's company you want to dazzle. Halve the recipe to serve two when romance is your intention.

Tender leg of lamb takes splendidly to Asian-style stir-frying. A spectacular Mongolian Lamb on Snow delights the eye and the taste buds with its exciting array of textures, tints, and flavors.

LAMB CHOPS WITH GARLIC-HERB PURÉE

Nothing is quicker or more flavorful than rapidly broiled or grilled lamb chops. Allow two 1-inch-thick rib or loin chops (or double chops) per person, or one thick chop for each calorie counter.

> 6 *thick (or double) rib or loin*
> *lamb chops*
> *Oil, for greasing rack*
> *Salt and freshly ground*
> *pepper, to taste*
> 6 *slices premium-quality bacon*
> *(optional)*
> 1 *teaspoon (approximately)*
> *olive or peanut oil (optional)*
> 1 *quart water*
> 2 *large (2 oz each) bulbs garlic*
> *(about 40 cloves), peeled*
> 1 *tablespoon yogurt or*
> *sour cream*
> 2 *tablespoons minced fresh*
> *herbs of choice (basil, mint,*
> *tarragon, chervil, marjoram,*
> *or parsley, or a combination)*
> *or* 1 *teaspoon dried herbes de*
> *Provence*

1. Remove chops from refrigerator about 1 hour before cooking. Preheat broiler or prepare charcoal grill, oiling the rack in either case. If desired trim excess fat from sides of chops and season meat lightly with salt and pepper. If desired wrap a strip of bacon around outside of each chop, securing with toothpicks or turkey-trussing skewers, or rub meat with a little olive or peanut oil.

2. Bring the water to a boil. Drop garlic cloves into boiling water, decrease heat to low, and simmer 25 minutes. Drain garlic and purée in blender or food processor with yogurt and herbs.

3. Place chops about 4 inches from heat source. Broil 8 to 10 minutes on first side, about 4 minutes on second side for rare, longer on second side for medium. Top nearly cooked chops with garlic-herb purée, return to broiler, and broil until purée begins to brown (2 to 3 minutes). Let rest about 5 minutes before serving.

Serves 3 or 6.

FRESH MINT SAUCE

Mint sauce is an ideal accompaniment for lamb chops or almost any broiled, grilled, or baked lamb dish.

> ½ *cup chicken stock or water*
> ¼ *cup sugar*
> ¾ *cup chopped fresh mint leaves*
> ½ *cup white wine vinegar or*
> *malt vinegar*
> ½ *teaspoon crushed chile*
> *(optional)*

1. In a heatproof bowl pour boiling stock over sugar and stir until dissolved. Stir in mint and vinegar. Cover and let stand at room temperature for at least 2 hours (preferably overnight).

2. Strain mixture if a clear sauce is desired. If a spicy sauce is preferred, stir in chile. Serve sauce at room temperature.

Makes about 1½ cups.

MONGOLIAN LAMB ON SNOW

This dish is as beautiful as it is delicious, with strips of red chiles and green pepper mixed with lamb, all resting on crisp-fried white noodles. Serve with cooked rice to fill out the meal. Or rest the meat mixture on boiled, thin Chinese wheat noodles or even vermicelli that have been lightly dressed with dark sesame oil.

> 1½ pounds boned leg of lamb
> ¼ cup soy sauce
> ¼ cup Shaoxing, sake, or dry sherry
> 2 tablespoons hoisin sauce
> ¼ cup Poultry Stock (see page 17)
> ½ tablespoon sugar
> 1 tablespoon slivered fresh ginger
> 1 tablespoon slivered garlic
> 3 tablespoons dark sesame oil
>   Peanut oil, for deep-frying
> 2 ounces (approximately) Chinese transparent noodles (rice noodles or bean threads)
> 1 quart water
> 6 to 8 green onions, plus more for garnish
> 1 cup bean sprouts, heads and stringy tails snapped off
> 1 large and 1 medium green bell pepper, trimmed, seeded, deveined, and cut into ⅛-inch-thick slices
> 2 to 4 small hot red fresh chiles, trimmed, seeded, deveined, and cut into ⅛-inch-thick slices
> 2 tablespoons minced fresh coriander, plus more for garnish
> 1 tablespoon cornstarch mixed with 1 tablespoon water

1. Trim fat from lamb, separate into muscles, and trim away tendons and membranes. (This will make lamb extremely tender.) Slice lamb into strips ⅛ inch thick by ½ inch wide, and about 1½ inches long. Mix soy sauce, wine, hoisin sauce, stock, sugar, ginger, garlic, and 1 tablespoon of the sesame oil. Add lamb to mixture, cover, and marinate about 1 hour at room temperature (or refrigerate overnight).

2. Have ready a serving platter and tongs. In a wok or deep, wide saucepan, heat about 3 inches of peanut oil to about 350° F. (It will be smoking slightly and very fragrant. To test, drop in 1 transparent noodle. If noodle puffs up immediately, oil is ready.) Break up noodles into handfuls. Drop 1 handful into hot oil. As soon as sizzling stops, using tongs, carefully turn noodles over and fry other side, gently pushing noodles into oil to make sure all of them puff up. With tongs remove noodles to platter, draining excess oil back into pot. Repeat until platter is covered with a bed of puffed noodles about an inch thick. Let oil cool until it can be safely poured out of wok.

3. Bring the water to a full boil. Meanwhile slice all but two of the green onions in 2-inch slices, including green tops. Place bean sprouts in a colander in sink and slowly pour boiling water over them. Immediately cool sprouts under cold running water. Mix sliced onions with drained bean sprouts. Separately mix sliced peppers and chiles. Mince the 2 remaining onions in a third bowl; mix with cilantro and reserve. Arrange all ingredients, in a line, convenient to the stove. Drain lamb, reserving marinade.

4. Wipe out wok and film with remaining 2 tablespoons sesame oil. If using a gas stove, remove burner plate and gently place wok directly on burner. (With electric stove place wok on preheated burner plate set to highest heat.) Heat oil until fragrant. Add lamb and, stirring and flipping constantly, fry until meat loses its pink color (about 1 minute). Add pepper mixture and fry, stirring and flipping, until peppers soften (about 1 minute). Add bean sprout and onion mixture and fry until onions soften (about 30 seconds longer). Pour in reserved marinade and stir. Pour in cornstarch mixture and stir until thickened. Remove from heat and place lamb mixture over bed of noodles. Scatter minced green onions and coriander over lamb and serve.

Serves 4.

LAMB STEWS

For stewed and braised dishes, lamb's tougher and fattier parts excel. In all the recipes that follow, lamb shoulder, shank, and neck are interchangeable.

LAMB PRINTANIÈRE

Fresh mint seasons the lamb in this glistening stew.

> 3 pounds boneless lamb leg or shoulder, fat trimmed, cut into 1-inch cubes
>   Salt and freshly ground white pepper, to taste
> 3 tablespoons butter or margarine
> 2 teaspoons salad oil
> 3 shallots, finely chopped
> 1 clove garlic, minced or pressed
> 1 large carrot, sliced about ¼ inch thick
> 3 or 4 sprigs fresh mint
> 1 cup chicken stock
> 1½ cups dry white wine
> 1½ to 2 cups shelled fresh peas

1. Sprinkle lamb lightly with salt and pepper. In a large, deep frying pan or Dutch oven, melt 2 tablespoons butter with the oil. Add lamb, a third at a time. Brown well, removing lamb as it browns. When all lamb is done, add shallots, stirring until soft and lightly browned. Add garlic and carrot. Return lamb to pan. Add mint, stock, and wine. Bring to a boil, cover, reduce heat, and simmer until tender (45 minutes to 1 hour).

2. Remove lamb and keep warm. Strain cooking liquid, discarding carrot and mint. Skim away surface fat. Return liquid to pan and boil over high heat. Cook, stirring, until slightly reduced and syrupy. Add salt if needed. Mix in peas and cook, stirring, for 1 to 2 minutes. Cut remaining 1 tablespoon butter into pieces. With pan off heat, stir in butter, one piece at a time, until melted. Warm dinner plates in oven. Return lamb to sauce. Spoon lamb into center of plate. Surround with sauce and peas and serve.

Serves 6 to 8.

Step-by-Step

MAKING LEAN GROUND LAMB

Why bother making ground lamb at home? The answer lies in the fat content: Supermarket ground lamb is 30 percent fat, the same as sausage or the cheapest grade of ground beef—but both pork fat and beef fat are much more pleasant in flavor than lamb fat. (Lard and beef suet are both cooking fats, but lamb fat is good for nothing.)

Furthermore, the melting away of fat during cooking leaves the cook with merely two thirds the amount of meat purchased, and worse, what fat remains gives lamb its reputation for greasiness. Admittedly, shoulder of lamb, deboned and scrupulously trimmed of fat, will also lose a third of its weight under the knife, but what's left is pure, lean meat, clean in flavor and low in calories. If some fat is desired, it can be ground, too, in exactly the percentage that the cook requires.

1. Start with lamb shoulder chops, either blade or round bone. Buy enough to compensate for the loss of about one third the total weight. First remove all fat and attached membrane surrounding the chop using a sharp, small knife. (A boning knife is ideal.)

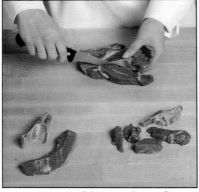

2. Cut meat off bones, discarding bones (or reserving them for stock). Cut away any veins of fat and connective tissue. This will leave small pieces of very lean meat.

3. Grind meat in a meat grinder or shred in a food processor with metal blade, including precisely as much fat (cut in small pieces) as you desire (15 to 20 percent is more than ample for any lamb dish). If a food processor is used, pick over the meat, removing any white clumps of fat or gristle that have survived the shredding. Using a food processor will produce a particularly silky, finely grained ground meat that's especially suitable for Middle Eastern and Indian ground meat dishes. (In both areas meat is usually ground twice and then kneaded, but shredding in a processor takes care of the entire procedure.) Wrap the meat very thoroughly to store before use (for example, in plastic wrap and then in a zip-top freezer bag); refrigerate for up to 4 days or freeze for up to 4 months.

MOROCCAN LAMB SHANKS WITH HONEY

Based on the exotically flavored *tajines*, or stews, of Morocco, these lamb shanks go well with pilaf made, for a change, with coarse-milled bulgur wheat (available from natural foods stores or packaged as couscous) substituting for the rice. Follow with a simple salad liberally strewn with fresh herbs in a tart oil and lemon dressing.

> 1 tablespoon butter or margarine
> 1 tablespoon olive oil or salad oil
> 2 medium onions, thinly sliced
> 1 clove garlic, minced or pressed
> 1 teaspoon salt
> ½ teaspoon each *ground turmeric and ground ginger*
> ¼ teaspoon each *ground allspice and ground coriander*
> ¾ cup water
> ¼ cup honey
> 2 cinnamon sticks, each about 3 inches long
> 4 to 5 pounds lamb shanks, cracked
> 1 lemon, thinly sliced
>   Pilaf (see page 63) made with bulgur wheat

1. Preheat oven to 350° F. In a large frying pan heat together butter and oil. Sauté onions until limp but not browned. Add garlic, salt, turmeric, ginger, allspice, and coriander and stir to coat onions; simmer about 2 minutes. Mix in the water, honey, and cinnamon sticks; bring to a boil, then remove from heat.

2. Arrange lamb shanks in a deep casserole just large enough to hold them in a single layer. Pour on onion mixture. Arrange lemon slices over lamb. Cover and bake until lamb is very tender (about 2 hours).

3. Remove lamb and lemons to a serving dish and keep warm. Skim fat from cooking liquid; boil liquid to reduce and thicken it slightly. Pour over lamb and serve with Pilaf made with bulgur.

Serves 4 to 6.

BALKAN SUMMER LAMB STEW

Here a sophisticated casserole balances the richness of the meat against poignant herbal flavors, the sweetness of long-cooked, well-tamed garlic, a nip of spiciness, and the cleansing bite of lemon juice. (For a switch fresh mint can substitute for dill.) Serve with Pilaf (see page 63) or warm French bread to sop up the extra sauce.

>   3 to 3½ pounds lamb shoulder
>   with bones, cut in chunks,
>   or cracked lamb shanks,
>   trimmed of excess fat
>   2 medium onions, peeled and
>   coarsely chopped
>   3 large bell peppers (preferably
>   a mixture of colors), trimmed,
>   seeded, and chopped into
>   2-inch pieces
>   12 small red new potatoes,
>   scrubbed, eyes removed
>   2 large tomatoes, cut into
>   eighths
>   1 bunch green onions
>   (including green tops), roots
>   trimmed, sliced into 1½-inch
>   lengths
>   1 small bulb garlic (about
>   1 oz, with about 8 cloves),
>   cloves separated, crushed,
>   and peeled
>   1 cup snipped fresh dill or
>   3 tablespoons dried dill
>   1 tablespoon hot Hungarian
>   paprika or ½ teaspoon
>   cayenne pepper, or to taste
>   Salt and freshly ground black
>   pepper, to taste
>   ¼ cup olive oil
>   ⅓ cup water
>   3 yellow summer squash or
>   yellow zucchini, ends
>   trimmed, thickly sliced
>   ¼ cup green beans, ends
>   trimmed, cut in 1½-inch
>   lengths
>   2 tablespoons lemon juice,
>   or to taste
>   Warm French bread or Pilaf
>   (see page 63), for
>   accompaniment

1. Preheat oven to 350° F. Place lamb in a large (6-quart or more) ovenproof casserole or Dutch oven and add onion, bell pepper, potatoes, tomatoes, green onion, garlic, dill, paprika, salt, and black pepper. Pour on olive oil and then the water. Cover and bake 2½ hours.

2. Scatter squash and green beans on top of other ingredients and add a little more water (about half a cup) if the stew looks dry. Bake 30 minutes longer.

3. Remove casserole from oven, leaving oven turned on if serving stew the same night. Pour off (or tilt casserole and spoon off) most of the liquid into a bowl. To liquid add lemon juice, tasting carefully and correcting seasonings. *To serve the same night:* Spoon off all visible fat from liquid or, better yet, place bowl in freezer until fat congeals on top (about 20 minutes). *To serve the next day:* Refrigerate liquid separately from remaining ingredients. Remove and discard fat from top of liquid.

4. Whichever technique is used, before serving pour remaining degreased liquid back into casserole (see Note). Cover casserole and reheat in oven until liquid is bubbling slightly (about 20 minutes if chilled, 5 minutes if unchilled). Serve in large soup bowls with French bread on the side or on large plates over a bed of Pilaf.

Serves 4.

<u>Note</u> For a thicker, creamy sauce, stir ¾ cup yogurt into liquid just before reheating.

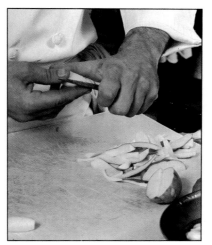

GROUND LAMB AND "SECOND HELPINGS"

Different spice mixes confer wholly different flavors on ground lamb. Use home-ground lamb (see page 60) for lamburgers (see opposite page) so you can control the fat content. (Supermarket ground lamb is 30 percent fat.) The taste benefits of making your own ground lamb will far outweigh the extra effort required.

SHEPHERD'S PIE

This old English favorite using roast lamb (or lean ground lamb) is very simple and unfailingly wonderful. Accompany it with any steamed, lightly buttered, seasonal green vegetable.

>   3 cups mashed potatoes
>   3 tablespoons unsalted butter
>   ½ to ¾ cup milk, as needed
>   Salt and pepper, to taste
>   2 cups trimmed, finely diced
>   cooked lamb or 1 pound lean
>   home-ground lamb (see page
>   60), browned over high heat
>   in a skillet, fat poured off
>   1½ cups (approximately)
>   Flour-Thickened Pan Gravy
>   for Roasts (see page 13)

Preheat oven to 350° F. Mix mashed potatoes with butter and enough milk to make smooth. Stir in salt and pepper to taste. In a well-greased casserole or deep baking dish, or in 4 small, individual casseroles, make a bottom crust of half the mashed potatoes. Cover potatoes with lamb and gravy. Cover or dot lamb with puffs of mashed potatoes. Bake until top crust is touched with brown, crisp spots (about 20 minutes). Serve hot.

Serves 4.

SKINNY PEPPERED LAMBURGERS IN HERBED PIZZAIOLA SAUCE

Accompany these lamburgers with Tomato, Green Pepper, and Cucumber Salad (see opposite page) made without oil for a meal of under 400 calories per person. Each pound of lamb will serve 3 or 4 (or 2 big eaters) as a main dish or 6 to 8 as an appetizer.

> 1 teaspoon salt, plus more to taste
> 1 pound very lean (under 10 percent fat) home-ground lamb (see page 60)
> 2 tablespoons cracked black peppercorns
> 2 cups water
> 1 bulb garlic (approximately 14 cloves)
> 1 tomato, peeled, seeded, and minced
> ½ cup finely chopped fresh basil, mint, or parsley
> 1 tablespoon butter, cut into 4 pieces

1. Mix salt with lamb, shape meat into 4 patties, and coat both sides of patties with peppercorns, pushing peppercorns into meat with the heel of the hand. Let stand at room temperature for 1 hour.

2. Meanwhile bring the water to a boil. Drop garlic cloves into boiling water; lower heat and simmer until garlic is very tender and mild (about 25 minutes). Drain garlic and peel, reserving water.

3. Heat a heavy, nonreactive or nonstick medium skillet until waves of heat ripple up. Sear lamb patties in dry skillet for 2 minutes per side. Transfer to warmed platter. Add to skillet poached garlic, ¼ cup water from the garlic, tomato, and basil. Reduce sauce rapidly to a glaze, stirring constantly. With pan off heat, whisk butter into warm sauce a piece at a time. Season with salt to taste and pour sauce over lamb.

Serves 4.

ARMENIAN SHISH KEBAB DINNER

Roast Eggplant With Garlic and Dill

Armenian Shish Kebab

Pilaf

Tomato, Green Pepper, and Cucumber Salad

Young, Fruity Red Wine, such as Beaujolais, or Mint Tea

The rich but fresh-tasting cuisine of Armenia is a special variation of Middle Eastern food. Lamb is overwhelmingly the favorite meat of Armenians, and they treat it with supreme expertise. This exotic dinner is a sensual treat, from the first course to the last. The roast eggplant appetizer, a contemporary version of an Armenian folk recipe, can be served warm or chilled, but it's best at room temperature. This menu serves four.

ROAST EGGPLANT WITH GARLIC AND DILL

Salt draws the juices out of other substances. With eggplant, this is a desirable effect: Salting the slices draws the bitterness from the seeds, leaving the flesh sweet-tasting and receptive to flavoring.

> 1 large eggplant
> Salt, as needed
> ¾ cup (approximately) olive oil
> 4 to 6 cloves garlic
> 2 tablespoons minced fresh dill or 1 tablespoon dried dill
> 2 tablespoons pine nuts
> 2 tablespoons balsamic or red wine vinegar

1. Preheat oven to 400° F. Peel eggplant, slice ¼ inch thick (it will look prettiest sliced on the bias into ovals), and spread slices in a single layer on a drying rack, colander, or large roasting rack. Sprinkle with salt. Let stand 30 minutes. Droplets of brown liquid will appear on eggplant slices. Place slices in a colander, rinse off well in cold water, and shake colander to rid eggplant of excess water.

2. Film a large baking pan with about 2 tablespoons of the olive oil. Place eggplant in pan in a single layer. Lightly crush garlic cloves with flat of a knife, peel them, and cut them into slivers. Scatter garlic slivers evenly over eggplant (each piece should be topped with at least 1 sliver). Sprinkle eggplant with dill and drizzle ½ cup of the olive oil evenly over slices.

3. Place baking pan in top third of oven. Bake 20 minutes. If eggplant seems to be drying out, drizzle on a little more oil. Scatter pine nuts over eggplant and bake, checking every few minutes, until pine nuts are golden, garlic is brown, and eggplant is tender with some charring at edges of slices (about 10 minutes longer).

4. Immediately remove eggplant slices to individual appetizer plates or to serving plate and drizzle vinegar evenly over them. Let cool at least 5 minutes before serving.

Serves 4.

ARMENIAN SHISH KEBAB

The secret of preparing clean, greaseless shish kebab meat is to bathe chunks of perfectly trimmed leg of lamb in a very simple marinade in which olive oil replaces all the fat of the lamb. To get perfect skewers of meat and vegetables all cooked at the same time, partially cook all the elements except the tomatoes first, then put them together in classic shish kebab order on skewers and finish broiling. For this recipe you'll need at least four metal skewers.

> 2 pounds boneless leg of lamb (from a 4-lb half leg of lamb), trimmed of all fat and sinew and cut in 2-inch cubes
> ½ cup olive oil
> 2 tablespoons fresh lemon juice
> 3 large cloves garlic, peeled and crushed
> 1 teaspoon dry white wine
> 1 small bay leaf
> Small pinches of salt, freshly ground pepper, dried oregano, and crumbled dried rosemary leaves
> 2 large onions, peeled and cut into 8 wedges each
> 2 large green bell peppers, cut into 8 pieces each
> 12 medium-large mushrooms, stemmed and wiped clean
> 2 large tomatoes, stem bruises removed, cut into 8 wedges each

1. Place lamb in a large container with a cover. In a medium bowl mix olive oil, lemon juice, garlic, wine, bay leaf, salt, pepper, oregano, and rosemary. Pour marinade over lamb cubes, stir thoroughly, and refrigerate, covered, at least 24 hours, stirring occasionally.

2. About 1 hour before serving time, preheat broiler. Drain lamb kebabs, reserving marinade. Thread separate skewers of lamb, onion, green pepper, and mushrooms and place on a broiling tray. Baste vegetables with some of reserved marinade. Broil about 4 inches from heat, turning frequently, as follows: lamb and green pepper, about 7 minutes; onions, about 12 minutes; mushrooms, about 3 minutes. Remove skewers and allow to cool slightly, until ingredients and skewers can be handled. Leave broiler on.

3. Remove skewers from ingredients and rethread 4 or 8 skewers (depending on size of skewers) so that each one includes, in alternating pieces, some lamb, onion, green pepper, mushrooms, and tomato. Baste again with any remaining marinade. Return skewers to broiler and, turning frequently, broil until meat is reheated and cooked medium-rare, vegetables are slightly blackened in spots, and tomatoes are very tender but not yet falling off skewers (5 to 7 minutes more). To serve, bring skewers to the table and push meat and vegetables off them onto each plate individually. Accompany with Pilaf.

Serves 4.

PILAF

In this invaluable and basic rice preparation—common (with small changes in seasoning) to southern France, Greece, Armenia, Turkey, the Middle East, India, and Latin America—the rice is sautéed gently in butter with onions or thin pasta before liquid is introduced. In fine Armenian restaurants each portion is topped with a tiny piece of skinless broiled tomato borrowed from the shish kebab.

> 3 tablespoons butter
> 1 small onion, minced, or 1 tablespoon dry vermicelli, broken into 1-inch pieces
> 1¼ cups long-grain rice
> ⅛ teaspoon ground allspice
> 2½ cups Poultry Stock (see page 17)
> ¼ teaspoon salt (if stock is unsalted)
> Skinless broiled tomato pieces, about ¼ inch square, for garnish (optional)

1. In a heavy, medium-sized saucepan with a tight-fitting lid over medium heat, melt butter. Add onion and sauté gently over medium-low heat until onion is softened. Add rice and allspice and continue sautéing, stirring occasionally, until rice is transparent. (If using pasta, omit onion and add pasta, rice, and allspice all at once; sauté as above.)

2. Add stock and salt (if used) and bring to a boil over highest heat. Stir once, cover, and simmer 25 minutes without uncovering pot. Remove from heat and set, if possible, over pilot light on center of stovetop (or another warm place on the stove). Let stand, covered, about 10 minutes. At serving garnish each portion, if desired, with broiled tomato pieces.

Serves 4 to 6.

Variation Coarse-milled bulgur wheat may substitute for rice. Preparation is identical.

TOMATO, GREEN PEPPER, AND CUCUMBER SALAD

This simple, refreshing salad can be served at the same time as the shish kebab (or any other lamb dish) or afterward to cleanse the palate before dessert. Dieters may even omit the oil, if desired.

> 3 medium-sized ripe tomatoes, diced
> 1 small green bell pepper, diced
> 2 medium cucumbers, pared and very thinly sliced
> ½ cup minced parsley
> ¼ cup minced fresh mint leaves (optional)
> 3 green onions, including some crisp green parts, thinly sliced
> ¼ cup fresh lemon juice
> ¼ cup olive oil
> 1½ teaspoons salt

Place tomatoes, pepper, cucumber, parsley, mint (if used), and green onion in a salad bowl. Beat together lemon juice, olive oil, and salt; pour over vegetables, toss, and serve.

Serves 4.

On a balmy weekend, the tropical flavors of this Asian-Style Summer Supper on the Patio are an exciting escape from the work world. Recipes start on page 78.

Pork

In many parts of the country, pork rivals beef as everybody's favorite meat, and little wonder. Pork is not only more economical than beef, but it is suited to a stunningly wide variety of treatments, ranging from delicate haute cuisine sautés such as Pork Mignonnes With Orange and Green Peppercorn Sauce (see page 73) to hearty braises such as Chile Verde (see page 75). A complete menu for an Asian-Style Summer Supper on the Patio starts on page 78, featuring Indonesian Pork Satay and Bananas in Cherimoya–Coconut Milk. This chapter also includes directions for breaking down a boneless blade pork loin (see page 70) and information on Asian ingredients (see page 77).

CUTS OF PORK

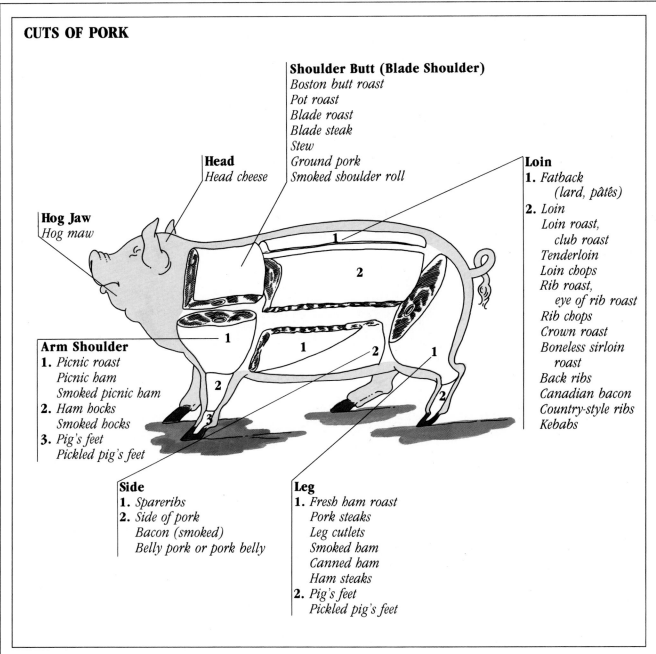

Shoulder Butt (Blade Shoulder)
Boston butt roast
Pot roast
Blade roast
Blade steak
Stew
Ground pork
Smoked shoulder roll

Head
Head cheese

Hog Jaw
Hog maw

Loin
1. *Fatback*
   (lard, pâtês)
2. *Loin*
   Loin roast,
      club roast
   Tenderloin
   Loin chops
   Rib roast,
      eye of rib roast
   Rib chops
   Crown roast
   Boneless sirloin
      roast
   Back ribs
   Canadian bacon
   Country-style ribs
   Kebabs

Arm Shoulder
1. *Picnic roast*
   Picnic ham
   Smoked picnic ham
2. *Ham hocks*
   Smoked hocks
3. *Pig's feet*
   Pickled pig's feet

Side
1. *Spareribs*
2. *Side of pork*
   Bacon (smoked)
   Belly pork or pork belly

Leg
1. *Fresh ham roast*
   Pork steaks
   Leg cutlets
   Smoked ham
   Canned ham
   Ham steaks
2. *Pig's feet*
   Pickled pig's feet

Pork has fewer primal or wholesale cuts than beef, and a smaller variety of retail cuts are found at the market. The choices for preparing each cut are less exacting than with beef—even the tough parts of the pig are relatively tender.

Shoulder Butt (Blade Shoulder)

The economical pork shoulder butt (also called Boston butt) has relatively dark, flavorful meat, divided into many small muscles, each sheathed with a thin coat of fat and divided by thicker streaks of fat and sinew. Pork shoulder makes the most luscious of all roasts and steaks at first taste—it seems like the pig's answer to beef prime rib—until one encounters streaks of sinewy fat.

Thus the shoulder is often braised to dissolve these portions, and its sauce carefully degreased (see page 28). Shoulder meat can also star in a Szechuan-style stir-fry or be cut into kebabs or stew, and it's a perfect cut for making homemade country sausage. As a roast the shoulder is best enjoyed in the company of family or close friends.

Arm Shoulder

The picnic portion of the arm shoulder is the foreleg of the pig. It is mainly sold smoked as a small ham. When found fresh it can be treated much like the shoulder butt. The ham hock is the bottom end of this cut. Typically the fresh picnic shoulder is roasted, but it can also be braised or cut into kebabs, and the hocks (which are nearly always smoked) are flavor boosters for beans, greens, and meat stews. The feet of the pig are both fatty and bony and are definitely a developed taste. They are usually pickled.

Leg

The cut sold as leg of pork is the hind leg, which is usually smoked for ham. When sold unsmoked it's commonly labeled fresh ham and may be marketed with or without the bone. As a roasting cut it's just the opposite of the Boston butt—its meat is pale, very lean, and fine-grained, but somewhat dry, tending to toughness when roasted.

A roast fresh ham makes a spectacular company dinner, but even with the best of care, it will not be quite as tender, cooked by dry heat, as the loin. Fresh ham is often braised to compensate for its lack of intrinsic moisture. It can, of course, be cut up for lean kebabs, stir-fries, and other dishes calling for cut-up pork. The ham butt section is the meatiest portion of a fresh ham; the ham shank is much bonier.

Side

The lower rib cage of a hog constitutes the spareribs and the side of pork. The side, the source of smoked bacon and salt pork, is rarely found unsmoked except in Asian markets, where it's called belly pork and is highly prized. (Italian *pancetta* is also a form of unsmoked side of pork.) Country-style ribs, by the way, are not thickly cut spareribs from this section, but are portions of the bony blade end of the loin.

Loin

The most prized cut, whether for roasting, barbecuing, braising, or rapid cooking as cutlets or in a stir-fry, is the loin. This is the source of most pork chops and pork steaks, along with the most elegant pork roasts, including the crown roast (which is a bone-in loin with the bones cracked and bent into a full circle).

Pork loin roasts and chops may be sold with or without bones; they may be divided in the market into a blade or rib, an end (the source of country-style ribs and pork rib chops), a center cut (source of the highest-priced pork chops and thus rarely

sold as a roast), and a sirloin end, which contains the pork tenderloin. The tenderloin may also be found in some markets sold on its own; it's a small strip of muscle, rounded at one end and pointed at the other, with a thin coating of fat. The tenderloin measures about 12 inches long and 3 inches wide at the widest point. It's a superb cut for rapid roasting or for scallops, medallions, *mignonnes*, cutlets, and stir-fries.

The opposite end of the loin, the rib end, also contains a tender, lean, and somewhat larger fillet piece. It's relatively easy to break down a boneless pork blade roast to separate this fillet from the fattier pieces; instructions are on page 70.

If you find pork tenderloin in the market, you may use it for a quick roast. Trim off the fat, but tie a layer of fatback on top and roast very briefly (about 20 minutes) at 400° F, until a meat thermometer indicates 160° F at the center. Remove fat, slice meat, and serve with a rich sauce, such as Quick Béarnaise Sauce (see page 14). Alternately, marinate the tenderloin overnight with the marinade for Polynesian Barbecued Suckling Pig (see page 70); use one eighth of the recipe and substitute honey for rum, baste, and roast very slowly, at 275° F until well browned and cooked through. This will give you Cantonese roast pork (*char siu*) to use in any stir-fry recipe.

The tenderloin may also be trimmed of any fat and sliced very thinly (¼ inch thick or less) for pork scaloppine or medallions (prepared as for either veal scaloppine recipe on page 45 or any recipe for chicken breast cutlets). The scallops, cut ¼ inch thick, may be pounded with a meat mallet into cutlets, lightly breaded with a favorite breading, and quickly fried.

The tenderloin may be sliced thickly (½ inch thick or more) for the pork mignonnes recipe on page 73. It also may be cut in chunks for Singapore Satay (see page 32) or stewed or sliced for stir-frying. Or it may be left in one piece, pounded to a long, thin steak, marinated, and quickly barbecued.

PORK TODAY

The pig is an adaptable animal that's relatively easy to raise to full size. Pigs will flourish in climates where cattle founder, and pigs are anything but picky eaters. Pigs produce, typically, two litters a year of six or seven piglets each. As a result the pig's meat is priced lower than that of the more demanding and less prolific beef cattle. Pork is just as nutritious as beef, however, and when well-trimmed, even less fattening.

Nonetheless, pork retains a reputation as a meat that's fattening and potentially dangerous, and it's often cooked badly under the illusion that the longer it's cooked, the safer the meat is. For adherents of two major religions that allow other meats to be eaten, pork is a dietary taboo.

That taboo may have arisen out of the danger of trichinosis from undercooked pork, but more likely it stems from disapproval of the pig's willingness to eat just about anything and its enjoyment of wallowing in mud. Today, however, pigs are raised scientifically in clean sheds with clean bedding and are fed grain rather than slops, so there's nothing unclean about a hog.

A fear of trichinosis (a disease of pigs, rats, and man, caused by a roundworm called *Trichinella spiralis*), along with inaccurate information about the hardiness of the trichina cyst, has prompted many Americans to cook pork until it's dry. In Europe, where trichinosis in hogs is extremely uncommon, pork is frequently roasted to medium-rare—an internal temperature of 150° to 160° F—rather than cooked to the typical well-done stage of American pork roasts (180° to 185° F).

In fact trichinae are killed at just 132° F. Cooking pork to an internal temperature of 137° F (the equivalent of a rare roast beef) will destroy every vestige of the parasite, if the pork is held at that temperature or higher for 30 minutes.

As for fat, the pork industry has been responsive to consumer demand and for the last 50 years has been breeding hogs for leanness, not fat. (Now that storebought cooking oils and soaps are readily available all over the country, hog fat is no longer a necessary resource.) Pig is usually marketed between the age of five and twelve months, specifically to avoid the higher fat content that develops in older animals.

In addition pork fat is concentrated in limited areas, surrounding the muscles rather than permeating them with heavy marbling. Thus a carefully trimmed pork loin or leg is a virtually fatless piece of meat, with fewer calories than the equivalent amount of Choice-grade beef and considerably less fat, less cholesterol, and fewer calories than the same amount of unskinned chicken breast.

At the same time, the pig's easy-going life produces relatively tender, juicy, subtly flavored meat from virtually every cut of the hog; pork can be afforded the widest variety of treatments of any meat. Pork can be prepared like veal (in delicate scaloppine) or like chicken breast; it can stand up to the strongest seasonings and yet will not overwhelm a delicate sauce. For an enthusiastic cook, pork can be approached with especial creativity and enthusiasm.

Pork, like beef, is graded, but with a numeric system. Grade 1 is the equivalent of Prime beef and is sold primarily to fine restaurants and specialty butcher shops. Grade 2 is the pork found in most good supermarkets, although grade 3 (mainly sold for commercial use and to institutions) may show up in a meat case as a "special." When buying pork choose finely grained meat with a light pink-gray color and streaks of creamy white, firm fat. Red pork and yellow fat are signs of an older animal; and in pigs, age does not confer flavor, but merely increases fat content. Extensive marbling of the meat isn't desirable in pork.

ROASTS AND BARBECUES

Virtually all the major parts of the pig take to roasting and barbecuing. Apparently, wallowing is not nearly as taxing as grazing: Even the front shoulder of a pig is relatively tender compared with the tough, powerful muscles in the chuck of a steer.

As noted earlier both the fresh ham and shoulder butt may be roasted, but with certain disadvantages (dryness in the ham, fat and sinew in the butt). The loin, with or without bones, remains the most accommodating and consistently successful of the pork roasting cuts. The loin, the spareribs, and even the butterflied shoulder butt all make superb barbecues, and a whole suckling pig is festive with either treatment.

Because pork is cooked to a higher internal temperature than is beef or lamb, it may be roasted at higher temperatures; its veins of fat will baste the lean parts throughout the roasting. When barbecuing, however, it's best to use a low fire, so that the exterior portions aren't overcooked before the inside is cooked tender.

As mentioned, pork is traditionally roasted in this country to well-done, but in Europe roast pork is served slightly rare and trichinosis is eliminated by bringing pork merely to 137° F. It's worth experimenting with roasting pork to a medium internal temperature of about 160° F, particularly for the leaner cuts (such as fresh ham and loin), which emerge much more tender and juicy when a touch of pink remains.

TUSCAN HERBED ARISTA OF PORK

An austerely elegant bone-in pork loin from the area around Florence, Italy, Arista derives its flavor from a generous infusion of garlic and herbs. To turn it into a festive crown roast, have your butcher bend it into a circle and fasten the ends (or do this yourself, using kitchen string to fasten). When roasting is complete turn roast bones up, place paper frills over ends of bones, if desired, and fill the center with vegetables of choice.

- 1 bulb garlic (about 12 cloves), peeled
- 3 tablespoons fresh or 2 tablespoons dried rosemary, plus fresh rosemary sprigs (optional)
- 1 teaspoon salt
- 1½ tablespoons coarsely ground pepper
- 2 tablespoons olive oil
- 1 bone-in pork loin roast, about 5 pounds

1. In a blender, food processor, electric minichopper, or clean coffee grinder (or by hand, using a garlic press and a mortar and pestle), purée together garlic, rosemary, salt, pepper, and olive oil. With a small, sharp knife, make slits through pork (at least 3 slits per rib). Insert herb purée into each slit. Tie fresh rosemary sprigs, if used, across pork. If possible let pork stand to reach room temperature and allow herb mixture to penetrate meat (2 to 3 hours).

2. Preheat oven to 350° F. Place pork, bone side down, on a roasting pan. Roast for about 17 minutes per pound (about 1½ hours total), until an instant-read meat thermometer inserted in the thickest part of the meat reads 160° to 165° F for slightly pink meat or 170° F for well-done. Remove pork from oven and let rest about 10 minutes before slicing. Serve hot, tepid, or cool.

Serves 6 to 8.

PORTED PORK ROAST

This simple and luscious pork roast, using a boneless pork loin, is the most adaptable of treats. Almost any vegetable and starch seem to complement it, so base your menu on seasonal vegetables treated in accord with the occasion—and baste the meat with a high-quality port (such as a Portuguese one).

> 1 boneless pork loin (about 4 lb)
> ½ cup port, or as needed for basting
> 2 large cloves garlic
> 2 teaspoons cooking oil
> ½ tablespoon dried rosemary
>   Pinch of salt
> 1 teaspoon freshly ground pepper, or to taste
> 1 cup veal or poultry stock

1. Rub pork all over with port; reserve remaining wine. Crush garlic with flat side of a knife and peel. With a small mortar and pestle or electric minichopper (or on a board, using the flat side of a knife), make a paste of garlic, oil, rosemary, salt, and pepper. Rub mixture into pork and let meat stand, if possible, until it reaches room temperature (2 to 3 hours).

2. Preheat oven to 500° F. Set pork on a rack, fat side up. Pour stock in roasting pan and place rack in pan. Place meat in oven and roast 20 minutes. Reduce temperature to 350° F and continue to roast for about 25 minutes per pound (including the searing period). With a bulb baster baste pork with reserved port every half hour until its internal temperature reads about 160° F on an instant-read meat thermometer. Use additional port if necessary, to keep liquid from drying out.

3. Remove pork to a cutting board and let rest. Tilt roasting pan and spoon off excess fat from drippings. Place pan over high heat on stovetop (using 2 burners if necessary), and stirring constantly and scraping bottom of pan, reduce liquid by about half, pouring accumulating juices rendered from resting pork into pan as reduction proceeds. Slice pork and place on serving dish. Pour into sauce the juices rendered during slicing. Correct seasoning of sauce and pour over pork. Serve hot.

Serves 6 to 8.

Florentines have enjoyed Tuscan Herbed Arista of Pork since the days of da Vinci. Bent into a crown and filled with a bouquet of seasonal vegetables, it looks like a work of art.

Step-by-Step

BREAKING DOWN A BONELESS BLADE PORK LOIN

Boneless loins from the blade (rib) end of the pig, sometimes called club roasts for their shape, are often sold on special at excellent prices. When on sale, however, they frequently include more streaky, fatty meat around the edges than when they're sold at regular prices.

Pork bones are heavy enough that their removal by the butcher may well pay for itself in money as well as time. Whole, boneless blade roasts make excellent roasting cuts, but they can also be broken down into several parts to obtain a long, lean fillet that is far less costly (and merely a little less tender) than the tenderloin, plus two fattier sections to use for stir-fries, sausage, lard, ground pork, and other purposes.

The fillet consists of smooth, pinkish meat at the center, with some small white lines of fat running lengthwise. This meat forms a long, slender cylinder that narrows down to a point at one end. The meat that will be trimmed off consists of any fat on top, the reddish meat with fat running in lengthwise streaks around the fillet on one side, and the meat with fatty streaks running horizontally on the other side.

While you are breaking down the boneless loin from the blade, save all the trims. See opposite page for ways to use these trims to best advantage.

If you do not want to break down the loin to extract the fillet, a boneless blade roast may simply be trimmed of the outer layer of fat and the remainder employed for pork steaks, cutlets, stews, satays, stir-fries, or *mignonnes*. Obviously it will not be as perfectly lean as a fillet or tenderloin used in the same recipes.

1. Place pork loin fat side down on cutting board. Starting on side with lengthwise streaks of fat, peel away entire streaky layer with your hands, using a small, sharp knife (preferably a boning knife) to detach fillet from fatty shell as needed. As you peel, open the two sections like a book and finish detaching with knife. Cut away area of meat with fatty streaks running sideways. The top layer of fat (which you'll have placed on the bottom, to start cutting) will come away with these other layers.

2. These cuts will leave a long, rough triangle of pinkish meat: the fillet. (A 3-pound boneless loin will trim down to about a 1-pound fillet.) The fillet can be roasted whole or cut into medallions (very thin slices, which may be cooked like veal scaloppine), mignonnes (somewhat thicker slices), and cutlets.

POLYNESIAN BARBECUED SUCKLING PIG

Suckling pigs are animals young enough to have been fed entirely on their mother's milk. At Tahitian and Hawaiian festivals, suckling pigs are cooked in special stone-pit barbecues—but virtually any large barbecue (or even a home oven) can suffice as long as the piglet is cooked slowly, basted attentively and, if on a barbecue, turned frequently.

   1 *fifth-sized bottle Shaoxing wine, sake, or dry sherry (about 3 cups)*
   1 *cup soy sauce*
  ½ *cup freshly squeezed lime juice (from about 4 limes)*
  ½ *cup firmly packed dark brown or palm sugar*
  ½ *cup dark rum*
   2 *tablespoons minced fresh ginger*
  ½ *bulb garlic (about 6 cloves), crushed and peeled*
   1 *suckling pig (12 to 25 lb), fully dressed*
     Cooking oil, as needed
   1 *small orange or mango*

1. Mix wine, soy sauce, lime juice, sugar, and rum. In a blender or food processor purée ginger and garlic, adding some marinade liquid, if necessary, or finely mince ginger and garlic and add to liquid (see Note).

2. If desired remove piglet's eyeballs with spoon and shut the eyelids. Poke about a dozen small holes, well spaced, in the piglet's skin along the sides of the backbone. Place piglet in a container large enough to hold it (for example, a plastic baby bath or a double set of large plastic garbage bags, with a wire tie to fasten). If using garbage bags, reserve about 2 cups marinade for basting, since it may be difficult to save marinade in bag when piglet is removed. Pour marinade over piglet, making sure some enters body cavity, and let stand for at least 3 hours (or refrigerate overnight), turning occasionally.

3. *To barbecue:* Prepare a large barbecue, placing a moderate amount of coals at outer rim, with a single, sparse line of coals running along center. Place grill well above coals. Burn coals down to white charcoal. Carefully remove piglet from marinade, reserving marinade for basting. Cover ears and tail with aluminum foil, place a wad of crumpled foil in mouth to hold it open, and rub skin with cooking oil. Place piglet on grill and, if possible, cover barbecue. About every 15 minutes baste with reserved marinade, and about every half hour turn piglet. Renew coals as needed. Piglet will roast in 3 to 4 hours. After 2½ hours insert an instant-read meat thermometer in thickest parts of meat (the ham and shoulder) at each baste. When temperature reads 160° to 165° F, remove piglet from barbecue and let rest at least 15 minutes before serving. If skin has charred from too close contact with heat source, simply slice it off and discard it. *To roast in oven:* Preheat oven to 450° F and place piglet in oven. After 15 minutes lower heat to 325° F. Roast until an instant-read meat thermometer inserted in several thick parts of the piglet reads 160° to 165° F, basting with reserved marinade every 15 minutes. Piglet may take as long as 30 minutes per pound to cook, but even a relatively large piglet should be checked, as above, with an instant-read meat thermometer at frequent intervals after it has been in the oven for 3 hours.

4. When ready to serve replace aluminum foil in piglet's mouth with an orange or mango. To carve, first remove forelegs and hams. Cut down center of back and separate ribs. As a special treat, serve a section of crisp skin to each person.

Serves 8 to 20, depending on size of piglet.

Note This marinade is also wonderful for barbecued pork loin. Use a fourth of a recipe for a 4- to 5-pound boneless loin.

PORK CHOPS, CUTLETS, AND SLICES

Most of the smaller cuts of pork are from the loin, although cutlets may come from the shoulder butt. Generally these cuts are cooked quickly by dry heat methods (panfrying, broiling, or grilling), but they are equally adaptable to slower cooking, such as smothering or baking. Care must be taken not to overcook small cuts of lean pork—they dry out easily.

SMOKED PORK CHOPS IN MUSTARD-CREAM SAUCE

This hearty but deluxe recipe from the Moselle area of France can also be made with unsmoked pork chops or cutlets or with sliced ham.

> 2 tablespoons cooking oil
> (sunflower or corn)
> 2 tablespoons unsalted butter
> 4 lean, thick, smoked pork chops
> (6 to 7 oz each)
> 1 cup whipping cream
> 2 tablespoons Dijon or other
> strong mustard
> ½ cup pickled cornichons
> (or small pickled gherkins),
> sliced thinly
> 1 tablespoon minced shallots
> or whites of green onions
> 1 tablespoon white wine vinegar
> Freshly ground pepper, to taste

1. In a large, heavy skillet, heat oil and butter together until butter is melted and mixture is hot. Add pork and sauté about 6 minutes per side, turning midway. Remove and reserve in warm serving dish. Pour oil out of skillet.

2. While pork cooks mix cream, mustard, pickles, shallots, and vinegar. Mixture will thicken slightly. When pork is done pour mixture into skillet and boil over high heat, stirring constantly, until thickened to coat a spoon (about 2 minutes). Add pepper to taste. Pour sauce over pork and serve hot.

Serves 4.

... ON USING THE TRIM FROM BREAKING DOWN A BONELESS BLADE PORK LOIN

After breaking down a boneless blade pork loin (see opposite page), you will find yourself with an ample supply of trims. These should not be thrown away since they have a wide range of delicious uses.

☐ The lean meat of the trims (about ¾ pound from a 3-pound boneless loin) can be used for Singapore Satay (see page 32) or thin cutlets. It can be ground to use in dishes calling for ground pork, such as Galloping Horses (see page 78) or Pork and Shrimp Potstickers (see page 78).

☐ The streaky, fatty meat (about ¾ pound from a 3-pound loin) is perfect for Homemade American Country Sausage (see page 88). It can also be turned into a rather fatty ground pork, like that sold at most supermarkets, and then mixed with leaner meat for meat loafs or meatballs, or prepared by a method that will render off the unavoidable excess fat.

☐ The rendered fat can be used for Homemade Lard (see page 73) or for covering homemade pâtés during baking, in place of the often difficult-to-obtain pork fatback called for in recipes.

☐ The entire amount of trim, which is about 30 percent fat, can be used for Homemade American Country Sausage (see page 88) or for ground pork that is equivalent to supermarket ground pork in its fat content; or the fat layer can be trimmed off and the remainder converted to a ground pork that is leaner than that in the supermarket.

When someone special drops in near dinnertime, these sophisticated Pork Mignonnes With Orange and Green Peppercorn Sauce are just right for an equally special, spontaneous feast.

SMOTHERED PORK CHOPS

No matter where they're served, smothered meat dishes are extremely popular (and remarkably similar) throughout the South. Chops are traditionally heaped high with sautéed onions and a spicy brown gravy. This Mississippi/Louisiana recipe borrows several New Orleans Creole techniques. Serve with mashed potatoes.

  2 tablespoons butter
  1 cup plus 2 tablespoons flour
1½ cups rich beef broth
    Pinch sage leaves, crumbled
    Salt and freshly ground
    pepper, to taste
  6 thick loin pork chops
  ½ cup lard
  3 large onions, sliced
  3 cloves garlic, minced
  ¼ cup celery, minced

1. In a small saucepan over medium-high heat melt butter; stir in the 2 tablespoons flour and cook, stirring constantly with a wire whisk, until lightly browned. Stir in broth and sage, mix well, remove from heat, and set aside. This mixture will be the sauce for your chops.

2. Add salt and pepper to the 1 cup flour; dredge chops in mixture. In a large, heavy skillet over medium-high heat, heat ¼ cup of the lard. Add chops and cook until browned. If there are too many chops to fit into skillet at one time, work in stages or use two skillets. Move browned chops to a large, ovenproof casserole with a cover. Preheat oven to 350° F.

3. Melt remaining lard in skillet over high heat. Add onions, garlic, and celery; lower heat to medium and cook, stirring frequently to avoid burning, until onions are golden (8 to 10 minutes). Remove vegetables with a slotted spoon and place over chops in casserole.

4. Pour off all lard from skillet. Add reserved sauce, raise heat to high, bring to a boil, and cook for 1 minute, stirring vigorously and scraping bottom of skillet. Pour sauce over chops in casserole, cover, and bake 30 minutes.

Serves 6.

PORK MIGNONNES WITH ORANGE AND GREEN PEPPERCORN SAUCE

This quick but aristocratic dish affords pork fillet slices the sort of treatment that's usually reserved for duck breast, with a sweet but tangy sauce that this fine cut fully deserves. If serving an appetizer first, make the sauce in advance, but don't start sautéing the pork until you're ready to serve it. Serve with sautéed potatoes and buttered peas or snap peas, cooked until barely tender.

    1 *large, seedless navel orange*
    1 *juice orange*
    5 *tablespoons unsalted butter*
    2 *tablespoons sugar*
    1 *tablespoon good-quality cooking oil (sunflower, corn, or peanut)*
 1½ *pounds lean, boneless pork loin, sliced ½ inch thick*
      Salt and freshly ground pepper, to taste
    1 *tablespoon orange liqueur (Grand Marnier preferred)*
    1 *teaspoon green peppercorns, drained and rinsed*
    1 *cup veal or beef stock, or canned beef bouillon (preferably low salt)*
      Parsley or watercress, for garnish

1. Remove zest (orange part only) from navel orange (reserving orange) and sliver in fine julienne. Blanch zest in boiling water to cover for 10 minutes, dropping whole juice orange into water during final minute to warm it (and maximize amount of juice yielded). Drain zest and juice orange and reserve. Squeeze juice orange to obtain about ⅓ cup juice. In a small, heavy, enameled or teflon-coated saucepan over low heat, melt 1 tablespoon of the butter. Stir in sugar until sugar melts and mixture turns golden. Add orange juice and zest and cook over low heat until sauce is thick. Reserve sauce.

2. Divide peeled navel orange into sections, and reserve sections at room temperature. In a large, heavy skillet, heat 2 tablespoons of the butter plus the oil until hot. Season pork with salt and pepper and, raising heat to high, sauté meat rapidly on both sides until browned and cooked through (about 2 minutes per side). Add liqueur; it will bubble and quickly reduce to a glaze. Remove pork from skillet, place in serving dish, and keep warm. (Tent with aluminum foil and place in a turned-off oven.)

3. Lower heat, add green peppercorns to skillet and crush them with the back of a spoon. Add stock. Turn up heat to high and, stirring constantly, rapidly reduce liquid to ⅓ cup. Add reserved orange sauce and salt and black pepper to taste; reduce heat to a simmer and cook 2 more minutes.

4. Cut remaining 2 tablespoons butter in small pieces and, with pan off heat, swirl into skillet one by one. Pour any juices yielded by pork into sauce. Place orange sections in sauce. Nap pork with sauce and orange sections and garnish with fresh parsley sprigs.

Serves 4 to 6.

HOMEMADE LARD

Homemade lard, greatly valued in Latin American cooking, is useful in pastries as well. The flavor of homemade lard is richer and porkier than that of packaged lard, the texture is softer, and the lard hasn't been subjected to the hydrogenation process that has been criticized by many doctors and nutritionists. The lard will keep for about 2 months refrigerated and for 6 months or longer frozen. To keep lard indefinitely at room temperature, pour it into a sterilized canning jar while it is still very hot.

    1 *pound pork fat*
  ½ *cup cold water*

1. Cut fat into small pieces and put through coarse grinder or shred briefly in food processor. Place in bowl, pour the water over fat, and let fat soak about 8 hours at room temperature.

2. Preheat oven to 225° F. Place fat and the water in heavy, cast-iron skillet. Over moderate heat on stovetop, cook until fat starts to sizzle and melt but does not brown (about 5 minutes). Transfer to oven and bake about 2 hours, adding a little more water after 1 hour if water has totally evaporated. When water evaporates again, leaving liquid fat and cracklings, remove skillet from oven. Strain liquid into an 8-ounce or 10-ounce jar (use a sterilized canning jar if lard is to be stored at room temperature). Lightly cover jar (for instance, with a sheet of aluminum foil) and let stand for 24 hours before sealing with lid and storing as desired. The cracklings left in strainer can be served over a salad, if desired.

Makes about 1 cup.

STUFFED PORK CUTLETS

A quick and simple recipe, this can be easily varied. For an Italian version similar to veal saltimbocca, stuff the cutlets with prosciutto and a good mozzarella (such as *bufalo*) or Bel Paese cheese. For a French/Swiss version, pair baked sliced ham with Gruyère or Emmenthaler cheese; and for an all-American version, use Cheddar or Monterey jack cheese with thinly sliced Smithfield or similar delicatessen ham. Serve as an appetizer or a main dish.

> 8 *boneless lean pork cutlets (from loin or butt), each about ¼ inch thick*
>
> 4 *thick (¼ inch) slices mild cheese of choice (4 to 6 oz total)*
>
> 4 *thin slices prosciutto, Smithfield, or baked ham (about 2 oz total)*
>
> 1 *egg, lightly beaten*
>
> 1 *to 1½ cups Italian-style seasoned dried bread crumbs (or mix 1 cup bread crumbs with 2 tablespoons grated Parmesan cheese, 1 tablespoon minced parsley, 1 teaspoon crumbled marjoram, and salt, freshly ground pepper, and garlic powder to taste)*
>
> ¼ *cup light olive oil or vegetable oil*
>
> 1 *lemon, cut lengthwise into 4 wedges, for garnish*

1. Trim away any fat or connective tissues from pork. Between 2 sheets of waxed paper, pound each cutlet with flat end of a meat mallet (or a heavy can) until flattened to about ⅛ inch thick. Trim cheese and ham to a size slightly smaller than cutlets. Top half the cutlets with a slice of cheese and a slice of ham. Cover with remaining cutlets and pound edges lightly to seal together.

2. Holding each sandwich together dip both sides in egg, then into bread crumbs to coat completely. Place on waxed paper.

3. In a heavy, 10-inch skillet over high heat, heat oil until rippling. Lower heat to medium-high, add cutlets, and cover with a spatter shield if desired. Cook until cutlets are cooked through (about 5 minutes per side). Remove from pan with slotted spatula, draining off oil, and serve hot, garnished with lemon wedges.

Serves 4.

PORK CHOPS WITH APPLES IN CIDER SAUCE

Here is a quick but casually elegant preparation that brings out the best in tender pork chops. Dry hard cider may be found in liquor stores, but in a pinch, unsweetened apple juice or cider will do nearly as well. Serve with buttered, parsley-sprinkled new potatoes or noodles or, for a special treat, with thinly sliced yams deep-fried until they are crisp.

> 2 *tablespoons (approximately) vegetable oil, to film skillet*
>
> 4 *thick rib or loin pork chops (about ½ lb each)*
>
> 2 *tablespoons unsalted butter*
>
> 2 *medium-sized red onions, peeled and cut into ¼-inch slices*
>
> 1 *tablespoon minced garlic*
>
> 2 *large sweet apples (such as Delicious), peeled, cored, quartered, and cut into ½-inch slices*
>
> 1 *tablespoon fresh sage, minced, or 1 teaspoon dried sage leaves, crumbled*
>
> ½ *teaspoon dried thyme leaves, crumbled*
>
> ¾ *cup dry hard cider or unsweetened apple juice*
>
> ½ *cup dry white wine Salt and freshly ground pepper, to taste*

1. Film a large, heavy skillet with oil and heat over a high flame until oil is fragrant. Pat pork chops dry, quickly brown on both sides in skillet, and remove to a plate.

2. Lower heat to medium and melt butter in skillet. Add onions and sauté, stirring occasionally, until softened. Add garlic and sauté until translucent (1 minute longer). Add apples and turn in butter just until completely coated.

3. Return pork chops to skillet, sprinkle with sage and thyme, and add cider and wine. Bring liquid to a simmer and cook over fairly low heat until chops are cooked through (20 minutes).

4. With a slotted spatula remove chops and apple mixture from skillet and keep warm. Reduce cooking liquid at a full boil over high flame, stirring constantly, until it has thickened to the consistency of light syrup. Add salt and pepper to taste, pour liquid over chops and apples, and serve hot.

Serves 4.

Pork (or Veal) Chops À la Normande Follow recipe above through step 2, using pork chops or veal rib or loin chops. When chops are returned to skillet, add 2 tablespoons Calvados (French apple brandy) or applejack. Making sure nothing flammable is near stove, heat briefly and, using a long match and great care, set Calvados aflame. When flames die down add cider and wine and proceed as above to point when cooking liquid is reduced to a syrup. Add 1 cup whipping cream and reduce at a full boil, stirring constantly, until liquid coats a spoon. Pour over chops and serve hot. Accompany with sautéed or French-fried potatoes, or rice.

BRAISED AND STEWED PORK

It's in braises and stews that pork shows off its adaptability. The loin, fresh hams, and juicy shoulder butt are excellent braising cuts. If there's time they benefit from a night in a marinade, such as Herb and White Wine Marinade (see page 9), and being braised in the marinade with, if necessary, enough extra liquid (stock, juice, or wine) to come about two thirds of the way up the meat.

CHILE VERDE
Mexican-style pork in hot green chile sauce

This savory, spicy-sour stew—the consistency of a thick soup—is set off by a fresh salad, warmed corn tortillas, and Pilaf (see page 63) made with a minced clove of garlic sautéed with onions and with allspice omitted. The stew is especially delicious if refrigerated overnight and served the next day so the flavors blend fully. Tomatillos, by the way, are related to the ground cherry, not to the tomato, so green garden tomatoes can't be substituted.

    3 pounds boneless pork
       (loin or butt)
    2 tablespoons lard or vegetable
       oil (peanut or corn)
    1 large onion, chopped
    1½ tablespoons minced garlic
    3 to 5 canned or pickled
       jalapeño or serrano chiles,
       cut into strips
    2 cans (10 oz each) tomatillos
    ½ cup loosely packed chopped
       cilantro, plus approximately
       1 tablespoon minced cilantro
       (for garnish)
    1 can (8 oz) mild green chiles
    1 bottle (8 oz) cactus strips
       (nopalitos tiernos en rajas),
       rinsed well (optional)
       Salt and freshly ground
       pepper, to taste
    1 ripe avocado (preferably
       Hass variety)
    1 tablespoon fresh lime
       (or lemon) juice

1. Cut pork into 2-inch cubes, trimming some, but not all, fat. Reserve.

2. In a skillet heat lard until rippling. Add onion and garlic; sauté until limp. Add jalapeño chiles, sauté 1 minute longer, and remove with slotted spoon to heavy, medium-large (about 2½ quarts) casserole.

3. Drain tomatillos, saving liquid. Purée tomatillos, the ½ cup cilantro, and about half the drained liquid in a blender (or just mash in a bowl). Add mixture to casserole along with mild chiles, cactus strips (if used), and pork. Season lightly with salt (the tomatillo liquid is salty) and generously with pepper. Over high heat bring mixture to a boil. Lower heat, cover, and simmer slowly until pork is tender (about 2 hours). If possible, refrigerate covered overnight and skim fat before reheating. If serving immediately, spoon off fat from top of liquid.

4. Just before serving, peel and slice avocado; sprinkle with lime juice and the minced cilantro and float on top of stew.

Serves 6.

Heady Chile Verde (pork in a rich green chile sauce) from south of the border will merit an "Olé!" It's even better if you can resist it long enough to serve it the next day.

PORK LOIN BRAISED IN MILK

This dish, a complete meal in itself, tastes rich, but is low in calories.

Salt and freshly ground pepper, to taste
2 *pounds loin of pork, in one piece*
Flour, for dredging
2 *tablespoons butter*
2 *tablespoons vegetable oil*
6 *carrots, peeled and halved, or 12 baby carrots, whole*
6 *small or 12 tiny new potatoes, well scrubbed*
2 *parsnips, peeled and thickly sliced (optional)*
2½ *cups whole or extra-rich milk*
2 *tablespoons warm water*

1. Rub salt and a generous amount of pepper into pork. Dredge pork lightly in flour. In a casserole just a little larger than the pork, over burner set to medium-high, heat butter and oil. When foam subsides add meat, fat side down. Brown all sides, lowering heat if butter browns.

2. With pan off heat, tuck carrots, potatoes, and parsnips (if used) around pork. Pour on milk and carefully bring mixture to a boil, taking care that milk does not boil over top. Lower heat and partially cover pan. Simmer until pork is very tender (1½ to 2 hours), turning meat halfway through. If milk evaporates too quickly, add a little more.

3. Remove meat to cutting board and vegetables to serving dish. Keep vegetables warm. In uncovered pot over high heat, cook remaining liquid until it darkens and coagulates into small, light-brown curds, which separate from watery, slightly yellowish fat. Tip pot and carefully spoon off fat (there will be quite a lot). Deglaze pan over high heat with the water, scraping bottom with a wooden spoon. Correct seasonings. Slice pork and arrange on serving platter with vegetables. Spoon sauce over pork; serve immediately.

Serves 6.

LIGHT PORK DISHES, GROUND PORK, AND "SECOND HELPINGS"

In two Asian recipes that follow, pork reveals its ethereal side, in slivers or ground meat. For heartier appetites, there is a savory "second helping" dish, a South American potato pie in which a small amount of pork (starting out as either roast pork or raw ground pork) flavors a satisfying main dish. Supermarket ground pork is as high in fat as sausage is (about 30 percent), so for true lightness (and far less waste), it's best to grind your own.

PASTEL DE PAPAS
Chilean roast pork and potato pie

A surprise hides in the center of this zestful South American version of shepherd's pie.

1 *tablespoon paprika, plus more for garnish*
3 *tablespoons oil*
1 *large onion, chopped moderately finely*
8 *ounces roast pork, finely diced, or 12 ounces lean ground raw pork or beef*
2 *tablespoons raisins, soaked in warm water 15 minutes, drained*
¼ *teaspoon dried oregano*
½ *teaspoon freshly ground black pepper*
¼ *teaspoon cayenne pepper*
⅛ *teaspoon ground cumin seed*
½ *cup meat gravy or 1 tablespoon flour plus ½ cup milk or meat stock*
1 *chopped hard-cooked egg*
15 *oil-cured black olives (such as Kalamata), pitted and halved*
2 *large baking potatoes, peeled and halved*
2 *tablespoons butter, or as needed*
½ *cup milk, or as needed*
Salt and white pepper, to taste
1 *egg, beaten*

1. In a 10-inch skillet sauté the 1 tablespoon paprika in oil until oil turns red (about 2 minutes). Let paprika settle briefly, then carefully drain through a fine strainer, saving oil. Discard paprika. Return oil to skillet.

2. Heat oil; add onion and sauté over medium heat, stirring occasionally, until onion is translucent (about 10 minutes). Add pork, raisins, oregano, black pepper, cayenne, and cumin. Raise heat and cook, stirring, until meat is browned and flavors blended (about 2 minutes for cooked meat, 7 minutes for raw). If using supermarket ground pork, tilt pan and spoon off some of excess fat. Add enough gravy to moisten (or sprinkle with flour, stir in milk, and cook over low heat until thickened). Remove mixture from heat and fold in chopped egg and olives. Cover and let stand for 2 hours at room temperature or overnight in refrigerator, if possible.

3. Preheat oven to 350° F. Drop potatoes into boiling, salted water to cover and boil until tender (about 30 minutes). Drain and mash with butter and milk, whipping until texture is fluffy. (Add more butter and milk if needed.) Stir in salt and white pepper to taste. Add beaten egg and stir vigorously until mixture thickens slightly. If mixture is watery transfer to a pot and beat over low flame until extra moisture evaporates.

4. Place half the potatoes on bottom of a small (about 1½ quart) casserole, cover with meat mixture, and spoon the rest of the potatoes on top. Sprinkle lightly with paprika and bake, uncovered, until heated through and lightly browned (about 25 minutes).

Serves 3 or 4.

SIAMESE PORK SHREDS WITH CABBAGE

From Thailand comes this clear-flavored, spicy dish, which is quickly made once the pork has marinated. This recipe serves two as a full main course accompanied with rice; in a multicourse Asian meal, it will serve more.

- 1 tablespoon fresh coriander root, minced (reserve leaves for another use)
- 1 teaspoon minced garlic
- ½ teaspoon sugar
- 2 teaspoons vegetable oil (peanut, sunflower, or corn)
- ½ pound boneless pork, sliced about ¼ inch thick
- 1 small, dried hot chile, trimmed and seeded, or 1 teaspoon Thai (not American) hot-pepper flakes
- ½ stalk fresh lemongrass or 1 teaspoon lemon juice
- 2 small bay leaves
- 2 cups chopped cabbage
- 2 to 4 fresh small, hot chiles, preferably red, seeded and sliced thinly
- ½ cup unsweetened coconut milk
- 2 tablespoons peanut (or other) oil
- ½ teaspoon fish sauce (nam pla, patis, or nuoc mam) or salt
- 20 fresh basil leaves

1. In a mortar and pestle (or electric minichopper), grind together coriander root, garlic, and sugar. Blend in oil.

2. Place pork slices between sheets of waxed paper and pound thin (to ⅛ inch thick) with flat end of a meat mallet. Cut slices into thin strips and place in a bowl; add coriander root mixture and rub in until all pork strips are coated. Cover and let stand at least 1 hour at room temperature, or 3 hours or longer in refrigerator.

3. In mortar and pestle or electric minichopper, pulverize dried chile, lemongrass, and bay leaves. (If lemon juice is used, reserve.)

4. Bring about 1 quart water to a rolling boil. Add cabbage and boil until softened but not mushy (about 3 minutes). Drain and cool immediately under running water and reserve. Add fresh red chile to pork mixture. (If lemon juice is used instead of lemongrass, add juice to coconut milk). Arrange all ingredients near stove.

5. In a wok or large, heavy skillet over burner set to high, heat peanut oil until fragrant and rippling. Add lemongrass–dried chile mixture and sauté, stirring constantly, until chiles darken (about 2 minutes). Add pork mixture and stir and flip constantly until no red color is visible in meat (1 to 2 minutes). Add coconut milk. Lower heat to medium and cook about 3 minutes to blend flavors. Stir in fish sauce and basil and continue to cook just until basil wilts.

6. Lay bed of cabbage on a serving plate and pour contents of pan over it. Serve immediately.

Serves 2.

PORK AND SHRIMP POTSTICKERS

This always popular Chinese appetizer is appetizing indeed.

¾ pound ground pork

¼ pound small, raw shrimp, peeled and chopped finely

½ cup green onions (both whites and crisp greens) or Chinese chives, finely minced

½ pound fresh or drained canned water chestnuts, peeled and cut into very fine dice

3 tablespoons light soy sauce

3 tablespoons Shaoxing wine, sake, or dry sherry

1 teaspoon minced fresh ginger

1 tablespoon cornstarch

1 teaspoon sugar

2 teaspoons dark sesame oil

1 package (10 oz) wonton skins
Peanut oil, for filming skillet

¼ cup water
Vinegar, soy sauce, and Chinese-style hot chile oil, for dipping

1. In a large bowl mix pork, shrimp, green onions, water chestnuts, light soy sauce, wine, ginger, cornstarch, sugar, and sesame oil. Have a small bowl of cold water handy. Place about 2 teaspoons filling in middle of each wonton skin. Dip finger in water and moisten edge of wonton skin, fold in half over filling to form a crescent shape, and pinch edges together to seal. As potstickers are completed, lay in 1 layer on a sheet of waxed paper.

2. Film a large, heavy skillet with peanut oil and heat over burner set to medium until oil is fragrant. Place 1 layer of potstickers in pan, seam side up, and fry gently until bottoms are golden brown (about 6 minutes). Pour in the ¼ cup water, immediately cover pan and reduce heat to low, and cook 10 minutes. With a slotted spatula place potstickers on serving platter and keep warm. Repeat until all potstickers have been cooked. Place vinegar, soy sauce, and hot chile oil on table. Serve potstickers, letting each person mix dipping sauce on his or her plate.

Makes about 48 potstickers, serves 4 to 8.

78

ASIAN-STYLE SUMMER SUPPER ON THE PATIO

Galloping Horses

Indonesian Pork Satay With Peanut Dipping Sauce

Thai Beef Salad (see page 31) or Singapore Satay (see page 32)

Bananas in Cherimoya–Coconut Milk

Thai Iced Tea

Chilled Asian Beer, or Chilled Gewürztraminer Wine

Here's a leisurely menu for a patio barbecue on a warm summer's evening with a combination of piquantly exotic dishes from Southeast Asia that is sure to perk up heat-jaded appetites. All the dishes but the barbecued satay can be made in advance and served at room temperature (except the dessert, which should be reheated slightly just before serving). This menu, to serve six to eight, includes two main dishes that normally serve four apiece. Consider the size of your barbecue grill when choosing the second main course (Thai Beef Salad or Singapore Satay).

GALLOPING HORSES
Thai pork and fruit appetizer

Here a savory, spicy, ground pork mixture rides atop a slice of orange or pineapple.

1 pound lean pork or 1¼ pounds ground pork

2 tablespoons peanut oil

¼ cup minced onion or shallot

2 tablespoons minced garlic

½ cup roasted peanuts, preferably unsalted, roughly crushed

1½ tablespoons sugar

2 teaspoons ground coriander

2 teaspoons fish sauce (nam pla, patis, or nuoc mam)

1 teaspoon light soy sauce

2 to 3 small, fresh, hot chiles, preferably red, thinly sliced

2 large navel oranges, peeled and sectioned (about 20 sections)

1 can (12 or 14 oz) pineapple slices, drained
Fresh mint and fresh coriander, for garnish

1. If grinding your own meat, finely grind pork. (A food processor may be used, although it shreds rather than grinds meat. Pick over shredded meat and remove any unshredded streaks of connective tissue.)

2. In a large skillet over medium-high heat, warm oil; sauté onion and garlic until wilted (about 2 minutes). Stir in pork, breaking up meat, and cook until pork is lightly browned. If using storebought ground pork, pour off excess fat. Reserve meat in pan.

3. Add peanuts, sugar, coriander, fish sauce, soy sauce, and chiles to skillet and cook over medium heat until chiles wilt (3 to 4 minutes). Mixture will remain rather loose.

4. Slice each orange section lengthwise along spine of thick side, almost but not quite all the way through. Open two attached pieces like a book, to make a circle. Alternate orange circles with pineapple slices on serving platter. Place equal amounts of meat on each fruit and top with a mint leaf and a coriander leaf. Serve at warm room temperature.

Makes about 30 appetizers, serves 6 to 10.

INDONESIAN PORK SATAY WITH PEANUT DIPPING SAUCE

Marinate this rich, nutty satay overnight, if possible. The meat is delicious when barbecued, but it may also be broiled in an oven.

- ½ cup roasted, unsalted peanuts
- 1 tablespoon crushed coriander seeds
- ½ tablespoon minced garlic (about 2 cloves)
- ½ teaspoon hot-pepper flakes, or to taste
- 1 medium red onion, chopped
- 4 teaspoons firmly packed dark brown sugar
- ½ teaspoon fish sauce (nam pla, patis, or nuoc mam)
- 2 tablespoons fresh lime juice
- 2 tablespoons soy sauce
- ¼ teaspoon freshly ground black pepper
- ⅓ cup orange juice
- ¼ cup peanut oil or melted butter
- 1 pound lean pork cut into 1-inch cubes

Peanut Dipping Sauce

- 1 cup unsalted, roasted peanuts
- 1 cup chicken broth
- 3 tablespoons firmly packed dark brown sugar
- ¼ cup fresh lemon juice, strained, or ½ tablespoon tamarind paste, dissolved in 4 tablespoons hot water
- 1 to 2 tablespoons hot-pepper flakes
- 5 cloves garlic, minced (about 2 tablespoons)
  Salt, to taste

1. In a blender or food processor, grind peanuts to a coarse meal. Add all remaining ingredients except the pork and purée. Place in a saucepan and heat just to a boil. Let cool. Pour cooled sauce over pork, mix to coat all cubes, cover, and let marinate at least 3 hours at room temperature or overnight or longer in refrigerator. If grilling on bamboo skewers, soak skewers (1 or 2 per person) in water to cover for the same length of time.

2. Prepare barbecue, if used, and light fire about 30 minutes before you intend to start cooking. Drain meat (reserving marinade), thread meat on skewers, and place skewers on barbecue, close to white-hot coals. Barbecue rapidly, basting frequently with marinade and turning skewers every few minutes, until meat is well-browned all over and just cooked through. (Avoid overcooking.) Meat may also be broiled in oven or electric broiler about 2 inches from heat source. Serve on skewers with Peanut Dipping Sauce.

Serves 4 (8 in buffet menu)

Peanut Dipping Sauce

1. Grind peanuts very finely in a blender or food processor (or with a rolling pin). Reserve.

2. In a heavy enameled or stainless steel saucepan over medium heat, bring broth and sugar to a boil, stirring. When sugar has dissolved completely, add lemon juice, hot pepper, garlic, and salt. Return mixture to a boil. Transfer to a bowl and serve hot. (Sauce may be refrigerated and reheated just before serving.)

Makes about 2½ cups.

BANANAS IN CHERIMOYA–COCONUT MILK

This warm, tropical dessert will be welcome when the evening breeze picks up on the patio. It is a variation on a popular Thai-Hawaiian dessert (made on Oahu with small, local apple bananas, which have an apple flavor and a tough texture), with a cherimoya added for an especially luxurious flavor. If you can't find cherimoya, omit it; the dish will still be lovely.

- 8 slightly unripe bananas or 16 ripe apple bananas
- 4 cups unsweetened coconut milk
- ¼ cup firmly packed turbinado or light brown sugar
  Pinch of salt
- 1 large, soft, ripe cherimoya

1. Peel bananas, cut in half lengthwise, and cut halves once crossways. In a large saucepan bring coconut milk, sugar, and salt to a boil. Add bananas and immediately reduce heat to a simmer. Simmer, uncovered, until bananas are tender and liquid has reduced slightly (about 40 minutes; longer for apple bananas).

2. Meanwhile peel cherimoya, pick out and discard all seeds (this is somewhat laborious), and purée fruit in a blender or food processor. (Purée may be covered and refrigerated until ready to use.)

3. Just before serving add purée to warm coconut milk mixture and heat briefly until just warm (not hot). Serve dessert at approximate temperature of a warm bath or the summer seas of Waikiki.

Serves 8.

THAI ICED TEA (OR COFFEE)

Rich and refreshing, this drink provides a welcome thirst-quencher on warm summer evenings. Use a highly caffeinated tea or coffee to perk your guests up after their evening meal. Sweetened condensed milk will provide all the sugar most people need.

- 1 cup strong Asian tea (such as oolong) or strong, dark-roasted coffee (such as French roast or espresso)
- 2 cups boiling water
- 3 tablespoons sweetened condensed milk
  Ice cubes

Mix tea or coffee with the boiling water. Add sweetened condensed milk and swirl in. Pour into tall glasses filled with ice cubes.

Makes 8 glasses.

For a festive party, try the exotic make-ahead menu of An Informal Dinner Party in Rio—your guests will start dancing a samba. Recipes begin on page 94.

Preserved Meat

Hams and sausages come in a vast variety, each having its own distinctive flavor and special uses. Few foods speak of hospitality quite as clearly as Cider-Baked Country Ham (see page 85) at a holiday dinner—but an equally generous sight is Feijoada Completa (see page 94), a stunning array of mixed meats with black beans. For family fare, Italian Sausage Sandwiches (see page 88) or Country Ham Slices With Red-Eye Gravy (see page 85) can perk up weekday meals. Special features on pages 86 and 90 will guide you through the many kinds of ham, bacon, and sausage available, and an invaluable list on page 83 provides mail-order sources for hard-to-find items.

HOW HAM, BACON, SAUSAGE, AND CORNED MEAT ARE MADE

Today we eat smoked meats for their intense flavor, but ham, sausage, and bacon all arose out of the need to keep meat safely for more than a day or two, before refrigerators and freezers were invented. No farm family could justify killing their fattest hog just to get one or two meals out of it.

Bacon and sausage also proved to be a way to use odd parts of the hog that might otherwise be too fatty, tough, or sinewy for good eating on their own. When people lived by hard physical labor, the high calorie count of a plump, fatty sausage was vastly desirable.

Ham This cut is usually from the hind leg of the hog; when it is from the shoulder, it is known as smoked picnic ham. Processing begins with curing, accomplished in one of two ways: Hams are either cured in salted brine for several days or else are rubbed with salt, sugar, sodium nitrate, and other spices and hung for several days to dry-cure.

Nitrate acts as a preservative, preventing the growth of botulism bacteria, and in the days before refrigeration its use enabled the leg of a hog slaughtered in September to be eaten safely in January. The deep pink color of most hams comes from the nitrate cure; fresh leg of pork is pale pinkish gray like other cuts of uncooked pork.

With some especially prized types of ham (such as Parma, prosciutto, and Westphalian), processing consists entirely of curing; the hams are neither smoked nor steamed, but are dry-cured long and carefully enough at controlled temperatures to be safely ready to eat at purchase. Wet-brined hams are often steam-smoked (with steam produced by water over a wood fire), and dry-cured smoked hams are usually smoked dry, in special chambers where the heat and the amount of smoke are gradually increased until the ham is done.

Commercial hams (especially canned ham and ready-to-eat sliced ham) are usually wet-brined and then steam-smoked or may even be injected with brine and water (and in some cases, smoke flavoring) and steamed over gas or electric heat; these processes increase the weight of hams by increasing the water content. The price of such ham is relatively low, but the consumer is buying a lot of water along with the meat.

Genuine dry-cured smoked or unsmoked hams are more expensive not only because the processing is slow and costly, but also because the hams shrink considerably during processing, rather than expanding from the introduction of water. The flavor of dry-processed ham is much more intense. Especially as a cooking ingredient to enhance other foods, dry-cured ham and smoked ham (wet- or dry-cured) may be ultimately a better value than commercial ham: A small amount packs a great deal of flavor.

Wet-cured hams, whether smoked or not, are ready to cook at purchase. Dry-cured smoked aged hams (such as southern-style country ham or Smithfield ham) must be soaked before cooking (see page 84).

Bacon The belly meat of the hog may be processed in several ways. Unsmoked pork belly may be made into salt pork or Italian *pancetta*. Bacon, however, is belly meat that is usually dry-cured with sugar, nitrates, and salt. Then, if it is packaged commercial sliced bacon, it may have water and smoke flavoring injected rather than undergoing a full dry-smoking over wood.

Bacon with water injected can be recognized during cooking because, as the water is rendered, it spatters in the pan, and the bacon shrinks considerably. Genuine smoked bacon is dry-smoked entirely, developing a much stronger smoke flavor and shrinking and spattering far less during cooking.

Like dry-smoked ham, fully smoked bacon especially justifies its often higher price when it's used as a cooking ingredient flavoring other foods; to use commercial sliced bacon in a recipe such as Feijoada Completa (see page 94) or in a pot of greens, the amount of smoked bacon called for should be doubled.

Sausage Generally made of pork, sausages consist of finely or coarsely chopped meat that is mixed with varying amounts of fat and distinctive blends of herbs, spices, and seasonings. Soybean protein or nonfat dry milk may be added to bind (and stretch) the meat.

With the exception of country sausage (or the butcher's pork sausage meat, which is merely unspiced, coarsely ground pork), the meat and flavorings are then stuffed into a casing of hog or sheep gut, thin collagen made from cattle hide, or plastic (this latter being used for salami, bologna, and similar meats). Depending on the tradition of how a particular type of sausage is made, the sausage may or may not be mechanically tied into links.

Except for fresh sausages (such as country sausage, Italian sausages, chorizo, and bratwurst), virtually all sausages are cured with a sodium nitrate blend to prevent deadly botulism bacteria from developing during air-drying, low-heat steaming, or low-heat smoking; the cure is what changes the meat from the pale pinkish gray of pork to the familiar brownish red. Potassium nitrate (saltpeter) may also be used in the cure.

As with hams some sausages (including most pepperoni and hard salami) are dry-cured but unsmoked. Others (such as kielbasa, *andouille*, and some *chaurice*) are slowly smoked over smoldering wood chips in special smoking chambers at temperatures between 90° and 160° F.

Still others (especially German sausages such as frankfurters and most commercial kielbasa) are steamed or steam-smoked. Some commercial "smoked" sausages are injected with smoke flavoring to save the manufacturer the time and expense of having them actually smoked over wood.

Corned meat These whole cuts of meat (such as beef round, brisket, or tongue) are wet-brined with plenty of salt. Corned meats may (as in pastrami and smoked tongue) or may not (as in corned beef) be smoked after brining. They differ from pickled meats (such as pickled pig's feet) in that corning uses a water brine rather than vinegar and does not include cooking the meat. Typically corned meats come from rather tough parts of the animal and require long, slow, moist cooking.

KEEPING DRY-CURED HAMS

Dry-cured whole hams need not be refrigerated before cooking, but they should be hung in a cool, dry area. They may be kept for as long as desired. The skin of the ham may be covered with a mold. This is not a cause for alarm. The mold is harmless, and the skin will not be eaten. (Aged prime beef also develops a mold, which the butcher scrapes off before the meat reaches the meat case.) Some country-ham suppliers furnish packages of sliced ham as well as whole hams. Although the packaging is sufficiently airtight that it is safe for several days for shipment at any time of the year, you should refrigerate or freeze slices until ready to use them. After cooking, leftover ham, well wrapped, will keep about three weeks refrigerated and about three months frozen.

MAIL-ORDER SOURCES FOR HAM, BACON, AND SAUSAGE

Many of the finest preserved meats are available only by mail or phone order, unless one can conveniently visit the production site. Frequently prices at sources such as those listed below are barely higher than those of much inferior packaged versions from a supermarket refrigerator case.

Aidell's Sausage Company
618 Coventry Road
Kensington, CA 94707
(415) 420-1737

Alewell's Country Meats
Route 3, Box 5
Hagerstown, MD 21740
(816) 463-2215

Roi Ballard's Mahogany-Smoked Meats
Meadow Farms Smokehouse
Box 1387
Bishop, CA 93514
(619) 873-5311

Bacon Champs
Burger's Country Hams
Highway 87 and South Route 3
California, MO 65019
(314) 796-3134

B & B Food Products
Route 1
Cadiz, KY 42211
(502) 235-5297

Casa Moneo
210 West Fourteenth Street
New York, NY 10011
(212) 929-1644

Early's Honey Stand
Rural Route 2
Spring Hill, TN 37174
(615) 486-2230

Harrington's
618 Main Street
Richmond, VT 05477
(802) 434-3411

Heid Meat Service
427 Edgewood Drive
Kaukauha, WI 54130
(414) 788-4888

J Bar B Foods
Box 7
Waleder, TX 78959
(800) 242-0064 or (512) 665-7511

Lawrence's Smoke House
RR 1, Box 28
Newfane, VT 05345
(802) 628-7751

Luter's Hams
Smithfield Packing Co.
Smithfield, VA 23430
(804) 357-4321

McArthur's Smokehouse
Litchfield on the Green
Box 190
Litchfield, CT 06759
(203) 567-4593

Nodine's Bacon and Sausages
North Street, Route 63
Goshen, CT 06756
(203) 491-3511

G. B. Ratto's
821 Washington Street
Oakland, CA 94607
(800) 325-3483 or (800) 228-3515 in California

Scimitar Meats
Box 340
Canby, OR 97013
(503) 266-5781

Smithfield Collection
Box 487
Smithfield, VA 23430
(800) 628-2242

Southampton Supply Company
Box 419
Franklin, VA 23851
(804) 562-5111

Weaver's
Box 725
Lebanon, PA 17042
(712) 272-5643

Cider-Baked Country Ham trims hours off regular cooking time because the ham steams and bakes at the same time. The sweetness of cider is a perfect complement to the salty ham, and a splash of bourbon adds a true southern accent.

COOKING DRY-CURED HAMS

Dry-cured hams are extremely salty and are coated with pepper as well as with any mold that develops during aging. To remove some of the salt and soften the coating, soak the ham at room temperature for 12 to 36 hours in several changes of water. Then scrub the outside with a stiff brush to remove the mold and coating.

Cover the ham with cold water and simmer it (do not boil) until the meat is partly tender but still firm (about 20 minutes per pound). Allow ham to cool enough to handle, then carefully remove the skin, leaving a thick coating of fat on the ham. Score the fat in diamond shapes;

glaze the ham with brown sugar, corn syrup, or maple syrup (thinned, if desired, with cider or pineapple juice); then bake in preheated 400° F oven for just long enough to set the glaze (about 15 minutes).

Alternatively the simmering can be omitted, and the ham can be baked in a preheated 350° F oven, allowing 20 minutes per pound. Put water or cider in the pan. In this case when ham is nearly done, remove it from the oven and let it cool a little; then remove the skin, score and glaze the fat, and continue to bake the ham until the glaze is browned. If you prefer soak the slices in water or milk for 1 hour and panfry them.

CIDER-BAKED COUNTRY HAM

In this treatment the ham is baked with cider so that no simmering on the stovetop is needed.

1 Smithfield ham or country
    ham (12 to 14 lb)
4 cups apple cider
½ cup bourbon
    Brown sugar, for glaze

1. Soak ham in several changes of cold water for at least 24 hours. Scrub under cold running water with a stiff brush and wipe dry.

2. Preheat oven to 350° F. Place a long sheet of heavy aluminum foil in the bottom of a shallow roasting pan (foil should be long enough to fold around and make a tent for ham). Place ham on foil, pour on cider, and seal foil around ham. Bake until ham is cooked through and tender (about 4 hours).

3. Remove ham from oven and allow it to cool until it can be handled. Discard aluminum foil. Remove drippings and save fat if desired. Gently and carefully remove skin, leaving a thick layer of fat. Score fat in a diamond pattern with a sharp knife and return ham to oven for 15 minutes to heat surface. Slide out oven shelf so that ham is fully exposed. Heat bourbon in a small saucepan, pour it over the ham and, using a long match *and great caution*, set bourbon alight. *Be sure* that nothing flammable is near the oven opening. When flames die down spread brown sugar over fat and return ham to oven until sugar forms a dark, melted glaze (about 15 minutes).

Serves 8 to 10.

HAM AND LEEK OR ASPARAGUS ROLLS IN CHEESE SAUCE

This graceful, quick lunch or light dinner may be accompanied by warmed French bread, sweet butter, and chilled dry white wine. It multiplies easily to serve more than two. Sautéed mushrooms or finely chopped sautéed zucchini may be added to the rolls, if desired, for more substance.

¼ cup each *grated Parmesan
    and Gruyère cheeses*
2 heaping teaspoons snipped
    fresh chives
    Freshly squeezed lemon juice,
    to taste
    Salt, white pepper, nutmeg,
    and cayenne, to taste
6 leeks, trimmed and washed
    well, or 6 thick spears aspara-
    gus, trimmed
6 thin slices cooked ham

White Sauce

1 tablespoon butter
1 tablespoon flour
1 cup milk

1. Preheat oven to 400° F. Over low heat, stirring constantly, melt together White Sauce and cheeses. Remove from heat and add chives and lemon juice. Season carefully with salt, white pepper, nutmeg, and cayenne to taste.

2. *If using leeks:* Trim off tips, slit in several places along white section, and cut in lengths the same size as ham slices. Rinse once again to remove sand, drop into lightly salted boiling water, lower heat, and simmer until barely tender (about 10 minutes). Drain well. *If using asparagus:* Snap off tough bottoms, drop into skillet of boiling, salted water, lower heat, and simmer until crisp-tender (about 4 minutes); drain thoroughly.

3. Wrap each leek or asparagus stalk in a slice of ham. Butter an oven-proof, shallow baking dish long enough to hold leeks or asparagus. Place ham-vegetable rolls in dish, pour on cheese sauce, and bake until bubbling and golden (about 20 minutes).

Serves 2 for lunch or light supper.

White Sauce Over low heat melt butter. Add flour, stirring until golden (about 5 minutes). Add milk, mixing continuously until thickened.

Makes 1 cup.

COUNTRY HAM SLICES WITH RED-EYE GRAVY

Ham slices from the butcher will be enlivened by this surprising sauce. The secret is black coffee.

4 slices (each ½ in. thick) coun-
    try ham, cooked or uncooked
    (see Note)
4 tablespoons rendered
    drippings from baked ham,
    or vegetable oil
¼ cup firmly packed light
    brown sugar
½ cup strong black brewed
    (not instant) coffee

1. Score through fat at edges of ham slices to keep them from curling. In a large, heavy skillet, heat drippings. Add ham and sauté over medium heat, turning several times, until lightly browned on both sides (20 to 25 minutes for uncooked slices, about 10 minutes for cooked slices).

2. Remove ham and keep warm. Stir sugar into pan juices and cook at low heat, stirring constantly, until sugar dissolves. Add coffee and simmer until gravy turns rich brown (about 5 minutes); do not boil. Pour gravy over ham and serve.

Serves 4.

<u>Note</u> If you are using uncooked slices of a salty, dry-cured ham, add 1 cup water to skillet along with ham. The ham will absorb all the water by the time it is cooked through; add more water if the original amount is absorbed too quickly.

CROQUE-MONSIEUR
Old-fashioned French grilled ham and cheese sandwich

It's difficult to find this quick lunch (or midnight supper) dish made well in Paris any more (nowadays you'll spend a fortune for a mere ham and cheese on white bread), but you can easily make it at home: It's warmed ham and melted cheese encased in French toast. This is a romantic version just for two.

> 4 tablespoons (approximately) butter, at spreadable temperature
> 4 slices good white bread or wide French bread, crusts trimmed
> 1 egg
> ¼ cup milk, half-and-half, or whipping cream
> 2 slices (¼ in. thick) mild cheese of choice (such as Cheddar, fontina, Tybo, Gruyère, or Emmenthaler) cut a little smaller than bread
> 2 slices cooked ham of choice or 4 slices cooked bacon

1. Butter one side of each slice of bread, reserving at least 2 tablespoons butter for pan. In a wide soup bowl, lightly beat together egg and milk. Place a slice of cheese and a slice of ham (or a slice of bacon, broken in half) on two of the pieces of bread, cover with the other pieces, and dip both sides of sandwich in egg batter, letting it rest there long enough for batter to soak in a little (about 20 seconds per side). Pinch edges of bread together as best you can without breaking bread.

2. In a skillet large enough to hold both sandwiches, over medium heat melt remaining butter. Add sandwiches and fry, turning midway, until bread is golden brown and cheese is melted and oozing out the sides of the sandwiches.

Serves 2 as snack, lunch, or light supper.

GLAZED HAM SLICES

For a quick family meal, slices of ordinary ham can be covered with a tasty glaze and rapidly broiled. Serve with coleslaw or salad and yams, rice, potatoes, or warmed rolls.

> 1 pound sliced ham
> ¼ cup honey
> ¼ cup soy sauce
> 1 teaspoon Dijon or regular mustard

Preheat broiler. Place ham slices on broiler rack set in broiler pan. Stir together remaining ingredients and spread on ham slices. Broil ham, glazed side up, 5 to 6 inches from heat source until slices are heated through (3 to 4 minutes).

Serves 3 or 4.

Ham With Lime-Mustard Glaze
Mix ¼ cup dry mustard with 2 tablespoons each cold water, white wine vinegar, and lime juice. If glaze is too nippy, add a little olive oil and a pinch of sugar. Spread glaze on one side of each ham slice and broil, glazed side up, 5 to 6 inches from heat source until slices are heated through (3 to 4 minutes).

Ham With Tarragon-Mustard
Glaze Mix ¼ cup dry mustard with 1 to 2 tablespoons each cold water and tarragon wine vinegar plus ½ teaspoon dried tarragon. If glaze is too nippy, add a little olive oil and a pinch of sugar. Spread glaze on one side of each ham slice and broil, glazed side up, 5 to 6 inches from heat source until slices are heated through (3 to 4 minutes).

Cranberry- or Chutney-Glazed
Ham Spread about ⅓ cup cranberry relish or chutney on one side of each ham slice. Broil, glazed side up, 5 to 6 inches from heat source until slices are heated through (3 to 4 minutes).

A SAMPLER OF HAM AND BACON

There are many types of ham, ranging from mild, fork-tender Italian appetizer hams to the fiercely peppered hams of Louisiana—and more than one type of bacon exists, too.

Here is a guide to the meats such as those pictured on page 87 that you may find in a fine delicatessen or at the deli counter of an ethnic grocery. Good-quality preserved meats are widely available at well-stocked delicatessens, particularly those specializing in Italian, German, or Latin meats. They may also be purchased by mail order (see page 83) or by visiting production sites.

Baked ham Any mild ham that has been baked until fully cooked is considered baked ham. The finest flavored baked ham comes from dry-cured, smoked hams rather than commercial hams (such as canned hams) that have merely been injected with brine and smoke flavoring. Baked ham may be wrapped tightly and refrigerated for about five days if wet-brined, or for three weeks if dry-cured (which eliminates moisture that promotes spoilage). Baked ham may be cut in conveniently sized chunks for future use, wrapped very well, and frozen for three to six months. The meat will deteriorate rapidly once defrosted (even partially), however, and cannot be refrozen.

Boiled ham Mild ham that has been boiled until fully cooked is boiled ham. Packaged, thinly sliced ham is boiled ham and contains a great deal of water; if the package indicates the presence of potassium nitrate, the ham has been colored pink with saltpeter. The best flavor is obtained by buying uncooked ham and boiling it at home. Boiled ham may be stored like baked ham.

Country ham Southern-style country ham is slowly dry-cured, smoked, and aged, using no artificial methods to speed up the process, and keeps well both before and after cooking due to its relative dryness. Southern-style country ham must be soaked before cooking. (See pages 83 and 84 for instructions on keeping and cooking dry-cured ham.) New England- and Pennsylvania-style country hams are moister, being wet-brined before they are dry-smoked.

Kentucky ham A dry-processed southern ham, Kentucky ham comes from the state of Kentucky.

New England ham A slightly sweet, moist ham, New England ham is wet-brined with maple sugar and smoked over hickory or corn cobs.

Pancetta Thinly sliced, unsmoked Italian bacon that has been salted, cured, and lightly spiced, *pancetta* is mild-flavored and very tender. It can be safely eaten without cooking. It may be frozen, well-wrapped, for three to six months. Once defrosted pancetta should be used within a few days, since it turns rancid quickly due to its high fat content.

Parma ham This exquisite aged, salt-cured, ready-to-eat ham from Parma, Italy, comes from hogs fed on the whey rendered during the manufacture of Parmesan cheese. Sliced thinly, Parma ham is translucent.

Pennsylvania ham Typically ham processing in Pennsylvania begins with wet-brining, but continues with heavy dry-smoking.

Prosciutto ham Salt- and air-cured ready-to-eat ham, prosciutto is similar to Parma ham but often somewhat saltier. Much of the prosciutto in the United States is imported from Italy, where hogs for this ham are fed on chestnuts. Sliced thinly, prosciutto is often served with ripe melon or fresh figs as an appetizer and is a valuable cooking ingredient—small quantities lend a lot of flavor. Prosciutto is readily available in Italian and international delicatessens, but if it is not in stock, country ham makes a passable substitute.

Smithfield ham Similar to Southern-style country ham, a Smithfield ham must, by law, have been cured and smoked in Smithfield, Virginia. These hams come from free-ranging hogs fed on acorns, hickory nuts, and peanuts to lend the meat a nutty flavor. The hams are dry-cured in salt and coated with pepper. The flavor is intense and salty. (See page 84 for instructions on cooking Smithfield hams.)

Smoked bacon Genuine smoked bacon has been dry-cured with sugar, salt, and (usually) nitrates and then smoked entirely over an aromatic wood (such as hickory, apple wood, or mahogany) or, in some cases, corn cobs, dried apples, nut husks, and similar fruit and vegetable products. Smoked bacon may be sold with or without a thick, aromatically smoky rind.

Some sides of smoked bacon with a full rind left on (typically those from southern meat processors) may be hung for months in a cool place without spoiling, but they will drip fat as they hang. It is usually easier to cut the slab into convenient pieces (many recipes call for about 6 ounces)

and freeze the blocks, well-wrapped, for up to six months.

The rind must be removed before cooking unless the bacon is only for flavor and will be removed from the dish before serving. In cooking, salt pork is often used as a substitute, but salt pork is not smoked; it contributes the salt and fattiness of bacon but not the smoky flavor.

Tasso A heavily smoked Cajun ham made from lean pork shoulder seasoned with cayenne, *tasso* is always used as a seasoning meat rather than served on its own.

Virginia ham Essentially a Smithfield ham, Virginia ham is a country ham that has been processed outside of Smithfield proper.

Westphalian ham This German ham is similar to Parma ham and prosciutto, but comes from pigs fed on sugar beet mash and is smoked with juniper brush. Westphalian ham is sliced thinly and eaten raw.

York ham Although from England, York ham is similar to both America's Smithfield ham and the legendary hams of central China. York hams are usually boiled, or boiled and then also baked.

SAUSAGE

Sausages are not health foods, except in terms of whatever health benefits that pleasure confers. They are generally high in fat, but also vibrant in flavor, each variety seasoned differently than the next. The following recipes are a brief round-the-world survey of sausage dishes, ranging from elaborate party feasts to quick, tasty snacks.

Sausages are wonderful grilled at a barbecue, in an assortment of meats (see Patagonian Parillada Mixta on page 103), sliced into cooked lentils, or laid over polenta, covered with tomatoes and cheese, and baked as a gratin. They can also be sautéed with apples and onions like pork chops (see page 74).

ITALIAN SAUSAGE SANDWICHES

In New York City these tasty sandwiches, cooked and sold in the streets during the Festival of San Gennaro, are available in sausage sandwich shops all year long. If you include the optional ingredients (and use hot sausages), you'll have a hot sausage sandwich, which is strictly home cooking and is regarded as a sure cure for colds.

- 3 medium-sized bell peppers, red and green (about ¾ lb total), or 1 jar (8 oz) roasted red peppers, drained
- 3 tablespoons olive oil
- 1 pound sweet or hot Italian sausages
- 2 medium onions, sliced not too thinly
- 2 tablespoons crushed garlic
- ½ teaspoon dried oregano
- ¼ teaspoon freshly ground black pepper
- 4 hot Italian frying peppers or other hot chiles (optional)
- 2 teaspoons capers, drained (optional)
  Italian bread (or French rolls) for 4 submarine sandwiches
- 8 bottled peperoncini peppers, drained and trimmed (optional)
  Anchovy paste or anchovy strips (optional)

1. Roast and peel fresh bell peppers (see page 101), seed, and cut into strips about ½ inch wide.

2. While peppers are steaming in bag, barely film heavy skillet with some of the oil and fry sausages over medium heat, turning frequently to brown, pricking skins occasionally. Drain on paper towels, slice lengthwise, and tent with foil to keep warm.

3. Meanwhile in another skillet over burner set to medium, heat remaining oil. Sauté onion, garlic, oregano, and black pepper, stirring occasionally, until onion is tender (about 8 minutes). Add frying peppers, if used, and sauté until tender (about 10 minutes). Add roasted bell peppers and cook another 5 minutes, stirring occasionally. Stir in capers, if used.

4. Cut bread crossways into 4 submarine sandwich–sized pieces, each a little longer than the sausages. Cut each piece lengthwise into 2 long halves. Make a bed of sautéed vegetables on 4 pieces of bread. Add *peperoncini* (if used). Top with halved sausage. Smear a thin coating of anchovy paste (if used), on the other 4 pieces of bread (or tuck anchovy strips in with sausages). Assemble into sandwiches and serve immediately, supplying forks to pick up stray bits.

Serves 4.

TOAD-IN-THE-HOLE

This English pub dish with a funny name hides small sausages in a light, puffy crust that's something like Yorkshire pudding, something like a popover. Serve with mustard on the side as an appetizer, snack, or the main course of a light supper.

- 1 tablespoon bacon drippings or cooking oil
- ½ pound pork link sausages (about 6 sausages)
- ¾ cup flour
  Pinch salt, plus more to taste
- ½ cup grated extra-sharp Cheddar cheese
- 1¼ cups milk
- 2 eggs
- 2 tablespoons minced parsley
  Freshly ground pepper, to taste

1. Preheat oven to 425° F. In a 9-inch ovenproof skillet (or a deep-dish pie pan), heat bacon drippings. Add sausages; roll them in fat and brown on all sides in oven (for about 20 minutes) or on top of stove, turning every 5 minutes.

2. Meanwhile sift flour and the pinch salt into a mixing bowl. Stir in cheese. In a smaller bowl beat milk, eggs, and parsley, and season generously with salt and pepper. Stir a small amount of milk mixture into the flour to make a smooth, very heavy batter and let stand 5 minutes before stirring in remaining milk mixture.

3. Arrange sausages like spokes of a wheel evenly spaced in pan and pour batter over them. Lower oven heat to 400° F and bake until batter is puffed and browned (about 30 minutes). Cut into wedges and serve while hot.

Serves 4 to 6 as appetizer or snack, 2 as light supper.

HOMEMADE AMERICAN COUNTRY SAUSAGE

Old-fashioned farmhouse cooks wouldn't think of throwing away fatty trim from pork, since trim is perfectly balanced for the mixed lean-and-fat of sausage—and country sausage takes just a few minutes and no special sausage-making equipment to make.

- ¾ pound pork (½ lb lean, ¼ lb fat)
- 1 tablespoon dried sage leaves, crumbled
- 1 teaspoon crushed red pepper, or to taste
- ½ teaspoon freshly ground black pepper, or to taste
- 1 teaspoon salt
- ½ teaspoon well-crumbled dried thyme leaves
- 1 large clove garlic, chopped

1. Grind meat twice in grinder with fine blade or chop fine with a food processor, using steel blade. (If using food processor pick over meat and remove any unground pieces of fat or gristle.)

2. Crush sage, red pepper, black pepper, salt, thyme, and garlic together with a mortar and pestle or in an electric minichopper or clean coffee grinder. Add spices to meat and mix thoroughly. To check seasoning pinch off a small piece of mixture, flatten it into a tiny patty, and fry it over medium heat until well browned on both sides; taste. Continue to correct seasonings in same way.

3. Form meat into a cylinder about 6 inches long. Wrap tightly in plastic wrap and refrigerate at least 24 hours

before using, to let flavors mellow. (Sausage may also be frozen after mellowing period; it will keep for about 5 months and may be sliced at will, frozen.)

4. To cook, cut sausage in slices about ¾ inch thick. Cook in a dry skillet over medium-low heat until well browned on both sides, pouring off fat as it accumulates. (For sausage with eggs or with biscuits and gravy, pour fat into another skillet and use it to cook eggs or as fat portion of pan cream gravy.)

Makes a 6-inch sausage to serve 4 to 6 for breakfast.

Buon appetito! Roast peppers and sautéed onions lend a luscious texture to the filling of Italian Sausage Sandwiches, which can be dressed modestly or as adventurously as the cook pleases.

89

A SAMPLER OF SAUSAGE

Sausages such as those pictured on page 91 fall into two categories: smoked (or dry) sausages—most of which are ready to eat (usually after some reheating, for palatability) and which can also be refrigerated for several days—and fresh, unsmoked (or moist) sausages, which are highly perishable and must be cooked fully before eating. The pink color of most dry sausages typically comes from nitrates; fresh sausages that are red (such as chorizo and Italian hot sausage) gain their color from paprika or hot red pepper.

Andouille Cajun sausage A heavily smoked, coarsely ground, spicy pork sausage, *andouille* is used primarily as a cooking ingredient. It can, however, be simmered or grilled and eaten as is. French andouille is a thick sausage cased in pork gut and filled with coarsely chopped pork chitterlings and stomach and is served cold, sliced, as an appetizer or as a snack.

Bangers Small, bland, English pork sausages, bangers are similar to pork links but with a high proportion of bread and dry-milk filler and a very light sage flavor.

Blood sausage (boudin noir) A mild sausage with a thick skin and very tender center, blood sausage is made from the blood of a steer or hog. French *boudin* includes chopped pork, onions, and parsley, and Italian blood sausage contains chopped pork and raisins. (Patagonian Parillada Mixta on page 103 calls for Italian blood sausage, which is similar to the Argentine version.) Slice and brown blood sausage in butter or barbecue it.

Bockwurst A highly perishable, finely grained, tender, usually unsmoked and uncured sausage, *bockwurst* is made of seasoned pork, veal, beef, milk, onions, chives, and eggs. Freeze it for storage of longer than two days. To prepare bockwurst, simmer it in water for 10 minutes, brown it in butter, or barbecue it. (Red-colored sausages identified as "bockwurst" are found in some markets and hot dog stands. These are cured sausages and may be treated like frankfurters.)

Boudin blanc In this country *boudin blanc* is primarily made in Louisiana and is rarely shipped outside that state because it is extremely perishable. Every grocery in Cajun country makes its own version of this delicate, piquant, uncured white sausage, mixing raw ground pork, ground cooked chicken breast, rice, garlic, green onions, cream, and spices in a fragile casing. If you are lucky enough to obtain some, simmer it in a skillet in a small amount of water for about 20 minutes, or if it has already simmered, very gently fry it in butter. The casings will inevitably break, spilling the contents of the sausages into the pan.

Bratwurst (Swiss sausage) This white, thick, tender, usually unsmoked and uncured sausage contains the same ingredients as bockwurst, minus the onions and chives. Bratwurst is very perishable and should be treated like bockwurst.

Braunschweiger A smoked German sausage, braunschweiger is made of pork by-products (such as snouts and liver).

Cervelat A cured, usually unsmoked sausage that originally contained pig brains, *cervelat* now consists of pork, beef, and bacon fat encased in beef gut. This sausage should be simmered gently for about an hour.

Chaurice A spicy Cajun pork sausage, *chaurice* is available smoked or raw and is usually flavored with parsley and onion. Cajun garlic sausage is a garlicky version of chaurice. Simmer chaurice about 10 minutes, or cut it up and use it as a flavoring meat for other dishes.

Chorizo A spicy red fresh sausage originating in Spain and common throughout Latin America, chorizo is made of coarsely ground, fatty pork seasoned highly with red pepper and garlic and colored by paprika. Hot Italian sausage or country-style Louisiana hot links can substitute in recipes.

Cotechino A salt-cured Italian sausage, *cotechino* is made from pork skins, ground pork, spices, and sometimes dry white wine that is colored red by saltpeter. It requires long simmering (about 2 hours).

Country sausage In the United States country sausage is a thick, coarsely ground pork sausage (two thirds lean, one third fat), either with or without a casing, spiced with sage and other herbs, with varying quantities of hot red pepper. It can be sliced and fried gently in butter for breakfast. It can also be broken up, fried, and used in stuffings.

Frankfurter This mildly spiced, very finely ground (emulsified) familiar sausage (usually lightly smoked as well as cured) may be all beef or beef and pork, with its distinctive flavor coming from cumin. Ready to eat, frankfurters can be reheated in simmering water or by frying or grilling. "Exposition frankfurters" are made from finely textured veal and pork.

Italian sausage Several types of unsmoked, uncured, fresh Italian sausage are available at Italian delicatessens. Italian garlic sausage contains coarsely chopped pork and pork fat, mixed spices, and lots of garlic. Italian sweet sausage, also called fennel sausage, is similar, with less garlic but plentiful whole fennel seeds (or, in some delicatessens, anise seeds) lending a slight licorice flavor; it's a favorite as the meat portion of Neapolitan-style pasta sauce. Italian hot sausage contains a heavy dose of hot-pepper flakes. All are perishable, and should be frozen if not used within two or three days. To prepare Italian sausage, simmer it 10 minutes, then slice and brown in a small amount of olive oil, or fry it whole, pierced with a fork in a few places, in a little olive oil. It may also be removed from the casing, broken up, and fried to serve as part of a stuffing or pasta sauce.

Kielbasa (Polish sausage) Kielbasa is a highly flavored, lightly smoked long sausage made of coarsely chopped pork with some beef and veal, spices, and lots of garlic. It may be simmered 15 to 20 minutes or may be broiled, grilled, or barbecued.

Knackwurst A lightly smoked, finely ground German sausage, knackwurst is made from emulsified beef, pork, pork fat, cumin, plenty of garlic, and saltpeter. Similar in taste to frankfurters, knackwurst are thicker. Poach knackwurst in water for about 10 minutes.

Landjäger A cold-smoked, pressed, ready-to-eat sausage, *Landjäger* was eaten by field troops in the German national guard (the *Landjäger*).

Linguiça (pronounced lin-*gwee*-sa) A coarsely ground, mildly spicy, Portuguese cured (but usually unsmoked) sausage, *linguiça* is made of pork, garlic, spices, and orange peel; it is moistened by either wine or vinegar. *Longaniza* (the Spanish version of linguiça), kielbasa, chaurice, Italian sausage, or a mild chorizo can substitute for linguiça in most recipes. Cook linguiça fully before serving.

Liverwurst A finely ground, spreadable, ready-to-eat cured sausage, liverwurst is made of mildly seasoned pork and beef by-products and soy protein.

Longaniza This Spanish sausage is a version of linguiça.

Luganega The milder Italian version of linguiça, dating back to the Roman Empire (mentioned by fourth-century writer Apicius as *lucanica*), *luganega* may include cumin, savory, bay, pine nuts, and parsley, with a little bite from both milled and cracked black pepper. Slice and gently fry luganega in olive oil or simmer it whole.

Louisiana hot links A widely available spicy pork sausage, Louisiana hot links come in two versions. Some hot links (such as those served at ball parks) are finely grained, lightly smoked, dry-cured sausages, like frankfurters but with the meat colored very red by paprika and cayenne. Others (such as those served in barbecue restaurants) are thick, coarsely chopped, very spicy country sausages. Traditionally grilled or barbecued, the dry links may also be simmered about 10 minutes.

Pork link sausages (breakfast links) Small, tender, unsmoked, and usually uncured sausages stuffed in thin sheep casings, pork link sausages are mildly seasoned along the same lines as country sausage and are perishable. Use them quickly after purchase; brown pork links gently in oil or grill them.

Salami (whole) A heavily cured, highly seasoned, ready-to-eat sausage, salami is coarsely milled but tightly packed, often in a synthetic casing that must be stripped off.

Summer sausage (includes mettwurst) Usually coarsely ground, summer sausage is a cured and lightly smoked but uncooked sausage made of pork, veal, or beef and soy concentrate. Summer sausage is quite perishable and should not be eaten raw.

Toulouse sausage A mildly seasoned, coarsely ground, fresh pork sausage, Toulouse sausage originated in southern France. Occasionally available in specialty delicatessens, Toulouse sausage is best known for its use in the French baked-bean casserole, cassoulet. Grill Toulouse sausage or brown it in butter.

Vienna sausages (cocktail franks) A kind of miniature frankfurter, Vienna sausages are mainly found bottled or canned. They are often served lightly grilled (or encased in batter and fried) and stuck on toothpicks at parties or else floating amid baked beans.

Cabbage isn't the only vegetable in Corned Beef and Cabbage, perfect for Saint Patrick's Day—or any other day. Add the vegetables when the meat is nearly done and they'll reward you with their succulence.

WINEY SAUSAGE-POTATO GRATIN

This delightfully simple casserole needs only a green salad to make a meal. If dinner is for two, this recipe can easily be halved.

> 2 large Idaho potatoes
> 2 tablespoons olive or vegetable oil, or as needed
> 1 pound spicy fresh sausage (such as Italian, chaurice, linguiça, chorizo, or Louisiana hot links)
> 2 large cloves garlic
> 2 medium red onions, minced
>   Salt and freshly ground pepper, to taste
> 1 scant teaspoon dried basil, herbes de Provence, or Italian seasoning mixture
> ⅔ cup dry white wine
> 2 small bell peppers, seeded and sliced thinly in rings

1. Preheat oven to 350° F. Peel potatoes, drop into saucepan with cold water to cover, and over high heat bring to a boil. Lower heat to medium and boil gently 5 minutes. Drain and cool.

2. Meanwhile heat 1 tablespoon of the oil in heavy skillet and brown sausages on all sides.

3. Split 1 clove garlic in half and rub all over bottom and sides of a 9-inch by 14-inch heat-resistant glass or ceramic baking pan or shallow, heavy, ovenproof casserole. Let garlic dry on casserole for a few minutes. Mince remaining clove garlic and add, with onions, to sausages. (If sausages have not rendered much fat, add a little more oil.) Lower heat and sauté mixture slowly until onions are tender. Remove sausages with tongs, slice thickly, and reserve.

4. Grease casserole lightly with oil. Slice potato ⅛ inch thick and layer with onion-garlic mixture in baking dish. Sprinkle with salt, pepper, and basil. Pour wine into dish and scatter bell peppers over potatoes. Top mixture with sliced sausage. Cover casserole with foil or a lid and bake 45 minutes. Uncover, bake 15 minutes longer, and serve while hot.

Serves 4.

CORNED MEAT

Corned meats generally appeal to those who like spicy, zestful food. One of the most popular corned meat dishes is that old Irish favorite, corned beef and cabbage.

CORNED BEEF AND CABBAGE

This is a one-pot, one-dish meal.

    3   to 3½ pounds corned beef
    2   bay leaves
    12   black peppercorns
    12   juniper berries
    12   to 15 medium red boiling
         potatoes, scrubbed
    12   medium carrots, pared and
         coarsely sliced on the bias
    12   parsnips, trimmed, pared,
         and coarsely sliced
    2   small cabbages, cut into
         8 wedges each, or 1½ large
         cabbages cut into wedges
         Dijon mustard (optional)
         Brown sugar (optional)
         Mustard and horseradish,
         as condiments

1. Rinse corned beef in cold water. Place in large pot. Cover with 6 inches cold water. Cover pot and bring to a boil. Taste liquid; if very, very salty, pour out water and begin again. When liquid is acceptable, skim off scum and add bay leaves, peppercorns, and juniper berries. Lower heat, cover, and simmer until meat is very tender but not falling apart (about 1 hour per pound, or 3 to 3½ hours).

2. About 45 minutes before meat is done, add potatoes, carrots, and parsnips. Return meat to a gentle boil, lower heat, and continue to simmer. About 15 minutes later, add cabbage wedges. Remove meat and slice before serving. If meat seems done before other ingredients, remove while other ingredients continue cooking. If desired sliced meat may be coated thinly with Dijon mustard and sprinkled lightly with brown sugar, then placed under broiler to glaze. Serve meat and vegetables with pot juices and mustard and horseradish on the table.

Serves 6.

"SECOND HELPINGS" OF HAM

"Second helpings" of ham left over from earlier meals can be used to prepare a wide range of appetizers and main dishes. To keep the leftover meat from spoiling, proper storage techniques are essential.

Storage

Pre-cooked ham, well-wrapped in the refrigerator, will keep for up to five days for wet-brined hams and up to three weeks for dry-cured smoked hams. For longer storage cut the ham into convenient chunks, wrap each chunk well, and freeze for up to three months (wet-brined) or five months (dry-cured smoked ham).

Defrost ham on the day of use, since hams deteriorate rapidly after defrosting. Save all drippings from smoked hams and bacon; for long storage freeze drippings (preferably in a metal or glass container), then scoop drippings out as needed with a heated metal spoon.

Preparation

Many good dishes can be improved by adding leftover ham for a richer flavor. Some suggestions follow, but feel free to use your imagination and improvise.

Basque dishes *For Basque chicken:* Sauté chicken in olive oil with sliced onions and bell peppers, coarsely chopped, peeled, seeded tomatoes, and diced baked smoked ham. *For a Basque omelet:* Sauté onions, peppers, tomatoes, and ham with fresh herbs of choice, pour on lightly beaten eggs, and cook slowly until eggs set.

Ham canapés Mix ground Smithfield or country ham with an equal amount of minced hard-cooked egg. Add cream or mayonnaise to moisten, season to taste with minced parsley and black or cayenne pepper, and spread on toast points or crackers. Or serve paper-thin slices of smoked ham on assorted breads spread with mustard; if desired, cover with a thin slice of cheese and place under broiler until cheese melts.

Ham in appetizers Fold ground Smithfield or country ham into batter of your favorite cheese soufflé, cheese omelet, or quiche, seasoning the remaining ingredients more strongly than usual with black or cayenne pepper, nutmeg, or fresh chiles.

Ham-stuffed peppers Substitute ground Smithfield or country ham for other meat in your favorite stuffed pepper recipe or mix 1 cup ground ham with ½ cup cooked rice, ⅓ cup each chopped celery and chopped onion sautéed in 3 tablespoons butter until soft, and 1 cup peeled, seeded, chopped tomato. Add minced parsley and pepper to taste and, if desired, some grated sharp cheese (such as sharp Cheddar). Blanch 4 green bell peppers for 2 minutes, cut off tops, seed, and stuff. Top with a thin coat of dried bread crumbs dotted with butter. Place stuffed peppers in a baking dish, add 1 inch of boiling water, and bake at 350° F for 35 to 40 minutes.

Ham with potatoes Add chopped or thinly sliced, cooked, smoked ham to potato gratin, potato *rôti*, or potato pancakes. Baked smoked ham is especially flavorful in *tortilla española* (Spanish potato omelet).

Soups and casseroles Smithfield ham can substitute for Chinese ham in Asian soups. Smoked hams of all types are also superb in soups or casseroles of lentils or beans.

Sliced country ham or other smoked ham is also delicious when reheated gently to substitute for pork in recipes for pork chops (such as Pork Chops With Apples in Cider Sauce on page 74, or Smoked Pork Chops in Mustard-Cream Sauce on page 71), or in any meat casserole that includes fruit or yams.

AN INFORMAL DINNER PARTY IN RIO

Feijoada Completa

Salsa Cruda (see page 27)

Farofa Garnish

Collard Greens in the Style of Minas Gerais

Rice a la Brasiliera

Caipirinhas

Hearty Red Wine (such as Zinfandel or Chianti) or Chilled Beer

This zesty dinner for a dozen is a celebratory union of the varied foods of the peoples of Brazil. Note that preparations for this meal must begin one to three days in advance. To start your party, hand each guest a frosty Caipirinha cocktail. When you're ready to serve dinner, the beans go over or next to the rice, the greens beside the meat and beans. Salsa Cruda is added as desired, and Farofa Garnish is lightly sprinkled over everything.

FEIJOADA COMPLETA
Black bean and mixed meat stew

You don't really need to have everything on the ingredients list to make this flavorful, hearty dish great. Kielbasa or chorizo can substitute for *linguiça,* and the Brazilian *carne seca* is recommended but not required. But do start well in advance. The preparation on day 1 will take about two hours. That on day 2 will take about four hours; this preparation can actually be completed the same day as the party if started by 10 a.m. (to serve at 8 p.m.), but doing so makes a very long day for the cook. On day 3 less than an hour is required to complete the stew.

- 4 cups black beans
- 1 smoked beef tongue
- 4 thick, smoked pork chops
- 1 pound Brazilian carne seca or other mild beef jerky (see Note, page 95)
- 1 slab smoked bacon (½ lb), in 1 piece
- 1 pound corned pork spareribs (if available) or fresh spareribs, cut into 4-inch pieces
- 2 pig's feet, split
- ½ cup white rum
- 1½ pounds linguiça or longaniza sausage
- 1½ pounds fresh mild sausage, such as breakfast links
- 2 pounds pork loin or beef bottom round in 1 piece, trimmed of excess fat
- 2 bay leaves
- 2 tablespoons olive oil or lard
- 2 medium onions, chopped
- 1 tablespoon minced garlic
- 1 cup Italian tomatoes, coarsely chopped
- 3 to 4 fresh or pickled hot chiles Freshly ground black pepper, salt, and aged hot pepper sauce (such as Tabasco), to taste
- 6 large navel oranges, quartered (peeled if desired)

Day 1

1. Cover beans with cold water to 2 inches above their surface and soak overnight. Place tongue, smoked pork chops, jerky, smoked bacon, and corned spareribs (but not fresh spareribs) in a large bowl, cover with cold water, and let soak 24 hours, changing water twice. (Soaking removes excess salt.)

2. Place pig's feet in saucepan; add cold water to cover. Boil, lower heat, and simmer 1½ hours. Refrigerate in cooking water.

Day 2

1. Remove pig's feet from jelly that will have formed around them. Place beans and pig's feet in a casserole or stockpot (about 8 quarts) large enough to hold all ingredients. Add rum and enough cold water to cover by 2 inches. Bring mixture to a boil, lower heat to a simmer, cover, and simmer 1½ hours. At the same time in another large pot, cover tongue, jerky, and bacon with cold water. Bring to a boil, cover, lower heat, and simmer 1½ hours.

2. Place spareribs (corned or not), smoked pork chops, and all sausages in another pot. Cover with cold water, bring to a boil, and immediately drain and reserve. This will remove excess salt.

3. After beans have cooked 1½ hours, remove jerky and bacon from pot with tongue (continue to simmer tongue) and add to beans, along with spareribs and beef bottom round (but not pork loin). Cover and simmer for another hour, adding hot water if needed to keep the beans covered with liquid.

4. Add sausages and pork loin (if used) to beans and simmer 30 minutes longer. (Add more hot water if needed to keep beans covered with liquid.) Finally add smoked pork chops and simmer for 30 more minutes. Beans and tongue will have simmered separately for 3½ hours.

5. Remove all meats from bean pot and drain tongue. Refrigerate separately if cooking will be continued the next day. Otherwise let cool until meat can be handled safely (about 1 hour). (Beans and meat may stand at room temperature for 2 to 3 hours before cooking is continued.)

Day 3

1. Preheat oven to 400° F. Peel and bone tongue and slice about ¼ inch thick. Bone all other meats (including pig's feet). Coarsely chop bacon and meat from pig's feet and stir into beans. Slice pork loin or beef round, coarsely chop meat from boned pork chops and spareribs into 12 pieces, and slice linguiça into 2-inch pieces. Arrange meats in large roasting pan, add about 2 cups liquid from beans, and cover with foil. Fifteen minutes before serving place mixture in oven to reheat.

2. Meanwhile add bay leaves to beans; reheat beans. At the same time heat oil in a large nonreactive (enameled, stainless steel, or non-stick) skillet and sauté onions and garlic until soft. Add tomatoes and chiles. Simmer until well blended (about 5 minutes). Season with black pepper. Remove about 2 cups of beans, mash with a fork (or purée coarsely in blender or food processor), and add beans to skillet. Mix well and pour contents of skillet into beans. Stir in and carefully correct seasoning, adding salt and hot pepper sauce to taste. (Beans should be spicy but not infernal.) Garnish with orange quarters.

Serves 12.

FAROFA GARNISH
Sautéed manioc flour

In the area around Rio, *farofa* accompanies nearly every meal as a table condiment, to be sprinkled freely over almost anything and everything. This garnish should be made on the day it is served.

- 2 cups manioc flour (also called mandioca, cassava meal, or farofa; see Note)
- 4 tablespoons unsalted butter, cut into bits

If flour seems coarse, briefly process in a blender, food processor, or best of all, in an electric minichopper or clean coffee grinder. Place flour in large, dry skillet over moderate heat and toast it, stirring constantly, until it is lightly browned (about 8 minutes). Add butter and, stirring constantly, cook until well combined and fragrant (about 5 minutes). Remove mixture to a serving bowl. Serve warm or at room temperature.

Makes 2¼ cups.

Note Farofa and carne seca are available from large Latin food stores and by mail order. (See mail-order information for Casa Moneo and G.B. Ratto's on page 83.)

COLLARD GREENS IN THE STYLE OF MINAS GERAIS

These aren't the long-stewed, soupy greens of the American South, but tender-crisp sautéed greens from much further south, the Brazilian state of Minas Gerais. No *feijoada completa* would be considered "completa" without them.

- 3 pounds (about 3 bunches) fresh collard greens or kale
- 6 tablespoons unsalted butter or bacon drippings (or a combination)
- 1 large clove garlic, minced

1. Trim stems from greens and shred greens finely. Wash well, then drop into a large pot full of boiling water. Cover to return swiftly to a boil, keeping an eye on the pot. Boil 3 minutes and drain immediately. (Collards may now be reserved at room temperature for several hours.)

2. In a large skillet over burner set to medium, heat butter. Add garlic and sauté until translucent. Stir in greens and sauté, stirring frequently, until warmed through and tender (10 to 15 minutes).

Serves 12.

RICE A LA BRASILIERA

This Brazilian version of pilaf has a subtle garlic flavor.

- 6 tablespoons unsalted butter
- 1 small onion, minced
- 2 large cloves garlic, minced
- 3 cups rice
  Freshly ground white pepper, to taste
- 5 cups Poultry Stock (see page 17), canned chicken stock, or water
  Salt, to taste

In a large (at least 4 quart) flame-proof casserole dish, melt butter. Stir in onion and garlic; sauté, stirring occasionally, over low heat until transparent (3 to 4 minutes). Stir in rice and white pepper; sauté until rice turns translucent (about 2 minutes). Add liquid and stir once. Cover tightly and cook over very low heat for 25 minutes. Let rest, covered, on a warm part of the stove for about 10 minutes. With a fork, stir in salt to taste and fluff rice.

Serves 12.

CAIPIRINHAS
White rum and lime sours

Serve just one *caipirinha* (pronounced ky-pee-*ree*-hya) to each guest, and your party will turn into a Brazilian fiesta.

- 8 limes
- 4 cups white rum or 2 cups each white rum and vodka
- 1½ to 2 cups superfine sugar
- 40 ice cubes, whole or cracked

Rinse and dry limes; trim off both ends. Cut limes (including skin) into small cubes and place in a blender or food processor (or use a large mortar and pestle). Chop limes coarsely, to release juices. Transfer to large, wide-mouthed bottle or cocktail shaker; add rum. Stir in sugar to taste, a half cup at a time. If necessary divide mixture into 2 wide-mouthed bottles. Add ice cubes and refrigerate for an hour or so or add cracked ice if serving immediately. Strain into cocktail glasses to serve.

Makes about 12 cocktails.

Caballeros, caballeras: Fire up the grill for this zesty, gaucho-style Argentine Picnic with a mixture of meats, each done to a turn. Menu starts on page 102.

Variety Meats

Variety meats—high in protein and minerals and low in fat—are delicious when cooked with skill, zest, and imagination in recipes such as Calf's Liver in Raisin Sauce (see page 102) or the wonderfully colorful Southwestern Grilled Sweetbreads (see page 98). A full menu for An Argentine Picnic starting on page 102 stars a bounteous Patagonian mixed grill—sausages, ribs, chicken, steak, and variety meats served with a fiery dipping sauce. This chapter also includes detailed instructions on preparing and cooking sweetbreads (see page 99) and preparing tongue (see page 100).

VARIETY MEATS: RICH FLAVORS AND HIGH NUTRITION

Variety meats are the subject of the strongest opinions and prejudices of virtually any food. Each cut has its fierce partisans, but even more detractors. Although organ meats are exceptionally good values in nutrition as well as price, many people reject them entirely, based on the look, smell, or texture of the meats or on their own often unfortunate childhood experiences with indifferently prepared variety meats. Admittedly, badly prepared organ meats can indeed be awful.

The secret to making organ meat delicious (rather than just "good for you," with all the suffering that those words imply) lies in careful preparation suited to precisely that meat. In some cases (such as with liver), this merely means serving the meat on the day it's purchased, trimming it carefully, and cooking it rapidly until rare. In other cases (such as with tongue, sweetbreads, and brains), the meat must be purchased several days before serving and then patiently put through processes that will tame the flavors, tenderize tough meat, and enable the cook to trim away objectionable parts.

The recipes that follow include a variety of luxurious treatments for these often-scorned meats—and for those who aren't sure which of the meats they'll enjoy, a Patagonian Parillada Mixta (see page 103) affords bite-sized samples of any or all of the variety meats.

SWEETBREADS

Sweetbreads (the thymus or sometimes the pancreas of a calf) have a small but enthusiastic following. When properly prepared the meat is fork-tender and mildly flavored.

SOUTHWESTERN GRILLED SWEETBREADS

This sunny combination of sweet and smoky flavors was inspired by the new southwestern cookery.

4 large or 6 medium red bell peppers, roasted and peeled (see page 101)
⅓ cup olive oil
1½ to 2 pounds sweetbreads, soaked, blanched, trimmed, pressed (see page 99), and cut into pieces about 3 inches square
Flour seasoned with salt and pepper or cayenne, to taste
12 slices bacon (preferably smoked bacon from delicatessen or mail-order source)
Cilantro sprigs, for garnish

Sweet Potato–Corn Pancakes

2 large sweet potatoes
1 can (4 oz) diced green chiles, drained
2 large ears corn (or one 8 oz can of corn kernels, drained)
Salt and freshly ground pepper, to taste
3 eggs, lightly beaten
4 tablespoons (approximately) yellow cornmeal, as needed
Butter, for filming skillet or griddle

1. Prepare batter for Sweet Potato–Corn Pancakes and reserve. In a blender or food processor, purée roasted, peeled red peppers with olive oil. Just before sweetbreads are to be cooked, in a small pot heat mixture gently until warm.

2. Prepare a grill with mesquite charcoal or other charcoal plus mesquite chips. Just before grilling sweetbreads, fry Sweet Potato–Corn Pancakes and keep warm in low oven.

3. Dust sweetbreads lightly with seasoned flour. Reserve excess flour. Place bacon slices on oiled grill about 4 inches over mesquite and grill briefly until they begin to brown (about 1 minute per side). Add sweetbreads to grill and cook uncovered until each side is browned and slightly crisped on surface and pieces are heated through, 2 to 3 minutes per side. (Do not overcook sweetbreads, or they will not be tender.) Remove from grill as done. To serve, place a bed of Sweet Potato–Corn Pancakes on each plate. Top with sweetbreads and bacon slices and drizzle red pepper purée over all. Garnish with a sprig of cilantro.

Serves 4 to 6 as main course, 8 to 12 as appetizer.

Sweet Potato–Corn Pancakes

1. Preheat oven to 400° F. Bake sweet potatoes until tender (45 minutes to an hour), puncturing skins in several places after 20 minutes of baking. Remove and cool. Scoop flesh of sweet potatoes into mixing bowl and mash with the chiles. Scrape corn kernels from ears into mixture. Season to taste with salt and pepper. Add eggs and stir strongly until fairly smooth. By tablespoonfuls stir in cornmeal to make mixture cohere loosely in a thick batter. Reserve.

2. Turn oven to 275° F. Film large skillet or griddle with butter and heat until fragrant. Drop pancake-sized lumps of sweet potato batter (about ⅓ cup each) onto hot surface, flatten gently with a spatula, and fry over moderately high heat until both sides are well browned (about 2½ minutes per side). As pancakes are done, transfer them to a lightly greased baking sheet and place in oven to keep warm. Grease skillet between batches.

Makes about 12 pancakes.

TONGUE

Tongue, one of the toughest meats before cooking, is among the tenderest when properly prepared.

TONGUE BRAISED IN RED WINE AND BALSAMIC VINEGAR

This treatment for tongue bathes the tender meat in a tangy wine sauce.

- 4 *tablespoons butter*
- 1 *cup minced onion*
- 1 *tablespoon minced garlic*
- ¾ *cup finely diced carrots*
- ¾ *cup finely diced celery*
- ½ *cup dry red wine*
- 1 *beef tongue, simmered and trimmed (see Preparing Tongue, page 100)*
- 2 *tablespoons balsamic or red wine vinegar*
- 2 *cups reduced tongue or meat stock, or as needed*
- 1 *tablespoon minced parsley*
- 2 *tablespoons minced fresh basil or 1 tablespoon dried basil leaves, crumbled*
- 1 *bay leaf*
  Salt and freshly ground pepper, to taste
- 1 *tablespoon fresh basil or parsley (minced), for garnish*

1. Preheat oven to 350° F. In a heavy, flameproof casserole with a tight cover over moderate heat, melt butter. When foam subsides stir in onion, garlic, carrots, and celery. Sauté, stirring frequently, until vegetables begin to brown (about 10 minutes). Add wine, raise heat, and boil until liquid reduces by about half. Remove from heat.

2. Slice tongue thinly and lay slices on top of vegetable-wine mixture. Pour in vinegar and stock and add parsley, the 2 tablespoons fresh basil, bay leaf, and salt and freshly ground pepper to taste. Stock should come nearly to top of tongue. If it does not, add more. Bring mixture to a simmer on top of stove. Cover tightly and bake in oven for 1 hour. Serve tongue with sauce and vegetables, garnished with basil.

Serves 4 to 6.

Basics

PREPARING AND COOKING SWEETBREADS

Most cooks find it more convenient to spread the work of preparing sweetbreads over two or three days. Within 24 hours of purchase, sweetbreads should either be frozen or given the preliminary preparation described below. Then you are ready to make the Southwestern Grilled Sweetbreads (see page 98) pictured above.

Preparing Sweetbreads

For all sweetbread recipes the following steps are necessary to tame the flavor by removing the blood (the aroma would otherwise be gamy), to soften the tough, fatty membranes that would ruin the texture, and to firm the meat to facilitate removing these undesirable membranes.

1. Defrost frozen sweetbreads, if used. Place in a bowl and cover with cold water; place bowl in refrigerator and soak sweetbreads for at least 2 hours or preferably overnight, changing water twice.

2. Place the sweetbreads in a pot large enough to hold them comfortably. Cover them with cold water extending one inch over meat. Add 1 tablespoon salt and 2 tablespoons white vinegar or lemon juice and bring slowly to a simmer. Simmer 15 minutes, drain, and immediately cool meat under cold running water.

3. Separate the 2 lobes of the sweetbreads and remove the tube between them. Using a small knife and fingers, peel off and discard membranes around the sweetbreads.

4. Recommended optional step: Place sweetbreads on a dinner plate and set another plate directly on top of them. Weight the top plate with several cans, or other heavy objects (use at least 5 pounds of weight, preferably more) for at least 1 hour. Pour off blood that accumulates around sweetbreads. This step mellows the sweetbreads, making them cleaner tasting and more digestible, as well as disposing of excess liquid. Refrigerate until ready to cook.

Cooking Sweetbreads

Devotees of sweetbreads often simply bread them lightly in flour, cornmeal, or crumbs and fry or sauté them in butter or broil, barbecue, or grill them. This meat can be braised very well, too. Whatever recipe is used care should be taken to cook sweetbreads only until done; their special tenderness is lost with overcooking.

Basics

PREPARING TONGUE

It's most convenient to break the preparation of tongue into two days (or else start the evening's dinner by noon). Nearly all tongue recipes, such as Tongue Braised in Red Wine (see page 99) pictured above, require simmering the tongue at length before final preparation starts. More than one tongue can be simmered at a time, with extras frozen.

BASIC SIMMERED BEEF TONGUE

Whether fresh or smoked, a whole, untrimmed tongue must be simmered until tender and then carefully trimmed before serving. This is the basic preparation, whether the tongue will be completed as a main course by additional cooking in a sauce or simply chilled and sliced for a delicatessen platter or for sandwiches.

Although beef tongue is the most commonly found tongue, smaller, more tender lamb, veal, and pork tongues are sometimes available. For veal and lamb tongue, cut simmering time to two hours; for pork tongue, which is rather strongly flavored, soak in acidulated water (as for sweetbreads) for two hours, then simmer two hours. Trim as noted in step 2, at right.

1 *beef tongue, fresh or smoked*
1 *large onion, quartered*
3 *large carrots, coarsely chopped*
2 *stalks celery with leaves, coarsely sliced*
2 *or 3 sprigs parsley*
2 *whole cloves*
1 *clove garlic, peeled*
6 *peppercorns*

1. In a large, heavy pot, cover tongue with cold water. Over high heat bring water to boil. Skim liquid well, lower heat, and add remaining ingredients. Simmer slowly for 3 hours, partly covered. (If tongue will be used "as is," with no further cooking, simmer an additional 30 minutes.) Drain tongue, reserve broth, and let cool.

2. Trim tongue by slitting the membrane that covers it and peeling membrane off with a small, sharp knife. Trim away fat from underside of tongue and remove small bones from the root. At this point, tongue is ready for final preparation. Keep tongue well wrapped and refrigerated (or wrap and freeze for later use); serve within 24 hours since the meat quickly absorbs refrigerator aromas.

Serves 6 to 8.

<u>Note</u> To use the tongue cooking liquid in any final preparation, strain, pour into deep pot, and while trimming the tongue, reduce broth by half over medium heat.

LIVER

A recent survey of food preferences discovered that liver ranked among America's five least favorite foods. Indeed, too often liver is cooked in ways that fail to enhance its flavor. For those with the courage to try liver, the recipes to follow will demonstrate that liver need not be nasty.

Any liver should be served within 24 hours of purchase. It does not take well to freezing (it develops a bitter off-taste and a tough texture). Look for livers of an even color, without phosphorescent greenish patches, and choose the lightest-colored liver available (which comes from the youngest animals).

If liver comes packaged in Styrofoam cups, avoid any in which liver is afloat in a deep pond of blood, which indicates package has spent too long in the meat case. Beef liver is tougher and stronger tasting than calf's liver, but cooked gently pink, it can be tasty indeed—and tender, juicy calf's liver may be a revelation to those willing to forget the past.

Beef Liver

Since the liver is an organ that rids the body of poisons, and since beef liver comes from mature animals that may have picked up some environmental toxins, beef liver may not be quite as good for you as you've been told. It is, however, packed with iron and other nutritious minerals.

Before cooking, trim the liver carefully: Cut off the thin membrane around the outside of the slices, or the meat will curl up into a half-shell as it cooks. Then, with the point of a small, very sharp knife (a boning knife is ideal), lift as many of the whitish clusters of fat and the thin, bluish connective membranes as you can and slide the knife between them and the flesh to remove them. Beef liver is best cooked rapidly to medium-rare, browned on the outside but pink at the center.

Calf's Liver

Many of those who find beef liver unbearable even when cooked properly (that is, medium-rare) are of an opposite opinion about calf's liver, which is far milder in flavor and tenderer in texture. (Those who enjoy poultry liver usually enjoy calf's liver, too.) Trim it carefully as for beef liver, above, and cook it rapidly until browned just at the surface and quite pink at the center.

POOKIE'S LIVER AND ONIONS

Even if you hate liver and onions, you'll find this tender, soulful version a revelation. If you *like* liver and onions, you're about to see starbursts. This recipe is based on a dish by brilliant chef Pookie Turner, who once told a customer raving about her soul food, "Soul food? What's soul food? If you're dying of thirst and I give you a glass of water, that's soul food, baby!"

> ½ pound beef liver, in one
>   thin cut
>   Salt and freshly ground
>   pepper, to taste, plus
>   ½ teaspoon each salt and
>   pepper
> 1½ teaspoons flour, plus flour
>   for dredging
> 2 tablespoons cooking oil
>   (preferably peanut, corn,
>   or sunflower)
> 2 tablespoons butter
> 2 green onions, minced
> 1 clove garlic, minced
> 1½ medium yellow onions, sliced
> 1½ cups beef stock
> ¾ teaspoon Kitchen Bouquet
>   seasoning sauce

1. Season liver with salt and pepper to taste. Dredge lightly in flour.

2. Over burner set to high, heat lightly oiled, heavy skillet until fragrant (about 1 minute). Add liver and fry until lightly browned (about 1 minute per side). Remove liver and reserve.

3. Clean skillet and on burner set to medium, heat it until dry. Add butter and heat until melted. Add green onion, garlic, and yellow onion; fry, stirring, until yellow onion is translucent (about 6 minutes).

4. Sprinkle the 1½ teaspoons flour over mixture and cook briefly—until flour turns golden and loses its raw aroma (about 1 minute); do not let flour brown. Stir in stock, Kitchen Bouquet, the ½ teaspoon salt, and ½ teaspoon pepper. Turn heat to medium-high and bring mixture to a boil. Cook, stirring, until liquid thickens slightly (about 6 minutes). Adjust seasoning, if necessary, to your own taste.

5. Return liver to pan and cook on both sides for 30 seconds each. (If liver is thick cook 90 seconds per side.) Remove from heat and serve immediately with boiled rice.

Serves 2.

. . . ON ROASTING AND PEELING FRESH PEPPERS

Roasting and peeling fresh peppers such as those pictured above can be extremely difficult and frustrating if not done properly. Here are a few tips to make the process a smooth and easy one.

☐ If possible, remove a burner from gas stove, or heat broiler of electric range.

☐ *With a gas stove:* Using long tongs or a long roasting fork, hold peppers (one at a time) directly over high flame, turning peppers until all sides are blistered and blackened. *With an electric range:* Place peppers close to heat source and broil, turning frequently, until blackened.

☐ Place blackened peppers in a paper bag. Seal top of bag and let stand for 10 minutes after final pepper went in.

☐ Remove peppers from bag and peel skin away with fingers (aided by a small, sharp knife, if necessary) under cold running water. Trim away stems, seeds, and heavy veins.

CALF'S LIVER IN RAISIN SAUCE

The ancestry of this sensual Parisian treatment of calf's liver is in a classic recipe for foie gras, the velvety, costly liver of a force-fed goose. This dish is quickly prepared (once the raisins have macerated for a few hours) but dressy in flavor. Accompanying dishes should be uncompetitive, such as steamed, buttered new potatoes.

    1   cup golden raisins
    1½   tablespoons Cognac
    ⅓   cup muscatel, dry Madeira,
         or Marsala
    1¼   pound calf's liver, cut in thin
         slices and trimmed
    ¼   cup flour, seasoned with salt
         and white pepper
    4   tablespoons unsalted butter
    ¼   cup meat stock, preferably
         homemade (if canned, dilute
         by half with water)
    1   tablespoon freshly squeezed
         lemon juice
    3   tablespoons minced parsley

1. Drop raisins into boiling water to cover, boil 10 seconds, and drain. Cover raisins with Cognac and wine; steep covered, at room temperature, for 2 hours or overnight.

2. Dredge liver in seasoned flour; shake off excess and place on waxed paper. In very large (12 inch) skillet (or 2 skillets) over high heat, melt 3 tablespoons of butter. When butter foams add liver slices and sauté at high heat until browned on outside but pink on inside (1 to 2 minutes per side, depending on thickness). Meanwhile slightly warm a serving platter with hot water; pat dry. Transfer liver to serving platter and tent with foil to keep warm.

3. Maintaining high heat add remaining 1 tablespoon butter to skillet. When it starts to brown, add raisin mixture and stock. Stir until thickened (about 2 minutes), scraping brown bits from bottom of pan. Remove from heat, stir in lemon juice, and pour over liver. Sprinkle with parsley and serve immediately.

Serves 3 or 4.

KIDNEYS

When sautéed quickly kidneys are delicious and tender, and when baked with other ingredients they contribute a zesty flavor.

STEAK AND KIDNEY PIE

A popular staple in British pubs, steak and kidney pie is one of the most enjoyed variety meat dishes.

    6   tablespoons flour
    1½   teaspoons salt
    ¼   teaspoon each freshly ground
         pepper, dried thyme, dried
         chervil, dried marjoram, and
         dried summer savory
    2   pounds boneless top round,
         cut into ½-inch cubes
    ½   pound beef or lamb
         kidneys, sliced
    ½   pound mushrooms, quartered
    2   tablespoons butter or
         margarine
    ½   cup dry red wine or regular-
         strength beef stock
    6   frozen patty shells (one 10 oz
         package), thawed
    1   egg, beaten with 1 teaspoon
         water

1. Preheat oven to 325° F. In a large bowl mix flour, salt, pepper, thyme, chervil, marjoram, and savory. Add steak cubes and kidney slices, coating well with flour mixture. In a skillet sauté mushrooms in butter until lightly browned. Place half beef and kidney mixture in a 2-quart, 2-inch-deep baking dish. Top with mushrooms, then with remaining meat. Pour on wine.

2. Arrange the 6 patty shells, overlapping slightly, on floured board or pastry cloth. Roll out pastry into slightly larger shape than top of casserole. Arrange over steak and kidney mixture; trim and flute edge. Pierce or slit top in several places.

3. Brush pastry with egg mixture. Bake until meat is tender (insert a long wooden skewer to test) and pastry is well browned (1½ to 2 hours). Serve immediately.

Serves 6 to 8.

AN ARGENTINE PICNIC

Patagonian Parillada Mixta

Salsa Cruda (see page 27)

*French Bread and Butter
of Your Choice*

Salad of Your Choice

Pears in Red Wine

*Dry Young Red Wine
(Such as Zinfandel or Chianti),
Lightly Chilled*

Iced Tea or Lemonade

This gaucho-style picnic is filled with wonderful, strong flavors—a fearless mixed grill accompanied by Salsa Cruda and a fiery dipping sauce so welcome in the cloudy, windswept climate of southern Argentina. Argentina is wine country, too, so for dessert, nothing could be more appropriate than pears poached in red wine.

PATAGONIAN PARILLADA MIXTA
Patagonian mixed grill

Argentine *parilladas* are quite different from the more refined English mixed grills. All parts of the animal turn up, and instead of bangers, Italian-style blood sausages play a central role. There's no grilled mushroom or tomato, no watercress garnish, no straw potatoes—merely meat, at least a pound per person—with two spicy dips, a tangy salad, and fresh French bread.

Argentine ranchers of the true pampas (northwest of Patagonia) also include sliced beef intestine (chitlins), udders, and testicles ("mountain oysters") in their mixed grills; include them if you can find them and would like to try them.

Recipe cooking times will produce rare to medium-rare steak and lamb. If authentic Patagonian cuisine is desired, continue cooking until well-done (about 2 more minutes on the second side).

      Olive oil, as needed
 6   *blood sausages (preferably Italian-style)*
 6   *beef short ribs*
 6   *small pieces of fryer or broiler chicken*
18 to 24 *ounces thick, tender steak (such as filet mignon or sirloin)*
 6   *small loin lamb chops (2 to 3 oz each) or 6 small pieces (about 3 oz each) flank or skirt steak (optional)*
12 to 18 *ounces sweetbreads, soaked, blanched, and pressed (see page 99)*
12 to 18 *ounces calf's liver*
 6   *veal kidneys (2 to 3 oz each), rinsed, halved, membrane and fat removed*
12 to 18 *ounces spleen or poached, drained tripe, rinsed and cut in strips about 1 inch wide (optional); see Note*
 2 to 3 *tablespoons dried oregano leaves, crumbled*
      Salt and freshly ground pepper, to taste

Spicy Dipping Sauce

 ¼   *cup olive oil*
 1   *cup red wine vinegar*
 3   *tablespoons cayenne pepper*
 4   *cloves garlic, peeled and crushed*
 1   *teaspoon freshly ground black pepper*
 1   *teaspoon dried oregano leaves, crumbled*
 ½   *teaspoon salt*
 ¼   *cup minced parsley*

1. Oil grill or broiler rack and place about 4 inches from heat source. Heat charcoal until starting to turn white, or pre-heat indoor broiler. Prick sausages in several places with a fork. Lightly sprinkle short ribs, chicken, steak, lamb chops (if used), sweetbreads, liver, kidney, and spleen (if used) with oregano and brush with a light coat of olive oil.

2. Place short ribs on grill first, rib side down. Grill for 10 minutes, turn, brush with oil, lightly sprinkle with salt and pepper, and grill about 30 minutes longer.

3. Six minutes after turning short ribs, add chicken to grill. Chicken will take about 12 minutes per side. Brush again with oil; sprinkle lightly with salt and pepper after turning.

4. Two minutes after turning chicken, add sausages and cook about 5 minutes per side. Immediately after turning sausages (about 5 minutes before ribs, chicken, and sausages are cooked through), add steak, lamb chops (if used), sweetbreads, kidney, liver, and spleen (if used) and cook about 3 minutes on first side. Turn, brush with oil, sprinkle with salt and pepper, and cook about 2 minutes on second side. Serve with Spicy Dipping Sauce and Salsa Cruda (see page 27).

Serves 6.

Spicy Dipping Sauce Whisk all ingredients together. Let stand at room temperature overnight (or for at least 2 hours) to mellow, or refrigerate for several days. Serve at room temperature.

Makes about 1½ cups, serves about 6.

<u>Note</u> If using tripe, first cover it with cold water, bring it to a boil, lower heat, and simmer until tender (25 minutes to 2 hours depending on whether it was precooked before reaching the market). Drain and pat dry before barbecuing.

PEARS IN RED WINE

This elegant, light dessert is simplicity itself. A fine ending to an Argentine meal, this dessert will satisfy your sweet tooth on other outings as well. Pack it into the ice chest to keep it cool for a picnic.

 8   *large, firm pears*
 1   *bottle dry red wine, such as Zinfandel or Cabernet Sauvignon*
 ¾   *cup sugar*
 2   *teaspoons ground cinnamon*
 1   *whole clove*
 2   *strips (about ¼-inch by 2-inches) orange rind*
 2   *strips lemon rind*
12   *black peppercorns*

Peel pears but leave stems on. In a deep, nonreactive saucepan or casserole, stir together wine, sugar, cinnamon, clove, orange rind, lemon rind, and peppercorns. Over high heat bring mixture to a boil to dissolve sugar; then add pears, lower heat to a simmer, and poach 15 minutes. Remove pears to a transparent, covered container and chill well before serving.

Serves 8.

East-West Broiled Squab, Orange-Scented Wild Rice, and Game Bird Crostini make a delectable and impressive dinner. Recipes on pages 117, 122, and 123.

Game

Rich in flavor, high in protein and nutritious minerals, and low in fat, game is as much a delight to the cook as to the diner. Among the imaginative recipes in this chapter are Garlic-Sage Marinated Grilled Quail (see page 114) and Stir-Fried Bison, Moose, or Venison in Shiitake Mushroom–Cream Sauce (see page 113). Step-by-step instructions on cutting up a rabbit (see page 107) and preparing rattlesnake (see page 108) are included, as well as recipes for accompaniments to game such as sage-flavored liver croutons (see page 123) and two versions of wild rice (see page 122). A listing of mail-order sources for all types of game is given on page 123.

OBTAINING GAME

Recipes in this chapter primarily use furred and feathered game. Finned game, which is not discussed, is not much different (only fresher and better) than fish from the market and can be cooked by the same methods. Some excellent game is available from commercial outlets, while other types of game are only available directly from hunters.

COMMERCIAL GAME

Both wildlife-protection and food-safety laws restrict the commercial sale of meat from America's wild animals. The only North American game animals that can be found readily in markets are those that have actually been farm raised, such as rabbit, bison, some deer, and the occasional raccoon or possum, along with numerous types of game birds.

However, game meats from other countries (especially New Zealand's wide variety of ranch-raised game), as well as farm-raised American game, are becoming increasingly available. Selected supermarkets are beginning to carry buffalo, venison, and boar, along with rabbit and game birds, in their frozen-food cases. Many butcher shops can provide game by special order, and the number of mail-order game suppliers is rapidly increasing. (For mail-order sources see page 123.)

Game prices are still generally higher than the equivalent cuts of feedlot-fattened domestic meats, in part because free-range, organically raised animals take longer than feedlot animals to reach salable weight. In addition farm-raised game is generally raised as a premium meat, without pesticides, insecticides, or growth hormones to fatten it quickly.

More important, for many thousands of years mankind has been selectively breeding domestic animals to furnish the greatest amount of meat—whereas game animals have been breeding themselves for the characteristics they need in the wild, such as speed and strength, rather than for rapid weight gain.

HUNTERS' GAME

The alternative to buying game is hunting it yourself or sharing a hunter's bounty.

Safety factors If you are cooking game obtained by hunting, it's important to understand how game should be handled for maximum wholesomeness and safety.

Most wildlife experts counsel against eating animals that have been trapped. There's no way to tell if the animal was sick when it was trapped or became ill while it was captive.

The most tender game comes from animals killed by surprise with a single shot. Once an animal starts to run, its muscles grow tense, and adrenaline spreads through its body, toughening the meat.

Proper field cleaning methods are essential to ensure that the game is safe to eat. If an animal has musk sacs, these should be removed immediately, taking care not to puncture them. If the musk sacs spill on the meat, it will be inedible.

Next the organs and testicles should be removed. The gall bladder should be carefully cut away without breaking it, since if it spills on the meat or other organs, it will make them inedible.

Meat should be chilled as soon as possible after the animal's death and then should be kept cool by insulation until it reaches its destination. If meat is allowed to warm again after chilling, rotting may begin. The animal should be swiftly packed into a strong, very finely meshed cheesecloth game bag that should remain in place throughout aging, to prevent infestation by blowflies.

Aging and freezing Not all hunters' game needs aging. (Commercial game already has been aged as needed.) Neither game birds (except pheasant, which is ideally aged for two days) nor most small game require aging, and these animals are generally better without it, although they benefit from three or four days in the refrigerator before cooking.

Bear should be stripped of all fat in the field (unless you're fond of bear grease), but it needs no aging; antelope also needs little or none. Other large game (such as caribou, venison, moose, and bison) should be aged for 2 to 14 days (depending on type and size of animal) to tenderize the meat and enrich its flavor.

Aging takes place at a temperature of 40° F, within a total range between 38° and 42° F. If temperatures fluctuate much below that range, the meat will alternately freeze and defrost—a process that will ruin any meat. If temperatures rise much above the range, spoilage begins, and the meat will rot.

Dryness is also important to aging. Ideally game should be aged in a humidity- and temperature-controlled environment, such as a meat locker, which can be rented from a butcher or packing plant. A garage or garden shed is *not* appropriate for aging—least of all during the Indian summer hunting season, with its warm daytime temperatures.

Many hunters now swear by freezing as an alternative to aging: An animal frozen within 12 hours of its death will "age" in about a week in the freezer. In large pieces, well-wrapped meat can stay in the freezer for many months, or it can be defrosted after a week and cooked immediately.

If you receive meat aged by a hunter, find out how it was aged. Do not worry if there is some mold on the surface and a layer of blackened, dry meat just under the mold. These are harmless and can be cut or scraped off.

However, if the underlying meat smells rotten or has an iridescent greenish cast, it probably *is* rotten. A very bitter aroma or an intensely musky odor may indicate poor handling during evisceration. In any of these situations, be prepared to discard the meat, however regretfully.

Follow the same cooking guidelines for game as you would for beef: For tough meat use moist heat (braising, stewing, or sautéing in liquid); for tender meat use dry heat (pan frying, roasting, grilling, or broiling).

SMALL GAME

Rabbit is the most easily available small game. Cooking methods for rabbit apply to most other small game as well. This chapter also includes a recipe for rattlesnake—another animal that's widely available, although not at supermarkets.

RABBIT, HARE, AND SQUIRREL

Rabbits and hares are not quite the same species: Rabbits are white-meat animals, and hares are wholly rich, dark meat, with a lower ratio of flesh to bone. Squirrels may be cooked in much the same ways as rabbits and hares, although their meat may be tougher.

Both domestic and wild rabbits and hares can make excellent eating. Domestic rabbits are increasingly available in supermarkets. These come in two sizes: fryers, weighing up to three pounds, and roasters, weighing about four pounds. Roasters require longer, gentler cooking.

Rabbit meat is rather dry, and has a mild, pleasant flavor. The animal has very little fat, but what fat there is should be carefully trimmed away and discarded, since it has a soapy taste that many find objectionable. Inspect the central cavity, leg joints, and back and cut or pull off any fat found there. Also be on the lookout for small, yellowish, cystlike globules in these areas—these are musk glands that haven't been removed. Remove them without breaking them.

If the rabbit is a small, domesticated frying rabbit or young wild rabbit, at all costs avoid overcooking it, which will dry it out. Choose recipes in which the rabbit is cooked briefly, such as by frying or sautéing, or cut cooking time on braises to those you'd use for a tender chicken of the same size; for example, 45 minutes is ample braising time for a three-pound rabbit.

The tenderest part of a rabbit is the saddle, followed by the meaty hind legs. If several rabbits are available, the saddles and hind legs alone may be served; the front legs and bony breast may be removed, boned, and ground for terrine or meat loaf.

RABBIT LIVER PÂTÉ

Rabbit livers, which can taste rather gamy, turn gentle in this creamy pâté. However, any rabbit liver pâté should be served within 24 hours of preparation, since the livers rapidly grow strong-tasting again. Uncooked rabbit livers may be frozen, well wrapped, until you have enough for pâté. If you have only one liver on hand, make just a third of this recipe (using tiny pinches of the herbs) as an accompaniment to a main-dish rabbit and fry or toast just two pieces of diagonally halved bread; a third of the pâté will easily cover four toast points.

> 3 tablespoons unsalted butter
> 1 shallot, minced
> 1 clove garlic, minced
> 3 rabbit livers, trimmed well and halved
> 2 teaspoons Cognac or brandy
> ⅛ teaspoon dried thyme leaves, crumbled
> ⅛ teaspoon ground allspice
> Salt and freshly ground pepper, to taste
> 1 tablespoon whipping cream
> Toast points or croutons, for accompaniment

1. In a small, heavy skillet over medium-low heat, melt butter. Add shallot and garlic and cook, stirring, until tender (about 2 minutes). Increase heat to medium-high; add livers and sear rapidly on both sides, taking care not to overcook them. (Cook until centers are pink.)

2. Transfer contents of skillet to a food processor or blender. Add Cognac, thyme, allspice, salt, pepper, and cream and purée in pulses, scraping down sides of bowl frequently. Transfer pâté to a bowl, cover, and refrigerate for up to 24 hours. Allow to warm slightly before serving. To serve, spread on toast points.

Makes about 1 cup.

Step·by·Step

CUTTING UP A RABBIT

Cut a cleaned, skinned rabbit along center of breast from neck to tail. With a small, sharp knife, detach and remove all organs from the cavity. Trim away all tallowy fat in cavity, at leg joints, and along backbone. (It has an unpleasant taste.)

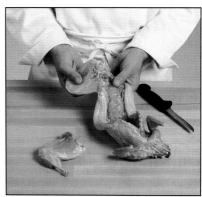

1. *Use both hands to dislocate front and hind leg joints by snapping them sharply away from body. Carefully sever with a knife or poultry shears.*

2. *With torso of rabbit held between both hands, cavity facing you, snap backbone between upper and lower back; finish by cutting along crack in bone. If desired, cut each torso piece in half by inserting knife along one side of backbone. If you wish, remove annoying small bones by snapping them away from breast bone. Use sharp yanks with fingers or needle-nose pliers to remove small bones from flesh.*

107

PREPARING RATTLESNAKE

To prepare a fresh-killed rattlesnake, first make sure that the snake is actually dead. Cut off the head (keeping your distance), bash the head to a pulp, and bury it deeply. Then proceed with steps 1 and 2 below.

If you obtain rattlesnake from a commercial outlet, it will already be skinned and eviscerated. Wash in cold water and proceed with step 2.

1. *To skin snake, make an incision the length of the belly; peel off skin. Scoop out all internal organs; wash meat in cold water.*

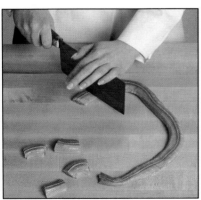

2. *If there is a tough, silvery skin over flesh, remove it: Place snake skin side down on a cutting board. Slide a thin, sharp knife between skin and flesh; pull snake up, away from skin. Soak snake in 1 quart water with 1 teaspoon vinegar for 2 hours, then refrigerate or freeze until ready to use. Chop as directed in recipe, using a hardened steel knife.*

JUGGED HARE WITH RABBIT LIVER PÂTÉ CROUTONS

This old Scottish recipe can be adapted to suit wild rabbit or domestic rabbit. If the rabbit is old or large, it may be marinated for 48 hours before cooking. If the rabbit has been obtained by hunting, the sauce may be thickened before serving by adding, off the heat, ¼ cup rabbit blood (to keep blood until use, mix with a spoonful of vinegar).

> 1 recipe Rabbit Liver Pâté (see page 107)
> ¼ pound smoked bacon, diced
> 1 large or 2 small hares or rabbits (3 to 4 lb total), trimmed of fat and cut into serving pieces
> Unsalted butter, as needed
> 1 medium onion, thinly sliced
> 1 large carrot, pared and cut into 1-inch slices
> 1 stalk celery, cut into 1-inch slices
> 1 cup White Veal Stock (see page 17) or Brown Meat Stock (see page 16)
> ½ cup port
> ½ cup Madeira
> ½ teaspoon dried thyme
> ½ teaspoon crumbled dried rosemary
> 1 bay leaf
> Salt and freshly ground white pepper, to taste
> 3 tablespoons oil or clarified butter, or as needed
> 4 slices white bread, crusts trimmed, halved diagonally
> Minced parsley, for garnish

1. Preheat oven to 325° F. Prepare Rabbit Liver Pâté (see page 107) and refrigerate, covered. Meanwhile, in a large, heavy, flameproof casserole, fry bacon over medium heat until crisp. Remove from pan with slotted spoon and reserve.

2. Add hare pieces to casserole (adding some butter, if necessary) and brown gently on both sides over medium heat (working in batches, if necessary, to keep meat uncrowded). Remove and reserve hare.

3. Reduce heat to moderately low. Add onion, carrot, and celery and sauté, stirring occasionally, until vegetables are softened and lightly browned (about 10 minutes). Remove with slotted spoon.

4. Pour stock, port, and Madeira into casserole and heat to a boil, scraping pan to loosen browned bits. Add thyme, rosemary, bay leaf, salt, and white pepper. Return hare and vegetables to casserole. Bring mixture back to a simmer, cover, and place in oven. Bake until hare is tender (about 40 minutes for small hares, 1¼ hours for a large one).

5. Remove hare from casserole again. Strain sauce, then return it to casserole and boil it until it reduces to about 1½ cups (about 20 minutes). Return hare to casserole and warm briefly.

6. Film a large, heavy skillet with oil. Heat, add bread triangles, and fry over medium heat until bread is lightly browned on both sides. Spread croutons with Rabbit Liver Pâté. Sprinkle hare with parsley and reserved bacon and serve hot. Pass croutons separately.

Serves 4.

RATTLESNAKE

Rattlesnakes are found all over North America, from the Catskill Mountains to the Berkeley hills. Suburbanites and vacationers as well as "desert rats" and old cowhands may find themselves killing and discarding rattlers without realizing that rattlesnake meat is not only edible, but uniquely delicious.

Rattlers do not, in fact, taste like chicken, but rather like the finest, most delicate frog's legs. The meat is bony, but makes fine finger food.

See Preparing Rattlesnake, at left, for preparation information. Rattlesnake is usually cut into bite-sized sections (using a strong knife of hardened steel) and fried as a light dinner or appetizer. In the South the snake is often soaked for a few hours in cold buttermilk (rather than vinegar water) and then dipped in flour and rapidly fried.

GERALD PROLMAN'S DESERT-STYLE RATTLESNAKE

This recipe comes from Gerald Prolman, founder of Night Bird, a major national game supplier. When prickly pear fruit (available in Latin markets in winter and early spring and often labeled *tuna*) is unavailable, use four peeled kiwi-fruits, make a purée from a large mango, or use any other exotic fruit that appeals to you. If you can't find any semihot chiles, substitute three small jalapeños, trimmed and seeded, and one additional bell pepper.

- 2 *peeled, halved prickly pears (the ripest have red-purple skin)*
- ⅓ *cup (approximately) golden tequila*
- ¼ *cup olive oil*
- 3 *medium bell peppers of mixed colors (red, green, gold, brown), trimmed, seeded, and cut into thin strips*
- 3 *medium semihot chiles (such as Anaheim, New Mexico, pasilla, or Italian frying peppers), roasted and peeled (see page 101), trimmed, seeded, and cut into thin strips*
- 1 *bottle (12 oz) sliced nopalitos (cactus), drained and rinsed*
  Scant ¼ teaspoon ground cumin seed
  Salt, to taste
- 1 *rattlesnake (about 1½ lb), skinned, cleaned, and chopped into 1½-inch lengths*
- ½ *teaspoon cayenne pepper, or to taste*
- ½ *cup flour, or as needed*
- 3 *tablespoons unsalted butter (preferably clarified), or as needed*
- ⅓ *cup minced shallots or whites of green onions*
  Juice of ½ ripe lime
- 3 *tablespoons minced cilantro*

1. Sprinkle prickly pears generously with about 4 teaspoons of the tequila and place in freezer for at least 1 hour.

2. In a medium-sized skillet rapidly heat olive oil. Add bell peppers and turn in oil over medium-high heat until peppers start to wilt (about 5 minutes). Add chiles and *nopalitos* and stir in cumin. Season with salt. Lower heat to medium-low and continue frying, stirring occasionally, until peppers are tender (about 10 more minutes).

3. Meanwhile pat snake dry with paper towels; dust lightly with salt (about 1 teaspoon) and cayenne. Dredge snake in flour, patting off excess. Place meat on a sheet of waxed paper handy to stove. Remove anything flammable from stove area.

4. Heat a large (12-inch), heavy frying pan until very hot. Melt butter. Place snake pieces in skillet meat side down. Brown rapidly, turn, and brown other side.

5. If using unclarified butter drain it off; clarified butter can remain in pan. Sprinkle shallots into pan and cook until wilted (about 30 seconds). Turn heat to low and, with a long match in your other hand, pour in remaining tequila. Standing well away from pan, immediately set fire to tequila. When flames die away squeeze on fresh lime juice and scatter on cilantro.

6. To serve, on each dinner plate place some of the pepper-cactus mixture, some of the fruit, and some of the snake and sauce. For a more substantial course, serve corn bread, corn muffins, or warmed flour tortillas on the side, with butter. To eat, treat snake as finger food. Alternate gnawing on snake (it is bony) and biting icy fruit and savory pepper mixture.

Serves 4 as a substantial appetizer or as a light main course.

BIG GAME

The most easily available large game animals in this country are deer and antelope of several species, buffalo, wild boar, and feral pigs. Feral pigs are ridgeback hogs that escaped from domestication and have continued to breed as wild animals; these may be treated like wild boar.

VENISON

The delicious meat of deer and antelope should certainly have a home on your range. Venison refers primarily to deer, but it's also a generic term for the meat of a group of animals including caribou, moose, elk, and antelope. Indeed most recipes for one can be used for the others, although their flavors differ.

The flavor of deer has a faint resemblance to that of the finest, best-aged, most greaseless lamb. Deer meat is becoming available, frozen, in some supermarkets and can be special-ordered from fine butchers as well. The leg is the easiest part to obtain commercially.

Moose is said to taste like the best beef. Due to wildlife laws American moose is virtually unavailable except by hunting, but farm-raised moose from other countries is available from some game-supply companies.

Antelope is often tougher than deer, and although lean, its meat tastes somewhat muttony or goaty and is best after marination. Recipes for lamb or veal can be used for antelope.

The meat of elk from North America is not too different from that of deer, but may be gamier and somewhat tougher. Elk meat commercially imported from New Zealand is actually from a species of deer that New Zealanders call elk and is tender and fine-flavored like other deer.

The tenderness of various cuts of all of these animals is similar to that of corresponding cuts of beef or lamb (see pages 20 and 50).

Saddle The saddle (including ribs, loin, sirloin, and tenderloin) of game has the tenderest meat but has much less of it (and with much less fat) than that of domestic animals of equivalent size.

Hind legs The hind legs make excellent roasts, particularly if they are marinated first to tenderize them. However, they must be either barded with a coating of fat (such as sheet beef fat, available from butchers) or at least rubbed generously with oil and basted again with oil during roasting, since there is no marbling in the meat itself.

Shanks The shanks are useful as marrow bones. Add these to a stew or a braise (especially those made with wine). When the stew meat is tender, remove these bones.

Front shoulders and legs The front shoulders and front legs contain hard-working muscles. These cuts may be roasted over liquid if desired (especially if first marinated), but are probably best stewed or braised, using any recipe for beef or lamb. The breast may be separated into riblets for barbecuing, stuffed and oven-braised like veal breast, or boned and ground. Large, boneless pieces from the breast area are leaner equivalents of beef brisket and may be braised or stewed.

ROAST MARINATED LEG OF VENISON WITH RED WINE SAUCE

This classic juniper-scented game marinade, excellent for all forms of venison and wild boar, will tenderize the meat—and then turn into a rich, elegant sauce.

- *1 leg of venison (about 7 lb boned, or 10 lb bone-in)*
- *⅓ cup olive oil, or as needed*
- *2 cups whipping cream*
- *1 cup port (preferably imported)*
- *4 tablespoons unsalted butter, at room temperature*
- *Salt and generous grinding of pepper, to taste*
- *2 tablespoons red currant jelly*

Red Wine and Port Game Marinade

- *2 medium onions, thinly sliced*
- *2 tablespoons minced fresh garlic*
- *1 large carrot, pared, and thinly sliced*
- *2 stalks celery, trimmed, and coarsely sliced*
- *1 teaspoon dried thyme*
- *1 teaspoon dried rosemary*
- *1 tablespoon black peppercorns*
- *1 tablespoon juniper berries, lightly crushed*
- *1 cinnamon stick (about 2 inches long)*
- *1 fifth-sized bottle (about 3 cups) dry red wine*
- *1½ cups port (preferably imported)*

1. Trim venison leg, removing outer membrane and any bits of fat. Place meat in a nonreactive container (such as glass or enamel-coated steel) large enough to hold meat and marinade.

2. Pour Red Wine and Port Game Marinade over meat. Cover and refrigerate 24 to 48 hours, turning meat several times. (Meat may be marinated at room temperature for 8 hours instead. If meat has not been aged, marinate 4 to 7 days.)

3. Preheat oven to 450° F. Lift meat out of marinade. Strain marinade, reserving solids separately. Film bottom of roasting pan with a little olive oil, scatter vegetables from marinade over it, and add ½ cup of the marinade to moisten and prevent burning. Pat venison dry. If meat is boneless tie roast into a thick cylinder with 3 or 4 lengths of kitchen twine. Rub venison all over with a generous amount of olive oil. Place venison on a rack over roasting pan. (If venison is definitely tough, omit rack and lay meat directly on solids.)

4. Place roasting pan in oven. Roast 20 minutes, then lower heat to 350° F. Roast for a total of 16 to 18 minutes per pound for rare to medium-rare, checking frequently with an instant-read meat thermometer inserted into the thickest part (120° F will be rare, 130° F will be medium-rare).

5. When venison has roasted for 1 hour, remove it from oven and place rack and meat over a container to catch juices. Place roasting pan over 2 burners on top of stove, pour in remaining marinating liquid, and bring mixture to a boil over high heat on both burners, scraping pan bottom to dissolve browned bits. Boil for about 5 minutes, then pour contents of roasting pan into a large, heavy casserole or saucepan (preferably enameled). Add juices rendered by meat.

6. Return venison and rack to roasting pan. Turn venison over, rub with more olive oil, and return to oven until cooked. When done remove from oven and let stand 20 minutes or more before carving.

7. Meanwhile place pan of sauce over medium-low heat and simmer until partially reduced (about 30 minutes). Pour through a strainer into a bowl, pushing on solids to extract juices. Return liquid to casserole, place over high heat, add cream and port, and bring to a boil. Boil until slightly thickened (about 15 minutes). Stir in butter until melted, then season to taste with salt and pepper. Stir in currant jelly. To serve, spoon some of the sauce over meat and pass remainder in a sauceboat.

Serves about 12.

Red Wine and Port Game Marinade

In a large bowl mix all ingredients. (Port, which adds richness and a certain sweetness, may be omitted to make a simple red wine game marinade for white-fleshed, mild-flavored game such as rabbit.)

Makes about 2 quarts marinade, for 6- to 8-pound boneless roast.

PAN-FRIED MEDALLIONS OF VENISON WITH MUSTARD SAUCE

Mustard and game are a wonderful match, and here vegetables sautéed with the meat absorb the drippings and, puréed, thicken the sauce. This sauce also goes well with roast venison (roasted over the same vegetables).

> 4 tablespoons unsalted butter
> 1 tablespoon olive oil
> 1 large onion, finely minced
> 2 pared carrots, finely diced
> 2 cloves garlic, minced
> 2 pounds thickly cut (about ¾ in.) medallions of venison (from leg or loin)
> 2 tablespoons flour
> ⅓ cup dry white wine
> 1 generous cup meat stock
> 1½ tablespoons Dijon mustard, or to taste
> ½ tablespoon Worcestershire sauce

1. In a large, heavy skillet, melt 2 tablespoons of the butter with olive oil. Add onion, carrots, and garlic and sauté gently over moderately low heat until softened (about 10 minutes). Push vegetables to sides of skillet and add medallions.

2. Increase heat to high and rapidly panfry medallions on both sides until just cooked through to rare (about 2 minutes per side). Remove meat to serving platter and tent with aluminum foil to keep warm.

3. Remove vegetables from pan and purée in blender or food processor. Place purée in a sieve over a small bowl and press gently on vegetables with a wooden spoon to extract juices and some puréed solids. Reserve.

4. In a medium-sized saucepan melt remaining 2 tablespoons butter. Add flour and stir over moderately low heat for 3 minutes. Stir in wine and stock and bring to a boil, stirring. Lower heat to medium and boil gently for 3 minutes. Stir in ½ cup of the sieved juices and solids. Stir in mustard, tasting carefully and adding more if needed. Stir in Worcestershire sauce. Nap meat lightly with this sauce and pass remaining sauce separately.

Serves 4 to 6.

Hearty, lean, and velvety venison marries well with assertive flavors. Pan-Fried Medallions of Venison With Mustard Sauce pairs a rich meat with a tart gravy.

Meals based on game meats need not be heavy—or traditional. Stir-Fried Bison in Shiitake Mushroom–Cream Sauce is a sparkling, luxurious dinner that can be made swiftly from even a less than tender cut.

BUFFALO

The meat of the American bison (or buffalo—the terms are interchangeable) and that of Asia's water buffalo taste very similar—both resemble the most flavorful beef. Had the pioneers in the West sampled a bit of this staple protein of the Plains Indians, they might well have tried to corral the animals, rather than allowing buffalo skinners to slaughter them to obtain their hides.

Fortunately a few bison were saved, and their herds were bred, both publicly (in national parklands) and by scattered private ranchers in Wyoming and the Dakotas. Today buffalo meat is increasingly available nationwide, and the animals are being bred and fed very much like organically raised beef cattle.

The cuts of buffalo are similar to those of beef (see page 20), so be guided accordingly in choosing a cooking method. The primary differences are that bison has a tender hump that can be roasted, and bison meat is almost fatless and therefore benefits by cooking with some liquid or added fat.

If you should obtain buffalo meat from a rancher who breeds a few range-fed bison as a hobby, odds are the meat will come from an extra bull in the herd, one who'd started getting too obstreperous to keep. The meat will very likely be as tough as it is tasty. These steaks will need strong pounding before cooking, and the stewing cuts will need an extra hour or so of simmering.

If the bison comes from a commercial source, however, it will be as tender as fine, grain-fed lean beef.

The steaks and roasts from tender cuts can be prepared just like those of beef, except that when roasting, you should rub meat well with oil before starting and brush with oil frequently during cooking, or else tie on sheet beef fat. Serve bison rare, since this lean meat will dry out if cooked even to medium. Buffalo steaks are among the best of all campfire meats, since their fine flavor is wonderfully complemented by a bit of smoke.

The buffalo recipe that follows uses the tougher parts of the animal.

STIR-FRIED BISON, MOOSE, OR VENISON IN SHIITAKE MUSHROOM–CREAM SAUCE

Mixing continental and Asian ingredients has become fashionable in urban restaurants. Sometimes the combinations can be shocking, but here game meat, cream, oyster sauce, and Asian mushrooms seem to be made for each other. Serve with noodles, pasta, or rice.

1½ pounds buffalo, moose, or venison steak (not necessarily tender)
1 tablespoon dark sesame oil
1 teaspoon light soy sauce
1½ tablespoons dry sherry or Shaoxing (Chinese rice wine)
2 large cloves garlic, crushed, peeled, and finely minced or pressed
1 ounce dry shiitake mushrooms Pinch sugar
2 tablespoons unsalted butter
1 tablespoon cooking oil (sunflower, peanut, or corn), or as needed
¼ pound fresh button mushrooms, wiped clean and sliced
1 cup whipping cream
1½ tablespoons oyster sauce
1 teaspoon balsamic vinegar

1. Cut meat very thinly against grain in ⅛-inch by ¼-inch by 1½-inch slices, trimming away any sinews or membranes and any fat. (This may be easier if meat is partly frozen.) Place meat in bowl. Stir together sesame oil, soy sauce, sherry, and garlic and massage mixture into meat to coat all pieces very lightly. Set meat aside to marinate about 30 minutes at room temperature or overnight in refrigerator.

2. Place shiitake mushrooms in a small saucepan. Cover with hot tap water and add sugar. Place on stove over lowest heat for 20 minutes, just to maintain the water's heat (not to simmer). Drain. (Liquid may be saved for use in sauces or soups.) Slice shiitake mushrooms thinly, discarding stems and, if necessary, the tough spot in the center of the cap where stem was attached.

3. In a large, heavy skillet, melt butter with oil. Add button mushrooms and over medium heat, sauté, stirring, until lightly browned (about 1 minute). Add shiitake slices and sauté until tender (about 1 minute longer). With a slotted spatula remove and reserve mushrooms.

4. Increase heat to moderately high. When fat in pan is sizzling, add meat. (More oil may be added to pan if mushrooms have absorbed too much.) Stirring and flipping constantly with a spatula, cook until meat is just cooked through (1 to 2 minutes). Remove with slotted spatula to a serving plate. Scatter mushrooms over meat and tent with aluminum foil to keep warm.

5. Pour off any excess fat from pan. Pour in cream and, stirring constantly, bring to a boil. Lower heat to a lively simmer and, stirring, reduce cream until thick enough to coat a spoon. Stir in oyster sauce and vinegar. Nap mushrooms and meat with sauce and serve immediately.

Serves 4 to 6.

WILD BOAR

Wild boar, a close relative of domestic hog, generally tastes like the finest pork, although meat from older boars may have a gamy undertone.

Boar is at its best between November and April, when it lives on a diet of acorns, lending the meat a nutty flavor. The parts of a wild boar correspond closely to those of a pig (see chart on page 66) and may be treated in much the same way.

Recipes for pork are equally suitable for boar. Try the marinade for Barbecued Suckling Pig (see page 70), which does wonders for wild boar roast.

WILD BOAR MEDALLIONS OR CHOPS WITH TANGY BERRY SAUCE

Swift and simple but luxurious, the sauce for the boar will also go with venison medallions.

1 pound medallions, ½ inch thick, cut from boar loin, or 4 thick boar chops (about 6 oz each)
Salt and freshly ground pepper
2 tablespoons cooking oil

Tangy Berry Sauce
¼ cup shallots
¼ cup balsamic vinegar
¼ cup dry red wine
¼ cup port
2 tablespoons honey Pinch cayenne pepper
¼ cup lingonberries or cranberries (fresh or frozen without juice)
2 tablespoons unsalted butter, cut into small pieces

1. Trim fat and silvery membrane from meat. Rub with salt and pepper and allow to stand at room temperature to develop flavor while sauce is prepared. For boar chops preheat oven to 300° F.

2. Heat oil over high heat in heavy skillet. Add meat and rapidly sauté on both sides until well browned. If using chops transfer meat to a 300° F oven for 20 minutes to complete cooking. Place meat on serving dish and nap with sauce.

Serves 4.

Tangy Berry Sauce Place shallots, vinegar, wine, port, honey, and cayenne in a small saucepan (preferably enamel coated). Stir well, then stir in berries. Bring to a simmer and cook over moderately low heat until liquid is very thick (about 20 minutes), stirring occasionally. Swirl in butter and serve hot.

Makes about 1 cup.

GAME BIRDS

The most apparent difference between game birds and domestic poultry is that wild game birds have virtually no fat under their skins. This gives their flesh a wonderful intensity of flavor, but also makes them somewhat more difficult to cook. Generally when cooking a game bird, you must stay closer to the stove than you would for, say, a plump chicken.

GETTING AND COOKING WILD BIRDS

Many farm-raised game birds (quail, partridge, and pheasant especially) are readily available from specialty markets and fine supermarkets and poulterers. Squab is no longer even considered a true game bird, since it is now raised domestically for meat on such a wide scale.

Wild turkey and wild goose are excellent roasted—but they should always be rubbed thoroughly with a fat of choice, or else sheets of fat or bacon should be tied over the breast.

HANDLING WILD BIRDS BEFORE COOKING

Except for pheasants, game birds are not aged. They may become more tender if refrigerated for several days or if frozen as soon as possible after their bodies have cooled.

Wild birds come with feathers on, and even one obtained from a commercial source may look like a fellow with a five o'clock shadow.

For a commercially obtained wild bird, if the bird still has many small pinfeathers, dry the skin with paper towels and singe the bird on a toasting fork, or place the bird close to the heat of a broiler very briefly.

Rub the bird with paper towels to remove feathers and, with strong tweezers, pull out remaining feather stubs, using a knife to cut away any stubborn clumps. Be sure to tweeze out any bird shot under the skin.

Cutting wild birds into serving portions before cooking will allow detection and removal of most of the bird shot from the meat. Biting into a lead pellet in an otherwise delicious bird is truly an unpleasant (and possibly tooth-breaking) gastronomic surprise.

QUAIL

There's little difference between wild and domestically raised quail. Despite their all-white meat and tiny size, quail are neither dull-flavored nor prone to dryness, and they turn out well even if slightly undercooked or overcooked. However, it takes two quail to make a light dinner, and they're bony enough to be finger food at home. The adaptable quail can be cooked quickly, by grilling or sautéing (or rapid roasting), or it can be braised at leisure. Quail may also be batter-fried like chicken (but for a briefer time) and finished off with a flavored cream sauce.

GARLIC-SAGE MARINATED GRILLED QUAIL

San Francisco Bay Area chef Tom Fox marinates quail in well-gentled cooked garlic and fresh sage and serves it as a first course. In the version of the dish presented here, the garlic is gentled by poaching (rather than the more risky roasting). Serve as a main dish or a first course.

- ½ *large bulb garlic (7 cloves, about 1 oz)*
- 12 *medium-sized fresh sage leaves, crumbled, or 1½ tablespoons crumbled dried sage; do not use ground sage*
- ½ *teaspoon salt*
- 3 *tablespoons olive oil, or as needed*
- 1 *teaspoon lemon juice, or as needed*
- 4 *quail, ready to cook*

1. Drop garlic cloves into boiling water to cover. Lower heat to a simmer and cook 25 minutes. Squish garlic out of peels into an electric minichopper or clean coffee grinder, if available, or into a blender or food processor. Purée briefly.

2. If using an electric minichopper or coffee grinder, add sage directly. If using a blender, first place sage leaves in a mortar and crush thoroughly, then add crushed sage to garlic purée. Add salt, olive oil, and lemon juice; blend until smooth. Taste carefully. If sage is a little bitter, add a little more oil and lemon juice. Rub mixture on quail; cover and marinate 3 hours at room temperature or overnight (or up to 72 hours) in refrigerator.

3. Quail may be rapidly grilled over red-glowing charcoal or wood, or broiled. If using a broiler (even in a gas oven), preheat for 12 minutes. Lift birds from marinade and place about 5 inches from heat source. Cook bony side first until browned (about 4 minutes). Turn and baste with marinade. Brown the other side. When pearls of juice appear on thinnest parts of quail, remove from heat. (If birds are not brown enough, cook a minute or so longer.) Serve hot.

Serves 4 as a first course, 2 as a main course.

SAUTÉED QUAIL WITH HAM AND MUSHROOMS

This simple recipe is adaptable to many accompaniments: Liver croutons, garlic toasts, and "Partly Dirty" Louisiana-Style Game Bird Rice (see page 122) are all suitable.

- 8 *quail*
- 1 *teaspoon salt*
- ½ *teaspoon freshly ground pepper*
- 1¼ *teaspoons dried thyme, crumbled*
- 6 *tablespoons unsalted butter*
- 2 *tablespoons cooking oil, or as needed (optional)*
- 2 *cups sliced mushrooms (chanterelles, oyster mushrooms, button mushrooms, or a combination)*
- ½ *pound cooked country or Smithfield ham (or other smoky ham) or 2 ounces prosciutto, cut into ¼-inch by 2-inch julienne*
- ½ *cup Poultry Stock (see page 17)*

1. Split quail by cutting along one side of backbone. If desired backbones and rib cages may be removed with a small, sharp knife to make eating easier. Flatten quail. Mix together salt, pepper, and thyme and sprinkle birds lightly on both sides with mixture.

2. In a large, heavy skillet over moderately high heat, warm butter and oil until foam subsides. Add mushrooms and quickly sauté, stirring frequently, until lightly browned. Remove with slotted spoon, draining fat back into pan. Reserve mushrooms and keep warm.

3. If necessary add sufficient oil to coat skillet. Add quail, skin side down, and ham. Cover and sauté until skin of quail is browned (3 to 4 minutes). Turn quail, cover again, and sauté until juices run clear (about 2 minutes longer). Arrange

quail on serving platter and sprinkle ham slivers over them and mushrooms around them.

4. Pour remaining fat out of skillet. Add stock, bring to a boil, and cook until liquid is somewhat thickened (about 1 minute), scraping up browned bits from bottom of pan. Correct seasoning and pour sauce over birds.

Serves 4 as a main course, 8 as an appetizer.

Quail Braised in White Wine For a slightly more luxurious main dish, do not remove quail and ham from skillet at step 3. Add 1 cup fruity dry white wine to skillet with stock. Bring to a boil, cover, and simmer until quail are falling-apart tender (about 25 minutes). Return mushrooms to skillet to reheat briefly. Serve hot.

Serves 4 as a main course.

Quail are dainty treats that are quick to prepare. In Garlic-Sage Marinated Grilled Quail, a savory marinade gives farm-raised birds a wild flavor.

115

SQUAB, WOOD PIGEON, AND GROUSE

Squab are young pigeons, but have little in common with the winged scavengers of the cities. (If you attempt to cook a city pigeon, you will not get a squab, but will probably get a disease.)

Squab lead a clean, soft life, eating corn or grain rather than street trash. Their flesh is a dark, rich-flavored delicacy. Since squab are farm raised, they contain just enough fat for roasting, grilling, or braising with no special caution; they may be cooked by any recipe for Cornish game hens.

However, squab are traditionally cooked only to rare: The flesh should be rosy when done, rather than brown. Typically one squab per person is served for a main course, although light eaters may well be satisfied with half a squab.

Wood pigeons (rather than city pigeons) are squab's wild cousins. They're far smaller, with dark red, lean, rather gamy flesh, but can be prepared in much the same fashion if cooking time is decreased.

If roasting, pigeons' breasts may be barded with strips of bacon or salt pork to maintain moistness; if grilled, pigeons should be basted frequently with oil or liquid. They may also be prepared like quail, which are light-meat birds of similar size. Like their domestic cousins wood pigeons are served rare, when the flesh is rosy. One wood pigeon makes an ideal light dinner.

Grouse can be prepared like either squab or partridge. They are lean, woodsy-flavored, light-meat birds, often much smaller than squab, so if roasting, bard their breasts with bacon or salt pork, pour a little liquid (water or stock) under the roasting rack, and roast carefully, decreasing cooking time to reflect the bird's smaller size. To grill, baste grouse frequently with melted butter or oil. Count on one large grouse or two small ones per person.

ROAST SQUAB WITH RICE-NUT STUFFING IN ROAST PEPPER–CREAM SAUCE

Squab roasts so quickly that this gala, summery recipe can be prepared in the same amount of time it takes to cook an everyday chicken dish. A premium rice will make the stuffing especially delicious.

> 1 cup Poultry Stock (see page 17) or water
> ½ cup high-quality rice (preferably basmati, Louisiana pecan, or a mixture of long-grain and wild rice)
> ½ cup pine nuts
> 2 tablespoons unsalted butter
> ¼ cup minced shallots or green onions
> 1 tablespoon finely minced garlic
> ¼ cup minced fresh basil leaves or ½ cup minced parsley
> ¼ cup golden raisins, soaked in warm water to cover
> Salt and freshly ground white pepper, to taste
> 4 squab (about 1 lb each), wood pigeons, or large grouse

Roast Pepper–Cream Sauce

> 2 medium-sized red bell peppers, roasted, peeled, seeded, deveined (see page 101), and thinly sliced
> 1 cup whipping cream
> 1 tablespoon minced fresh basil or 1 teaspoon dried basil
> Pinch cayenne pepper
> Salt, to taste

1. Preheat oven to 425° F. To make stuffing, in a small saucepan with a tight-fitting cover, bring stock to a boil. Stir in rice, cover, and simmer over lowest heat for 20 to 22 minutes. Reserve.

2. While rice cooks lightly toast pine nuts in a medium-sized, heavy skillet over medium heat, stirring frequently until nuts turn golden (about 5 minutes). Add butter and melt over medium-high heat. Stir in shallots, garlic, and basil and sauté, stirring frequently, until shallots are soft (about 3 minutes). When rice is

cooked stir it into shallot mixture. Drain raisins and stir into mixture. Add salt and white pepper and let cool a few minutes.

3. If desired squab may be boned to hold more stuffing and to make eating easier. To bone, place squab on cutting board breast side down. Slice through back along one side of backbone. With a small, sharp knife, begin at neck and cut flesh down and away from bones, removing rib cage, backbone, and finally breastbone. Leave thigh bones, leg bones, and upper wing bones intact. Trim off wing tips. (Bones may be saved to be used for stock.)

4. Lightly season birds' interiors with salt and white pepper. Divide stuffing between birds' cavities. Sew up openings with kitchen twine (or, if bird has not been boned, vents may be shut with turkey skewers and twine). Tie legs together. Place birds breast side down on rack in roaster just large enough to hold them. (If cooking wood pigeons or grouse by this method, pour some water under the rack.)

5. Roast birds until skins are golden (about 20 minutes), turning about halfway to brown breasts. (Wood pigeon may be done slightly earlier. Cut a slit in meat; meat should be rosy.) While birds roast make Roast Pepper–Cream Sauce.

6. To serve, remove twine from birds. Coat each dinner plate with some sauce and place birds on top.

Serves 4.

Roast Pepper–Cream Sauce
Combine roast bell peppers, cream, basil, and cayenne in a medium-sized, heavy skillet. Bring to a boil and cook until cream has thickened enough to coat a spoon. Transfer mixture to blender or food processor and purée until smooth. Return sauce to skillet and season generously with salt. Reserve. Just before birds are done, reheat sauce to a simmer.

Makes about 1½ cups.

EAST-WEST BROILED SQUAB WITH CANTONESE STUFFING

This dish is a spin-off from one of South China's greatest—but most laborious—dishes: minced squab on lettuce. Here the marinated, whole squab enjoys the same accompanying vegetables and condiments as a stuffing. Serve with cooked rice, if desired.

4 small or 2 large squab, preferably boneless

½ cup Shaoxing (Chinese rice wine), sake, or dry sherry

¼ cup light soy sauce

12 dried medium-sized shiitake mushrooms

3 tablespoons (approximately) diced Smithfield, country, or smoked baked ham

1½ teaspoons minced fresh ginger

1 cup water chestnuts, cut into ¼-inch dice

2 green onions (whites and crisp greens), minced
Pinch white pepper

1 tablespoon bottled Chinese-style oyster sauce

½ teaspoon sugar

5 tablespoons dark sesame oil, or as needed

2 tablespoons peanut or sunflower oil

2 egg whites

4 cups (approximately) iceberg lettuce, shredded (1 medium head)

2 tablespoons rice vinegar or other mild vinegar

1. Place squab in large bowl or sealable plastic bag. Mix together wine and soy sauce; pour over squab. Let birds marinate at room temperature 1 to 3 hours (or refrigerate overnight). Meanwhile soak mushrooms in warm water to cover.

2. Preheat broiler. Drain mushrooms (the soaking water may be used for cooking rice) and chop into ¼-inch pieces, discarding stems. Mix with ham, ginger, water chestnuts, and green onions and place near stove.

3. Mix together 2 tablespoons of the marinating liquid from the squab with the white pepper, oyster sauce, sugar, and ½ teaspoon of the sesame oil and place near stove. In a large, heavy skillet or wok, heat peanut oil until very fragrant. Add mushroom mixture and fry over very high heat, stirring, until mushrooms are tender (about 1 minute). Pour in liquid mixture, stir, and remove contents of wok to a cool bowl. Let cool for a minute, then stir in egg whites.

4. Stuff mushroom mixture into cavities of squab. Sew up openings with thin kitchen twine or white thread. Brush birds with a little of the sesame oil and broil 5 inches from heat, about 7 minutes per side for small birds, 10 minutes for large birds. Brush again with sesame oil after turning. Birds will cook to a very dark brown.

5. Meanwhile place shredded lettuce in a bowl and dress it with rice vinegar and 4 tablespoons of the sesame oil. Toss well. Divide among serving plates. When birds are done remove them from broiler and cut or tug out strings or thread. Place 1 small bird, or half a large bird, on top of lettuce bed on each plate and serve immediately.

Serves 4.

Richly flavored squab lends itself to a multitude of inventive stuffings that keep the meat moist during dry-heat cooking. Roast Squab With Rice-Nut Stuffing in Roast Pepper–Cream Sauce is a southwestern rendition.

An easy marinade tames the imperious pheasant. It makes the bird moist and tender, then imparts an intriguing flavor to the lively cream sauce of Marinated Grilled Pheasant Breasts.

PHEASANT

Although pheasants are larger than many other game birds, the methods for cooking them to maximize their tenderness are a model for use with any lean, wild, gallinaceous bird.

Most of the pheasant consists of plump, dense-textured, white-meat breast, attached to tiny, sinewy legs and small thighs. Domesticated pheasants have been bred for a very thick layer of fine-flavored fat under the skin all over the bird, whereas wild pheasants are far leaner (and more richly flavored). However, in both cases the breast meat is likely to toughen if a whole bird is roasted conventionally and without constant attention.

Pheasant breast should be cooked only until pale pink toward the center, not stark white. That old chestnut of pretentious restaurants, "roast pheasant under glass," always looked better than it actually tasted, because by the time the legs and thighs were cooked by dry heat, the breast was dried out.

A farm-raised pheasant, however, can be roasted whole. The cook's attentiveness will be rewarded with tender, succulent meat. Another way to ensure moist, delicate meat is to break down a pheasant (whether wild or domestic) into its separate parts and give each part the special treatment that so aristocratic and costly a bird deserves. (This process will also aid in discovering and removing the bird shot from a wild pheasant.)

The plump breast can be roasted, grilled, or sautéed. The small but tasty legs are an important component of the pheasant stock that's vital to the best sauces and to pheasant soup, and thigh pieces may be braised.

If you obtain more than one pheasant at a time, it's wonderful to serve in at least two courses: a savory pheasant soup or consommé followed by the roast or grilled breast, or a pheasant breast course followed by a braise of the thigh pieces.

STURDY PHEASANT STOCK

This wonderfully flavorful stock is the invaluable basis of both pheasant soup and most sauces for roast or grilled pheasant. Although it calls for the spare parts of two pheasants (to obtain enough broth for a soup), the recipe can certainly be halved if you have only one bird and need stock only for a sauce. Also, if you have a very fine strainer, you can drop herbs into the stock loose, rather than bothering with cheesecloth.

> *Legs, wings (or wing tips), backs, gizzards, and hearts of 2 pheasants, roughly chopped*
> 5 *to 6 cups poultry stock or water (see Note)*
> 2 *large carrots, pared and coarsely chopped*
> 2 *medium onions, peeled and coarsely chopped*
> 1 *large stalk celery, coarsely sliced*
> 1 *bouquet garni (6 sprigs parsley, ¼ teaspoon fresh thyme, and 12 white peppercorns, all wrapped and tied in washed cheesecloth)*

1. Place pheasant pieces in a heavy saucepan or casserole (about 2½ quarts), preferably enamel coated. Barely cover with stock. Bring just to a boil, lower heat immediately to a simmer, and skim scum from top.

2. Add carrots, onions, celery, and bouquet garni. Return mixture to a simmer and cook very slowly for 2 hours, skimming surface occasionally. Strain stock, pressing on solids to extract juices. Let cool to luke-warm, then cover and chill until fat forms a layer on top that's visible enough to remove. Degrease stock.

Makes 4 to 5 cups.

Note For best flavor use poultry stock (preferably a previous batch of pheasant stock) for the liquid if stock will be made into soup.

Brown Pheasant Stock Place pheasant pieces, carrot, onion, and celery in a large skillet filmed with 1 tablespoon rendered pheasant fat or butter. Gently sauté until all ingredients are browned (about 15 minutes). Remove all ingredients with a slotted spoon to a casserole or stockpot, as above. Barely cover mixture with poultry stock, add bouquet garni, bring to a simmer, and proceed as directed above.

Makes 4 to 5 cups.

MARINATED GRILLED PHEASANT BREASTS

Here is a savory but very easy recipe that not only emphasizes the flavor of pheasant, but gives the cook the greatest possible control over the doneness of the breast meat. (In addition skinning and boning the breast will allow most of the bird shot in a wild pheasant to be discovered and removed.) Note that two to three days are needed for marination. Serve the pheasant with the apple slices sautéed in butter, and, if desired, some tart cranberry sauce.

> 4 *pheasant breasts*
> 8 *juniper berries*
> 1 *teaspoon whole coriander seed*
> 2 *tiny hot red chiles, such as chile tepin, or ¼ teaspoon hot-pepper flakes*
> ¾ *cup olive oil*
> 3 *medium cloves garlic, crushed and peeled*
> 1 *sprig fresh thyme, torn apart, or ½ teaspoon dried thyme*
> 3 *tablespoons minced parsley*
> 2 *shallots or 3 green onions, minced*
> ¾ *cup dry white wine*
> 1¼ *cups Brown Pheasant Stock (see above) or Brown Poultry Stock (see page 17)*
> 1 *cup whipping cream*
> *Salt and freshly ground white pepper, to taste*
> 12 *thick apple slices sautéed in butter, for accompaniment (optional)*

1. Bone and skin pheasant breasts. (Reserve skin and bones for stock.) Place breasts in a shallow container with a cover.

2. In a small, dry skillet, toast juniper berries, coriander seed, and whole chiles until coriander starts to darken. With a small mortar and pestle, crush juniper mixture. Mix with olive oil, garlic, thyme, parsley, shallots, and wine. (If using hot-pepper flakes, add them now.) Pour mixture over pheasant breasts, turning breasts to coat both sides. Cover and refrigerate for 2 to 3 days.

3. About 40 minutes before starting to cook pheasant, preheat your broiler. In a small, heavy saucepan, simmer the pheasant stock gently until reduced to ¾ cup (about 30 minutes), skimming the surface occasionally. Remove breasts from marinade and place them on the rack of a shallow broiling pan. Add marinade to saucepan and over high heat rapidly reduce to ½ cup. Stir in cream, lower heat, and simmer until the sauce thickens enough to coat a spoon. Strain into a smaller saucepan, season with salt and white pepper, and reserve, covered.

4. Broil pheasant breasts no more than 2 minutes on the first side, about 1 minute on the second side, removing breasts from heat instantly when meat is pink at the center. Cut breasts into strips, place strips on a serving platter (with sautéed apples, if desired) and keep warm for a minute. Stir sauce and reheat slightly if cooled. Nap pheasant with sauce and prepare to serve immediately.

Serves 4.

PARTRIDGE

The most widely available partridge is the chukar, a relatively large bird (about 1 pound) that's raised commercially as well as hunted. Most other types of partridge or grouse are about half the size of a chukar, so adjust cooking times and portions. The wild versions of these birds are very lean, so if you are dry-heat cooking (roasting or broiling), baste birds with fat (or wrap breasts in bacon).

Partridge and grouse can be broiled and topped with a composed butter or roasted (follow any recipe for Cornish game hen), but they're at their most succulent when braised. Count on half a chukar per person in a complete, multicourse dinner, or a whole partridge or hazel grouse per person in a simple dinner. With the small wild partridge and grouse, two birds will be needed per person.

A PARTRIDGE IN A PEAR SEA

This lovely, lyrical dish not only plays on the words of the Christmas carol, but also justifies them: Partridge and pear are a wonderfully apt combination. Grouse, pheasant, or squab will also benefit from this treatment. Accompany with Pilaf (see page 63), wild rice, or sautéed potatoes. Serve vegetables as a separate course, since nothing should interfere with the subtle flavors of this dish.

6 *slightly underripe Bosc pears*
1 *cup Poultry Stock*
 (see page 17)
1 *slice orange zest (about*
 ½ inch by 2 inches)
 Salt and freshly ground
 pepper, to taste
4 *partridges, such as chukars*
 (12 to 14 oz each)
2 *tablespoons unsalted butter,*
 plus ½ cup additional
 unsalted butter, cut into
 small pieces, and chilled
2 *tablespoons oil (such as*
 sunflower, or corn)
4 *medium shallots, peeled*
 and minced
1 *teaspoon black peppercorns*
3 *cups dry red wine (preferably*
 Cabernet Sauvignon)
1 *tablespoon sugar*

1. Preheat oven to 375° F. Peel pears, reserving peel. Halve and core fruit, and place in bottom of a heavy, ovenproof, fireproof casserole large enough to hold birds. (An oval enameled or glazed 2½- to 3-quart casserole is ideal.)

2. In a small saucepan bring stock to a boil. Drop in pear peels and orange zest. Lower heat and simmer 10 minutes. Strain liquid and reserve; discard zest.

3. Lightly salt and pepper insides of birds. Pat skin dry and, using kitchen twine only, truss birds. (Tie together legs and loop string around body at wing level to tie wings close to body.) Heat the 2 tablespoons butter and the oil in a large, heavy skillet until foam subsides and brown birds on all sides. Nestle birds among halved pears.

4. Over high heat in fat remaining in skillet, quickly sauté shallots, stirring, until tender and slightly browned. Sprinkle shallots over birds. Sprinkle peppercorns over casserole contents. Pour wine, reserved stock mixture, and sugar into casserole and season lightly with salt and pepper. Bring to a simmer on top of stove, cover, and place casserole in oven. Bake until birds are tender (about 1 hour).

5. Using tongs or a large slotted spoon, carefully place birds and pears on a heatproof serving dish. Tent with aluminum foil and keep warm in turned-off oven. Place casserole over highest heat (or, if using ceramic dish, pour liquid into a saucepan) and reduce liquid by half, until somewhat syrupy, stirring frequently. Remove from heat and swirl in the ½ cup butter, piece by piece, until blended. Nap partridges and pears with sauce and serve additional sauce in gravy boat.

Serves 4 (or 8 in a multicourse dinner).

WILD DUCK

Wild ducks taste like intensified versions of their domestic relatives, but procedures for cooking them are just the opposite. With a plump Long Island duckling, the difficulty lies in getting the fat to melt wholly away by the time the meat is done. With wild ducks there's virtually no fat, and the challenge lies in keeping the flesh moist while also crisping the skin.

Mallards are medium-sized wild ducks, with rich-tasting dark flesh. Teals are much smaller than mallards and are considered special prizes. Mullards or moulardes are domesticated crosses between wild and domestic ducks, with flesh that is somewhat less fishy and somewhat more fatty than that of wild ducks. Muscovies are a large wild species from South America that are raised domestically in this country.

Wild ducks can be roasted very quickly at high temperatures—but if they're roasted without some liquid in the pan and without frequent braising, their flesh will turn to cardboard, and be tough and tasteless. All wild ducks need a moist vegetable or fruit in the cavity during roasting, a little liquid (or vegetables) underneath, and frequent basting.

Ducks may be browned briefly at very high temperatures and then completed in a moderate oven; this is often more effective than the traditional hunter's method of completely roasting the bird at a high temperature. Wild ducks also take beautifully to old-fashioned braised duck recipes, since there's no worry about fat turning the sauce greasy. One of the best ways to prepare wild duck is to separate the breast from the rest. The breast can be skinned, rapidly panfried, and finished with a fine sauce, and the remainder can be braised in a different rich liquid; then the entire duck served in two exciting courses.

WILD DUCK, CREOLE STYLE

Here wild duck is quickly sautéed in a spicy sauce that seems made to order. Serve with buttered cooked rice or a simple pilaf. This recipe is adapted from one by Bruce Aidells, a gifted San Francisco Bay Area cook.

    2   mallards or other wild ducks
        (about 1 lb each) or thigh
        pieces of 3 or 4 wild ducks
    ½   teaspoon dried crumbled sage
    ½   teaspoon dried thyme leaves
    ½   teaspoon dried crumbled
        oregano
    ¼   teaspoon cayenne pepper
    1   teaspoon paprika
    1   teaspoon salt
    1   teaspoon freshly ground
        black pepper
    1   tablespoon cooking oil
    2   tablespoons unsalted butter

Creole Sauce

    ¼   pound tasso (Cajun peppered
        ham) or baked ham, diced
    ¼   pound Cajun sausage
        (andouille, Cajun boar
        sausage, or chaurice) or
        other spicy sausage, diced
    1   medium onion, coarsely
        minced
    1   green bell pepper, finely diced
    2   stalks celery, finely diced
    1   bunch green onions, trimmed
        and chopped (including crisp
        greens)
    1   can (1 lb) Italian-style
        plum tomatoes in purée
    1   cup duck or poultry stock
        (see page 17)
    ¼   teaspoon crumbled dried sage
    ½   teaspoon dried thyme
    ½   teaspoon cayenne pepper
    2   fresh bay leaves or
        ½ teaspoon finely chopped
        dried bay leaves
    ½   teaspoon crumbled dried basil
    ½   teaspoon Worcestershire sauce
        Salt, pepper, and hot-pepper
        sauce, to taste (optional)

1. Cut ducks into serving pieces (wings, halved breasts, legs, and thighs with half of back attached to each). Pat skin dry with paper towels. Mix together sage, thyme, oregano, cayenne, paprika, salt, and black pepper and rub mixture into skin.

2. In a large (12-inch), heavy skillet, heat oil and butter together. When butter foam subsides, add duck pieces, skin side down. Lower heat to medium-high and fry duck until skin is browned. Remove duck and re-serve, draining fat back into pan.

3. Make Creole Sauce. Add duck pieces. Simmer 15 to 20 minutes longer, turning every 5 minutes. Duck is done when breast meat, cut with a knife, is reddish but not purple or bloody. (Stop cooking before meat turns pale, or it will be tough.)

Serves 4.

Creole Sauce Over medium-high heat fry *tasso* and sausage for 3 to 5 minutes in the fat that has been returned to the skillet after browning duck. Add onion and sauté 5 minutes at high heat, stirring. Add bell pepper, celery, and green onions and fry for 2 minutes to soften. Add tomatoes, stock, sage, thyme, cayenne, bay leaves, and basil. Over medium-low heat simmer vigorously until partly thickened (about 20 minutes). Just before serving stir in Worcestershire sauce. Add salt, pepper, and hot sauce (if desired).

Makes about 2½ cups.

A Partridge in a Pear Sea would be dazzling indeed at a festive December dinner—or in any other month when pears are at their best. Serve half a bird for an appetizer, or a whole one as a satisfying main course.

STARCH ACCOMPANIMENTS TO GAME

Game, with its intense flavors, is traditionally served with starch dishes that either are very smooth, light, and even comforting (such as rice or polenta) or are unusually full-flavored (such as the "Partly Dirty" Louisiana-Style Game Bird Rice recipe at right, the two wild rice recipes below, and the sage-flavored croutons on page 123).

BASIC WILD RICE

Wild rice is not rice at all, but a cereal grain native to North America. It goes exceptionally well with game birds of all sorts, both as a side dish and as a stuffing.

> 1 cup wild rice
> 4 cups cold water
> 1 teaspoon salt, or to taste
> Butter (optional)

Place wild rice in a strainer and wash well in cold tap water. Place in a 2-quart saucepan with the 4 cups water and salt. Bring water to a boil, reduce heat, cover, and simmer until rice has puffed and most of the liquid is absorbed (about 45 minutes). Drain off any excess liquid. Season as desired, stir in butter (if used), and serve.

Makes 4 cups, 4 to 6 servings.

Variations Wild rice may be prepared as for Pilaf (see page 63), using 3 cups poultry stock to 1 cup wild rice and extending cooking time to 45 minutes to 1 hour (until all stock is absorbed). Fresh seasonings of choice (garlic, thyme, marjoram, basil, or green onions) may be added freely along with the stock, for an herbed pilaf—or a plain wild rice pilaf can also be finished off as "Partly Dirty" Louisiana-Style Game Bird Rice (recipe at right). In addition wild rice can be tossed with diced mushrooms, celery, onion, green bell pepper, and poultry seasoning to taste, for use as poultry stuffing.

"PARTLY DIRTY" LOUISIANA-STYLE GAME BIRD RICE

An adaptation of a beloved Louisiana recipe called "dirty rice," this dish is "dirtied" by the addition of browned poultry gizzards and livers and ground meat. This version is only partly dirty—it centers on whatever organs you have from the game bird to be served for the main course. Gizzards and hearts may be used both in stock for a sauce and again for a dressing too.

> 2 tablespoons unsalted butter
> 1 cup long-grain rice
> Scant 2 cups Poultry Stock (see page 17)
> Game bird hearts (any amount up to ½ lb), if available, raw or cooked
> Game bird gizzards (any amount up to ½ lb), raw or cooked
> 2 tablespoons rendered chicken or duck fat or cooking oil, or as needed
> ¼ pound ground pork (optional)
> ¼ to 1 teaspoon cayenne pepper, to taste
> 1 teaspoon salt
> ¼ teaspoon freshly ground black pepper
> 1 teaspoon paprika
> ½ teaspoon dried thyme
> ¼ teaspoon crumbled dried marjoram
> 1 cup finely minced onion
> ½ cup finely diced green bell pepper
> 2 teaspoons minced garlic
> Game bird livers, finely minced (up to ½ lb; may be supplemented by chicken livers)
> 2 tablespoons water

1. In a medium-large, heavy saucepan with a cover, melt butter. Add rice and over low heat sauté, stirring occasionally, until translucent. Pour in stock, bring to a boil, stir once, cover, and simmer 25 minutes. Set aside, covered.

2. With a small, sharp knife, slice away tough outer membrane from hearts (if available) and gizzards, and mince or grind meat finely.

3. Heat poultry fat in a large, heavy skillet. Add pork, if using; if using raw hearts and gizzards, add these now too. Sauté over medium-high heat until browned, breaking up pork. Lower heat to medium. If using cooked hearts and gizzards, stir these in now. Add cayenne, salt, black pepper, paprika, thyme, and marjoram and stir over medium heat to coat giblet mixture. Stir in onion, green pepper, and garlic and over medium heat sauté until tender (about 5 minutes) adding a little more fat if needed. Add minced poultry livers and the water. Decrease heat to low and simmer just until the livers are cooked through but not toughened (about 2 minutes).

4. Stir reserved cooked rice into skillet, tossing to coat rice with giblet mixture. Serve immediately.

Serves 4 to 6.

ORANGE-SCENTED WILD RICE WITH ALMONDS AND PEAS

This dish goes especially well with A Partridge in a Pear Sea (see page 120). If using commercially dried orange zest, stir it in by teaspoonfuls, tasting carefully, since some brands have odd flavors.

> 3 tablespoons unsalted butter
> ½ cup slivered, blanched almonds
> 2 cups frozen tiny green peas (petits pois), defrosted but uncooked
> 4 cups cooked wild rice
> 1 tablespoon grated orange zest (preferably fresh or frozen homemade)

1. Preheat oven to 325° F. Melt butter in a 2-quart ovenproof casserole. Toss almonds lightly in butter, then sauté over lowest heat, stirring occasionally, until almonds are lightly toasted all over (about 10 minutes).

2. Add peas to almonds, then rice and orange zest, tossing together. Bake, uncovered, until heated through (about 14 minutes if starting at room temperature, 7 minutes if rice is warm).

Serves 6 to 8.

GAME BIRD CROSTINI
Sage-flavored liver croutons

This dish, based on a Florentine recipe for chicken liver toasts, is a delicious way to use just a few game bird livers. Don't worry about the anchovy; its flavor will disappear into the mixture, lending only a faint salty tang. Serve *crostini* as an appetizer or as an accompaniment to any simply prepared game bird, such as Garlic-Sage Marinated Grilled Quail (see page 114).

> 1 tablespoon olive oil, plus more as needed
> 3 tablespoons minced onion
> 1 small clove garlic, minced
> 1 small fresh sage leaf or ⅛ teaspoon dried sage
> ¼ pound game bird livers, trimmed of fat, and halved if large
> Salt and freshly ground pepper, to taste
> 1 anchovy fillet
> ½ ounce thinly sliced prosciutto
> 2 slices good white bread or 4 thin slices French bread

1. In a small saucepan heat the 1 tablespoon olive oil. Add onion and garlic and sauté gently until wilted. Add sage and livers, sprinkle with salt and pepper, and increase heat. Sauté over high heat, turning, until livers are barely cooked and still slightly pink in center.

2. Remove liver mixture to blender, food processor, or electric mini-chopper. Add anchovy and sliced prosciutto and whirl briefly to make a coarse purée.

3. Remove crusts from bread. If using white bread slice diagonally in half. Toast until light brown. Immediately brush each toast piece with some olive oil and spread liver mixture on top. Serve while still warm.

Makes 4 crostini, 2 to 4 servings.

MAIL-ORDER SOURCES FOR GAME

Nearly every type of game, including the wild boar used to make the Wild Boar Chops With Tangy Berry Sauce pictured above (recipe on page 113), is available by mail or phone order. However, many companies require a minimum order (usually $100 or $150); shipping charges may also be high. Get together with friends or neighbors for a joint order.

Czimer Foods, Inc.
Route 1, Box 285
Lockport, IL 60441
(312) 460-7152 or (312) 460-7293
Large selection of game animals and birds; exotics and smoked products.

D'Artagnan, Inc.
399–419 St. Paul Avenue
Jersey City, NJ 07306
(800) 327-2462
Venison, boar, rabbit, game birds, specialty domestic meats, foie gras, prepared foods. No minimum.

Durham–Night Bird Game and Poultry Co., Inc.
650 San Mateo Avenue
San Bruno, CA 94066
(415) 543-6508
Large selection of game animals and birds, including exotics.

Hayes Ranches
Box 1070
Hamilton, MT 59840
(406) 363-4090
Ready-to-eat game products (such as chili, pâté). Order by case only.

Iron Gate Products Company, Inc.
424 West Fifty-fourth Street
New York, NY 10019
(212) 757-2670
Selected game meats and birds in season. Case lots only.

Polarica, Inc.
Box 880204
San Francisco, CA 94188
(800) 426-3872
Very wide selection of game meats and birds.

Preferred Meats
2050 Galvez Avenue
San Francisco, CA 94124
(415) 387-4990 or (415) 387-9299
Game meats and poultry, some Northern European wild birds.

Scimitar Meats
Box 340
Canby, OR 97013
(503) 266-5781
Ready-to-eat, wine-marinated and alderwood-smoked game products. No minimum order; free shipping.

INDEX

Note: Page numbers in italics refer to photographs separated from recipe text.

Special Thanks

From Naomi Wise to:
Al Arikian, long-lost but not forgotten, for shish kebab secrets
Gerald Prolman, Night Bird (San Bruno)
Susan Patton, Preferred Meats (San Franciso)
Jim Noonan
Bob Steiner
Mr. Lum, retired butcher of 5th Avenue Market (San Francisco)
Affolter Brothers, Eureka Valley Meats (San Francisco)
Henry and Diana Chung, Hunan Restaurant (San Francisco)
Stu and Vicki Glauberman
Lois and Terry Link
Raul Loaiza
Dolores "Pookie" Turner
Gérard de Noel
Steve Aibell
Scott Peterson, Polarica, Inc. (San Francisco)
Terry Horn, Scimitar Meats (Canby, Ore.)

And especially to all the members of the Shakespeare Gang, for food-testing and suggesting, barbecue lending and computer mending:
Dave Blake
Shirley Bossier
Sam and Maura Hagerty-Hammond
Anita Monga
Peter Moore
Charley Pickel

Most of all, to:
Rita Golomb and the late Sam Golomb ("eating well is the best revenge") and Michael Goodwin for vast numbers of brilliant culinary ideas and 30 minutes a day of dishwashing.

From Karen Hazarian to:
Assistant Food Stylist Scott Gill
Arthur Shaw
Sebastien Gunningham
Saag's Products, Inc. (San Leandro, Calif.)
Kathleen Volkmann
Tom McGannon
Draeger's (Menlo Park, Calif.)

From Maria Winston to:
The Maxwell Galleries, for the loan of "Woodland Hearts," page 18, oil on canvas by William Keith; and "Los Olivos," page 36, oil on board by William Clapp
Harleen & Allen Fine Art, for the loan of "Lower Canyon IV," page 4, by Janet Jones
The Claremont Rug Company (Oakland, Calif.)
Paul Bauer (San Francisco)

U.S. MEASURE AND METRIC MEASURE CONVERSION CHART

	Formulas for Exact Measures				Rounded Measures for Quick Reference		
	Symbol	**When you know:**	**Multiply by:**	**To find:**			
Mass (Weight)	oz	ounces	28.35	grams	1 oz		= 30 g
	lb	pounds	0.45	kilograms	4 oz		= 115 g
	g	grams	0.035	ounces	8 oz		= 225 g
	kg	kilograms	2.2	pounds	16 oz	= 1 lb	= 450 g
					32 oz	= 2 lb	= 900 g
					36 oz	= 2¼ lb	= 1,000g (1 kg)
Volume	tsp	teaspoons	5.0	milliliters	¼ tsp	= 1/24 oz	= 1 ml
	tbsp	tablespoons	15.0	milliliters	½ tsp	= 1/12 oz	= 2 ml
	fl oz	fluid ounces	29.57	milliliters	1 tsp	= ⅙ oz	= 5 ml
	c	cups	0.24	liters	1 tbsp	= ½ oz	= 15 ml
	pt	pints	0.47	liters	1 c	= 8 oz	= 250 ml
	qt	quarts	0.95	liters	2 c (1 pt)	= 16 oz	= 500 ml
	gal	gallons	3.785	liters	4 c (1 qt)	= 32 oz	= 1 liter
	ml	milliliters	0.034	fluid ounces	4 qt (1 gal)	= 128 oz	= 3¾ liter
Length	in.	inches	2.54	centimeters	⅜ in.	= 1 cm	
	ft	feet	30.48	centimeters	1 in.	= 2.5 cm	
	yd	yards	0.9144	meters	2 in.	= 5 cm	
	mi	miles	1.609	kilometers	2½ in.	= 6.5 cm	
	km	kilometers	0.621	miles	12 in. (1 ft)	= 30 cm	
	m	meters	1.094	yards	1 yd	= 90 cm	
	cm	centimeters	0.39	inches	100 ft	= 30 m	
					1 mi	= 1.6 km	
Temperature	°F	Fahrenheit	5/9 (after subtracting 32)	Celsius	32°F	= 0°C	
					68°F	= 20°C	
	°C	Celsius	9/5 (then add 32)	Fahrenheit	212°F	= 100°C	
Area	in.²	square inches	6.452	square centimeters	1 in.²	= 6.5 cm²	
	ft²	square feet	929.0	square centimeters	1 ft²	= 930 cm²	
	yd²	square yards	8361.0	square centimeters	1 yd²	= 8360 cm²	
	a.	acres	0.4047	hectares	1 a.	= 4050 m²	

Proof-of-Purchase
0-89721-152-9